WITHDRAWN
UTSA Libraries

WITHDRAWN
UTSA Libraries

Making Cancer Policy

SUNY Series in Public Administration in the 1980s

Peter W. Colby Editor

Making
Cancer
Policy

Mark E. Rushefsky

State University of New York Press

LIBRARY
The University of Texas
At San Antonio

The author and publisher gratefuly acknowledge permission to reprint
Tables 5.1 and Table 5.2 from Robert A. Squire, "Ranking Carcinogens:
A Proposed Regulatory Approach," *Science* 214 (November 20, 1981),
pp. 877–880. Copyright © by the American Association for the Advance-
ment of Science.

Published by
State University of New York Press, Albany

© 1986   State University of New York

All rights reserved
Printed in the United States of America
No part of this book may be used or reproduced
in any manner whatsoever without written permission
except in the case of brief quotations embodied in
critical articles and reviews

For information, address State University of New York
Press, State University Plaza, Albany, N.Y., 12246

Library of Congress Cataloging in Publication Data

Rushefsky, Mark E., 1945–
    Making cancer policy.

√ (SUNY series in public administration in the 1980's)
    Bibliography: p.
    Includes index.
    1. Cancer—Government policy—United States—History.
2. Health risk assessment—Government policy—United
States—History. 3. Medical policy—United States—
History. 4. Environmental policy—United States—
History. I. Title. II. Series. [DNLM: 1. Medical
Oncology—United States—legislation. 2. Neoplasms—
history. 3. Public Policy—United States. QZ 200 R953m]
RA645.C3R87   1986   363.1'79   86-14387
ISBN 0-88706-406-X
ISBN 0-88706-407-8 (pbk.)

LIBRARY
The University of Texas
At San Antonio

Contents

Diagrams and Tables

Preface

Making Cancer Policy originated back in 1971 when I first became interested in environmental policy. Through the years, first as a graduate student, then as a professor in three different colleges and universities, that interest has matured in a series of articles and book chapters. The immediate impetus for the book dates back only to 1984, when I delivered a paper on risk assessment in cancer policy at the annual meeting of the Association for Politics and the Life Sciences (in conjunction with the American Political Science Association's annual convention). The paper (Rushefsky 1985) seemed barely to scratch the surface of the topic, which I thought deserved a considerably longer treatment.

This book is the result of that long process, ranging over some fourteen years. The purpose of the book is to examine the controversies over cancer risk assessment guidelines, or cancer policy. I offer one major explanation for those controversies: the incompleteness of the technical foundation of cancer policy. Others have pointed to this incompleteness, most recently Edith Efron (1984) in *The Apocalyptics*. Her conclusion is that risk assessment ought not be done in the face of scientific uncertainty, and I address her arguments in chapter 7. For the moment it suffices to say that agencies have issued and will continue to issue risk assessment guidelines anyway. Because of scientific uncertainties, cancer policies are colored both by the values of those promulgating them and of those seeking changes. Industry interests seek more relaxed or risk-tolerant policies because of economic considerations. The uncertainties are used to argue against rigid and "scientifically unsound" policies. Environmental interests exploit the same uncertainties to argue for prudent, risk-averse policies. Political values are thus intimately entwined with the scientific basis for the policy. The playing out of values is expressed through the science in disagreements with or support of a particular methodology or study.

A book on a controversial subject is itself likely to be controversial. Consider the reaction to Rachel Carson's *Silent Spring* in the 1960s or to Efron's *The Apocalyptics* in the 1980s. Both authors chose sides. Carson for risk-averse policies, Efron going beyond risk-tolerant policies to attack the whole enterprise of risk assessment. I have sought a more balanced course. My goal is not to advocate but to understand and explain the significance of various choices and the factors determining those choices. I am critical of those pursuing risk-averse policies as well as those promoting risk-tolerant policies. No side has a monopoly on truth, for the truth may never be known. We can only assume and go on from there.

A book, even by a single author, is a collaborative effort, and I want to thank those who, directly or indirectly, have helped me with this project. My biggest supporter has always been my wife, Cindy; but then I have always been her biggest fan. Her moral and editorial assistance has been unsurpassed. Al Teich was my mentor in graduate school, and from him I developed an interest in science policy. Though geographically distant, he remains a good friend. My former colleagues at the University of Florida (Albert Matheny, Tony Rosenbaum, and Ken Wald) were kind enough (after sufficient badgering) to read early drafts of the book and to make helpful comments. Dale Hattis and Nick Ashford aided my understanding of some technical points. Nick in particular has been very enthusiastic about this book, and I gratefully accepted his offer to write its introduction. I want to thank the three anonymous (sometimes semi-anonymous) reviewers for their comments. Finally, Michele Martin, my editor at SUNY Press, was a vigorous supporter of the book even before I had written a single word. She encouraged me to continue at a time when I was temporarily hesitant about the project. I commend both her and the staff at SUNY Press. Finally, some of the material in chapter 6 was based on a series of interviews in 1984 with very helpful and courteous people at the Environmental Protection Agency. I thank all those who have helped me through the years. Any mistakes that may appear in the book are, of course, my own.

Finally, I dedicate this book to my parents, Ben and Lillian, who may not always have agreed with me, but who have always supported me.

Introduction

Nicholas A. Ashford

There is hardly an area of regulation of health, safety and the environment frought with more controversy than the regulation of chemical carcinogens. The new and evolving science of the theory of carcinogenesis, and the attendant uncertainty surrounding both theory and data, have provided opportunities for vested interests to meddle mischievously in arriving at what they claim are science-based decisions. Professor Mark Rushefsky, trained as a political scientist, shows us how *political* science can be. He successfully challenges the notion that concerns about risks from chemical exposure can be clearly separated into decisions about risk assessment and decisions about risk management. The methodology and principles used in arriving at an assessment of risk can greatly alter the results in a particular case—and honest differences of opinion can receive the backing of reputable scientists. However, more or less conservative risk estimates can also be politically driven.

This book represents a scholarly and balanced attempt to explain and explore the values inherent in making societal decisions affecting technology under scientific uncertainty. The work is extensive and exhaustive, and provides a rich source of references and readings which are rarely found in the various polemics concerning the regulation of carcinogens. In a proper scholarly fashion, displaying impressive intellectual honesty, no point of view is ignored or left uncriticized.

The major thrust of the work addresses the role of uncertainty in science, the distinction between science judged by conventional

1

scientific standards and the legal standards of proof required for regulatory action, the identification of the key technical areas in dispute concerning the chemical origin of cancer, the historical evolution of federal cancer policy, and the rationale for government intervention through the performance of risk assessment and regulatory action.

At one point, Rushefsky steps back from the controversies to observe that not all the economic benefits of purported carcinogens are worth their continued use, i.e., a risk averse posture on the part of the government might cost us very little if we are clever about our choice of substitutes or changes in the industrial process. Thus, not all decisions to regulate a purported carcinogen need to be based on iron-clad science.

If one were to be critical of this work, it would have to be on the basis of its overzealous attempt at balance. Only peripherally is the question addressed whether all cancer policies are equally valid before the law. If industry sticks too rigidly to scientific standards of proof and if government at times stretches the gap between science and regulatory science in order to regulate, are the sins equivalent because the evidence is viewed either too narrowly or too broadly from a scientific perspective? Risk averseness reflecting the legislative mandates to protect public health by erring on the side of caution is what the law sometimes demands. Indeed, Rushefsky's account of political meddling in the Environmental Protection Agency in the case of formaldlehyde shows why the U.S. Courts of Appeal demand that both a choice of regulatory policy and a change in the course of that policy be fully justified. The initial protective course charted by the regulatory agencies and endorsed by the courts in the 1970s was illegally changed in the early 1980s. The courts forced the agencies to reconsider their ill-founded reversals. A regulatory policy based on strict scientific standards of proof is unlikely to have survived even if the regulatory agencies had begun that way. Such a policy would be clearly in violation of the legislative mandate provided in most environmental laws.

In addition to giving valuable historical accounting and analysis, this work provides the reader with understanding of the role of scientific advisory committees and blue ribbon panels in the formulation of regulatory policy. Both properly constituted and balanced advisory forums and close judicial scrutiny are necessary to ensure that political decisions are not clothed unjustifiably in the mantle of science. This work provides clear and valuable insight that can enable the critical analyst or reader to identify the hidden values affecting decisions in risk assessment and risk management, and to appreciate the difficulty in separating technical from policy determinations. Hopefully, this book will contribute towards creating a new respect for the challenging task of protecting the public from carcinogenic risks.

1

Science, Uncertainty, and Politics

Sure, you can show newspaper pictures of chemical swamps in New Jersey that ought to be cleaned up, but what do you do about the many new chemicals introduced into the marketplace each year? And is there enough knowledge in the scientific community to allow one to take current law and regulations, and move them forward?

--McGowan in "Examining the Role," 1983, p. 6

For the last ten years or so, various federal agencies have proposed and adopted policies designed to protect the population from exposure to those chemical substances that may cause cancer (carcinogens). These policies, known as generic cancer risk assessment guidelines,[1] or cancer policy for short, are documents telling those inside and outside the agency what kinds of evidence will be used to decide how and when carcinogens will be regulated. The guidelines have been a controversial subject of congressional review and of various interest groups' political action. This book examines those policies and the politics surrounding them. Because cancer policy is a highly technical and complex subject, I also focus on its scientific underpinnings, for science has become a surrogate for arguing over the policies themselves. I explore, then, scientific controversies, the politics underlying the policies and changes in those policies, and the content of the guidelines themselves.

5

The principal problem facing regulators is decision making under uncertainty, and the perspective of this book is on the choices facing regulators. My major argument is that the mixing of facts and values, science and politics, is inevitable in developing and applying risk assessment guidelines. Science, in its regulatory incarnation, is used to forward political goals by all sides in the disputes. Even those who seek a separation of the technical and political components of cancer policy do so for political purposes.

This chapter lays the groundwork for the book. Here, I examine four themes that will be woven throughout the book and that explain much of the rocky course in the development of cancer policy. The four themes are (1) scientific uncertainty, or the problem of imperfect knowledge, (2) controversies within the scientific and larger communities, (3) the mixing of science and politics in cancer policy, and (4) the political uses of science.

The Problem of Imperfect Knowledge

The uncertainty in the scientific basis for regulatory policy making is the first of our themes. Complete knowledge about the causes of cancer, cancer mechanisms, and the progression of cancer from initiation to observation of tumors is not currently available, though considerable progress has been made in recent years. The difficulty, from a policy standpoint, is that policymakers want "yes" or "no" answers, but science provides three answers: "yes," "no," and "maybe" (see chapter 2). The problem is how to translate the "maybe" answer into the two options that policymakers face ("Examining the Role," 1983). To bridge gaps in the scientific foundation, various assumptions must be made.

Given these uncertainties, how are regulators to act? There are some (e.g., Epstein, 1978) who believe that our knowledge base is sufficient to undertake prudent, conservative, protectionist policies. There are others (e.g., Efron, 1984) who assert that any protective action in the presence of uncertainty is unwarranted.

Case Study: The Broad Street Pump

This regulatory dilemma is well illustrated by the testimony of

Richard Bates during the Occupational Safety and Health Administration (OSHA) hearings on its generic cancer policy.

> A classic episode in the history of disease prevention took place in London in 1854. An epidemic of cholera occurred in the neighborhood around Broad Street. John Snow, the hero of the story, studied the habits of the victims and found that almost all obtained their water from the well on Broad Street. Swift action was taken; the pump was closed down and the epidemic rapidly subsided. This disease was caused by exposure to the bacterium *Vibrio cholerae*. (Occupational Safety and Health Administration, 1980, p. 5008)

Bates then described how critics might have countered the proposed action, given the lack of evidence about the cause of the cholera epidemic.

> Many scientists would point out that it had not been conclusively demonstrated that the water was the cause of the disease. They would be troubled because of the lack of satisfactory theoretical knowledge to explain how the water could have caused the disease. Furthermore, other habits of those who had become ill had not been adequately investigated, so it would not be possible to rule out other causes of the disease. The scientists would have been correct. Others would have pointed out that some members of the community who drank from the Broad Street well had not succumbed to the cholera. Thus, even if there were something wrong with the water, there must be other factors involved, and if we could control these we would not have to be concerned about the water. These conclusions are also correct. Some who consume water from the Broad Street well would have objected to closing it because the taste of the water from other wells was not as agreeable. Finally, if the pump had been owned by an individual who sold the water, he would certainly have protested against closing down his business on the basis of inconclusive evidence of hazard. (Occupational Safety and Health Administration, 1980, p. 5008)

LESSONS FROM THE CASE STUDY. Bates drew several conclusions from this story that apply to the regulation of chemical carcinogens. First, if a substance is in fact hazardous, exposure control may be necessary to save lives before conclusive evidence is available. The alternative, experiments on human beings, is unacceptable. Second, disease development in an individual is due to the interaction of a variety of factors. Third, the incidence of disease in a population can be reduced by decreasing either exposure or susceptibility, the option depending upon the state of knowledge at the time (Occupational Safety and Health Administration, 1980).

Bates's conclusions suggest that we apply the lessons of the Broad Street pump to chemical carcinogenesis. Certainly, his description of how some might react to a similar situation today characterizes many environmental disputes over the last fifteen years. Yet there are some critical differences between Bates's cholera example and cancer. For one thing, John Snow's effort was not quite the success that Bates described; the epidemic had already peaked by the time Snow's study led to closing off the pump (Goldstein and Goldstein, 1978). Moreover, cholera is an acute disease; the time from exposure to the onset of disease is fairly short. Turning off the Broad Street pump would have quickly eliminated the epidemic. But cancer is a chronic disease and develops only after a long latency period. There is only one cause of cholera, a particular bacteria; cancer is a variety of diseases with a variety of causes (Cairns, 1978). There is no pump that can be turned off to stop the spread of cancer. Even if there were such a "pump," the effects would not be seen for two decades or more because of the chronic nature of cancer. Establishing a clear cause-and-effect relationship between exposure to a substance and cancer is extremely difficult.

While Bates's story indicated the need, perhaps, to take precautionary measures even in the absence of complete knowledge, the case study also points up important differences that make defending prudent cancer policies formidable. The uncertainties that mark cancer policies, more burdensome than in the cholera case, permit scientific controversies to erupt and fester.

Scientific Controversies

Risk assessment is the characterization of possibly adverse human health effects. Because of the gaps in the scientific foundation of cancer, there are numerous points where assumptions and inferences must be made to complete a risk assessment. The totality of those assumptions and inferences are what may be called "risk assessment policy" (National Research Council, 1983). These assumptions lead to controversies, both within the "scientific estate" (Price, 1965; Hamlett, 1984) and in the larger society. The following case study illustrates the nature of these controversies and provides a brief but instructive example of the problems inherent in formulating generic cancer policy.

Case Study: Ionizing Radiation

Cancers may be caused by biological, physical, and chemical agents and also by radiation. The emphasis of this book is on chemical carcinogenesis, but the model for chemical carcinogenesis has been ionizing radiation. An assumption was made that radiation and chemical carcinogenesis were similar and that principles applicable to the former could be applied to the latter.[2] (See the early risk assessment documents of the early 1970s discussed in chapter 3.) Many of the questions about risk assessments of ionizing radiation have also been raised about those of chemical carcinogenesis.

Ionizing radiation is particle or wave radiation removing or adding charges from atoms and molecules. It has both natural and man-made sources. Natural sources include cosmic radiation, some radiation from sources on earth, and some from natural radioisotopes within the human body. Man-made sources include building materials, nuclear power reactors, television, medical diagnostic procedures, and fallout from nuclear weapons. It was the latter, and especially the bombing of Hiroshima and Nagasaki, that led to research in this field (Beebe, 1982).

The early studies of ionizing radiation led to concern about chronic or long-term biological effects from extremely small doses. A committee of the National Academy of Sciences (NAS) was formed to estimate the risk from radiation and to establish a basis for regulation. Its report, issued in 1972 and known as "BEIR I" (Biological Effects of Ionizing Radiation), adopted a "linear non-threshold dose-response model" (National Academy of Sciences, 1970). This model, which plays an important role in the regulation of chemical carcinogens, states that the incidence of cancer, the major biological effect of ionizing radiation (Beebe, 1982), is directly proportional to dose. One important implication is that there is no dose at which some effect might not occur. Radiation acts on DNA, and it is this change that produces neoplasms (malignant tumors); even a single exposure might initiate the process of carcinogenesis. This model challenged an earlier hypothesis that there was a threshold, a point of exposure below which no effects would occur. Because research failed to identify the threshold, the linear model was adopted by BEIR I and accepted in a second report, BEIR II (Council on Environmental Quality, 1978).

The controversy began with BEIR III in 1979. That report also adopted the linear nonthreshold model. The chairman of the NAS committee, Edward P. Radford, stressed that the model probably overstated actual impacts but that it was in general a reasonable estimation of dose-response effects. At the May 2 news conference announcing the report, however, it was clear that there was no unanimity within the committee. Six members dissented, asserting that injuries from exposure diminish more rapidly as exposure decreases (Marshall, 1979). This minority group, led by Harold H. Rossi, preferred an alternative, the quadratic model. Diagrams 1.1 and 1.2 illustrate the shape of the two models. By the end of May, a majority of the experts on the committee had written to the NAS asking for changes. In response, the academy formed a six-member subcommittee to resolve the controversy ("BEIR Report," 1979).

The subsequent subcommittee report (the subcommittee included neither Radford nor Rossi), issued July 29, 1980, offered a compromise. The report characterized the positions as two extremes, with the linear model at the upper end and the quadratic at the lower end. The resolution was to adopt a model midway between the other two, a linear quadratic model (Reinhold, 1980).[3] Diagram 1.3 illustrates the shape of this model.

LESSONS FROM THE CASE STUDY. This story illustrates a number of points that will be elaborated in this book. First is the problem of uncertainty. Despite the vast amount of research that has been conducted on ionizing radiation, there are still many unknowns. To deal with those unknowns, scientists and policymakers have made assumptions that bridge gaps in knowledge; those assumptions have policy implications. A risk-averse model, such as the linear model, implies a strict regulatory posture. A more risk-

DIAGRAM 1.1. Linear Dose-Response Curve

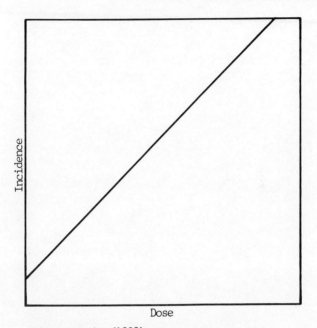

Source: Beebe (1982).

The linear dose-response curve suggests that
there is a proportional response to the dose:
as the dose increases or decreases, the tumor
response increases or decreases by the same
percentage.

tolerant one, such as the quadratic model, implies a more lenient
regulatory posture.

A second point is that scientists and science inevitably become
intimately involved in policy disputes. If science forms a basis for
policy, it becomes inherently political (see the discussion in chapter
8 of the NAS reports on diet and cancer and nutritional
guidelines).

Finally, the method of resolving the scientific (and policy)
dispute was a compromise that split the difference between two extreme positions. We expect compromise in a legislative or ad-

DIAGRAM 1.2.   Quadratic Dose-Response Curve

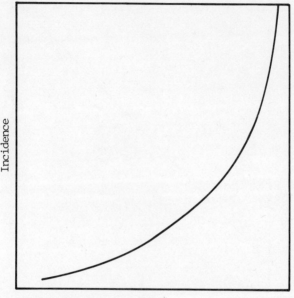

Source: Beebe (1982).

The quadratic dose-response curve suggests that
the change in tumor response at low dose levels
is smaller than the change of dose levels but is
higher at high dose levels than the change in
dose levels.

ministrative arena, but we are surprised to see negotiated compromise in the scientific arena. Its existence there reinforces the
point about the relationship between science and politics and also
indicates the peculiar problems inherent in mixing politics and
science. Each 'estate', or cluster of participants (Price, 1965;
Hamlett, 1984), has its own method of resolving disputes. Difficulties arise when political methods of dispute resolution are im-
posed upon scientific methods.

DIAGRAM 1.3.   Linear Quadratic Dose-Response Curve

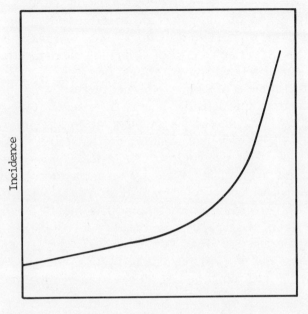

Dose

Source: Beebe (1982).

The linear quadratic dose-response curve suggests
a linear tumor response at low dose levels but a
more rapid tumor response change at higher dose
levels.

Mixing Science and Politics

Because of the uncertainties and controversies over cancer
policy, there is an inevitable mixture of science and politics. Yet
there are those, such as twice Environmental Protection Agency
administrator William Ruckelshaus, who advocate a strong
separation of "risk assessment" and "risk management" (though
in Ruckelshaus's case perhaps to protect an agency rocked by

scandal) (Ruckelshaus, 1983, p. 1027). *Risk assessment*, to repeat, is defined by the National Research Council (NRC) as "the characterization of the potential adverse health of human exposures to environmental hazards"; *risk management* is defined by the NRC as "the process of evaluating alternative regulatory actions and selecting them" (National Research Council, 1983, p. 18).[4] The former is presumed to be an objective, scientific process for estimating the potential hazard of a substance, action, or technology. Judging the acceptability of the hazard—deciding what is safe—is risk management, the subjective, value-laden, political aspect of risk control. EPA asserted this separation of science and policy in its recent reassessment of risk assessment policy (Environmental Protection Agency, 1984c). While those who write in this area admit the practical difficulties of separating the various stages, the separation is accepted, at least conceptually, as a goal to be achieved. Thus we have what Hadden (1984) calls the "two-stage model of risk regulation," with the technical or scientific portion providing the basis for (and preceding) the political decision.

Risk assessments are, however, mixtures of facts and assumptions, again because of insufficient data and theoretical gaps in the underlying science. The 1984 White House Office of Science and Technology Policy (OSTP) draft report distinguished among facts, consensus, assumptions, and science policy decisions. The distinctions among these four concepts demonstrate how the strict version of the two-stage model readily breaks down. For that reason, we consider these concepts at some length.

The OSTP report began with a statement of 31 principles (see appendix A and chapter 6). The principles were described in a revealing manner.

> Since there are gaps in the information available, differences in evaluations and in scientific opinion may exist about certain of the points highlighted as principles. However, these principles derive from a *weltanschauung* utilizing a balanced approach with an appreciation of all elements of the problem. (Office of Science and Technology Policy, 1984, p. 21597)

According to the report, *facts* are "statements supported by data" (Office of Science and Technology Policy, 1984, p. 21599).

An example of a fact is the statement that substance *x* produces a rate of cancer in mice greater than is expected by chance (with a probability level specified). An animal bioassay is conducted, it produces a certain result, and a conclusion is drawn from that experiment. Even here there might be controversy; critics might point to problems in the conduct of the study. A *consensus* statement is one that is "generally held in the scientific community" (Office of Science and Technology Policy, 1984, p. 21599). An example of a consensus statement is the first principle in the OSTP report: that carcinogenesis is a multistage phenomenon that is influenced by a variety of factors. *Assumptions* are "statements made to fill data gaps" (Office of Science and Technology Policy, 1984, p. 21599). An example of an assumption in cancer risk assessment is OSTP principle #8, which states in part that "agents found carcinogenic in animal studies . . . are considered suspect human carcinogens" (Office of Science and Technology Policy, 1984, p. 21598). Finally, there are *science policy decisions*, "statements made to resolve points of current controversy" (Office of Science and Technology Policy, 1984, p. 21599). An example of a science policy statement is OSTP principle #11, that it is appropriate to use high doses in animal bioassays because of the design limitations of those tests (the small number of animals used, usually 100).

OSTP thus provided a somewhat different description of risk assessment than that implied in the two-stage model.

> Because these issues and data gaps can be pivotal in the process, it may be necessary to make judgments about these unresolved issues and assumptions to adjust for deficiencies in the underlying data base that will permit risk assessments to be completed. These judgments and assumptions should be plausible and, to the extent possible, be based on the scientific information at hand. However, the validity of these judgments and assumptions often cannot be conclusively established, so the risk assessment process should not be viewed as strictly 'scientific' in the usual sense of the word. Instead, risk assessment involves a complex blend of current scientific data, reasonable assumptions and scientific judgments that permit decisions to be made in the absence of complete information. (Office of Science and Technology Policy, 1984, p. 21657)[5]

For that reason alone, the two-stage model is an inadequate description of risk assessment. Hadden (1984) offers four other reasons for the blurring of these lines. First, the temporal distinction between the two stages (assessment forming the basis for management) is fuzzy. She points to Congress's role in writing legislation that provides guidelines by which agencies may regulate risk. Thus, both the legislative and executive branches engage in scientific and political determinations. The second reason is the difficulty of separating technical values from other values. Different cultural values may determine which risks are the focus of attention (Douglas and Wildavsky, 1982; Majone, 1984; Rayner, 1984). Scientists can differ in their ideological viewpoints about technical hazards (Lynn, 1983; Rushefsky, 1977;), and they can also be influenced by epistemological differences (Robbins and Johnston, 1976; Rushefsky, 1982).

Changes in scientific information and capability are Hadden's third explanation for the blurred distinction between risk assessment and risk management. New information may trigger new rounds of decision making. For instance, in the case of the herbicide 2,4,5-T, the inadequacy of the monitoring equipment (with detection limits in the parts per million) inhibited the EPA from restricting the herbicide's use. Efforts by the EPA and industry to develop more sensitive equipment (detection in the parts per trillion) were instrumental in later efforts that eventually led to the withdrawal of the herbicide from the market.

The final factor that Hadden lists is the complex federal system and pluralistic interests. Risk assessment, indeed research itself, may differ depending upon who conducts it. Scientists for industry generally produce studies supportive of industry positions (von Hippel and Primack, 1971.)[6] Thus, the two-stage model suffers from both conceptual and practical difficulties.

That there is a mix of facts and values has been pointed out by others (Weinberg, 1972; McGarity, 1979; Whittemore, 1983). Weinberg gives the classic statement of this problem. He labels the types of issues discussed in this book as "trans-scientific": "questions which can be asked of science and yet *which cannot be answered by science*" (Weinberg, 1972, p. 209; emphasis in original). Strictly scientific issues can be settled through traditional scientific mechanisms of debate and peer review. Trans-scientific issues, on which scientists may and do offer opinions, are settled through political and adversarial proceedings. The confusion of factual and value judgements, combined with the uncertainties inherent in risk assessment, lead to political uses of scientific disputes.

> The large uncertainties endemic to toxicant risk data invite differing interpretations. While these interpretations often reflect the philosophical viewpoint of the interpreter, they are presented, criticized, and defended as scientific conclusions. (Whittemore, 1983, p. 28)

Risk assessment is thus only partially a scientific endeavor. Yet the two-stage model does seem to have been accepted by the Environmental Protection Agency in its latest cancer policy document. In chapters 6 and 8 I will again examine EPA's recent risk assessment initiative and the separation of facts and values.

The Political Uses Of Science

This discussion leads to the fourth, and final, theme of the book: the use of science to promote the political values of various actors. The cancer policy documents discussed in this book have a strong scientific or technical component. But some individual or organization must see the need for such a policy, and some regulatory agency must embrace it. The decision to recognize a problem and adopt a policy is a political one. For that reason alone, risk assessment guidelines are inherently intertwined with politics.

There is also a very close association between one's view about the need for a cancer policy and the strictness of that policy, and one's position on the various controversies over scientific assumptions. This association is pointed out in chapter 2 and is demonstrated in chapter 5. The Reagan administration, opposed to strong environmental programs, attempted to change cancer policies to a more risk-tolerant posture by using what it called new scientific developments as the basis for those changes. When this posture became caught up in the scandals surrounding the EPA in 1982–1983, those defending the older policies (1976–1980) asserted that the scientific basis had not changed and that there was a strong consensus on cancer policy. The recent risk assessment effort within the EPA and the insistence on the distinction between risk assessment and risk management seem to be an attempt to produce a somewhat less restrictive cancer policy, though the attempt is clearly not as determined as it was during the early Reagan administration years. As we shall see, the earlier periods of cancer policy development are also marked by those attempting to forward political views through science. Because those policies are, by definition, shaped by the political system, I must focus as much on the political as on the technical components.

Looking Ahead

The next six chapters develop these four themes in greater detail. In chapter 2 I examine the nature of science and compare it to something called "regulatory" science. I also look at a number of controversies that have marked cancer policy development and compare the success with which nine cancer policy documents issued during the 1976–1984 period resolved those controversies. Chapters 3–6 focus on the political and policy aspects of cancer policy. In chapter 3 I develop two models, one of agenda setting to explain why the federal government began to address the need for cancer policies and how those policies developed over time, and a second model to describe the interaction among the various estates. Chapter 3 also concentrates on the early, pre-1977 stage of cancer policy development. Chapter 4 describes the 1977–1980 period, when consensus among regulatory agencies was established. In chapter 5 I examine the 1981–1983 period, which was marked by an attempt to change cancer policy from risk-averse to more risk-tolerant positions. Chapter 6 describes the scandals surrounding EPA that afflicted the Reagan administration, and the partial return to the earlier consensus. In all four chapters, I explore the content of the policies themselves as well as their political context.

Chapter 7 addresses some larger issues and questions the underlying rationale for the existence of cancer policy. Is there a cancer epidemic that necessitates governmental action? Are chemicals an important, if not the most important, cause of cancer? Given the uncertainties in the scientific foundation, is risk assessment a valid enterprise? In particular, I look at the challenge to cancer policy given by Edith Efron (1984) in *The Apocalytics*, called by some the *"Silent Spring* of the counter-revolution" (Ames, 1984, p. 98). Chapter 8 summarizes our argument, describes the parallel and interactive development of science and policy, and offers some judgments about, and recommendations for, cancer policy.

2

Science, And Regulatory Science

> One of the things concerning us at *Environment* and at the
> Scientists Institute—something concerning many other people as
> well—is how one turns science into regulation, or how one turns
> what is known or not known in the scientific community into
> regulations that protect the health and safety of individuals and
> the environment, insofar as the environment can be separated
> from individuals.
>
> --McGowan in "Examining the Role," 1983, p. 6

Science's unquestionable benefits have come at a price. One source of concern is the possibility that chemical substances found in consumer products, the environment, and the workplace may cause cancer and other health problems. The pesticide DDT, for instance, has saved more lives than any other chemical; at the same time, it was found to bioaccumulate in the environment and the food chain, and has been implicated as a carcinogen. The mineral asbestos is an excellent insulator, but also a well-documented human carcinogen.[1] Similarly, although polychlorinated biphenols (PCBs) have been used for years as insulators in electrical equipment, they are some of the most toxic substances known. A 1982 fire in the state office building in Binghamton, New York, spread PCBs throughout the building and rendered it unusable. Science thus can simultaneously promote and threaten human welfare.

Cancer risk assessment (a form of technology assessment) is an attempt to anticipate and control one potentially harmful im-

21

pact of science and technology. In this chapter, I explore the technical basis for cancer policy and examine some of the problems created by that technical base. My tasks are threefold. First, I explore the nature of science, what I shall call "normal" science, and compare it to a sibling labelled "regulatory" science. Second, I describe the major elements of risk assessment and the gaps that require inferences, assumptions, and science policy decisions. Third, I look at ten specific risk assessment disputes and compare how the major cancer policies issued or proposed during the 1976–1984 period resolved them.

Normal Science and Regulatory Science

Normal Science

A thorough understanding of the nature of science would require delving into a number of different academic fields. To understand the problems of cancer policy, the requirements are fortunately fewer: we can select from academic fields only that which is useful to us. The purpose of this section is to show that many of the problems of cancer policy and the disputes surrounding it are rooted in the capabilities and limitations of science. Policymakers may assume for political purposes more certainty than the scientific foundation warrants. Some of those critical of cancer risk assessment, such as Efron (1984), have based their critique on a naive understanding of science, in both its normal and regulatory incarnations. I return to this point in chapter 7.

Goldstein and Goldstein (1978, p. 6) offer a useful definition of science. Science, according to them, has three distinguishing features:

1. It is a search for understanding, for a sense of having found a satisfactory explanation for some aspect of reality.

2. The understanding is achieved by means of statements of general laws or principles—laws applicable to the widest possible variety of phenomena.

3. The laws or principles can be tested experimentally.

If we substitute the term *theories* for *laws* and *principles*, the last feature requires some elaboration. Theories themselves are not tested; they cannot be directly confirmed or denied. Rather, predictions or implications derived from those theories are tested; this principle is called the "verification principle." If the predictions are confirmed, then we have more confidence in the theory. If the predictions are not confirmed, then we have less confidence. It is also possible that predictions cannot be tested because of lack of appropriate instruments or for other reasons. In that event, we withhold judgment until experiments can be made. The important point is that derivations from theories can, in principle, be tested.

Useful as this definition is in distinguishing science from other endeavors, it takes us only so far. Normal science has three other critical features: (1) it is a body of knowledge that accumulates and changes over time; (2) it is a process which operates on the basis of consensus and produces public knowledge; and (3) the knowledge produced is rarely deterministic but has greater or lesser degrees of uncertainty. I consider each of these features in turn.

A body of knowledge, an "archive" (Ziman, 1978), accumulates over time. That archive is both cumulative and revolutionary. It is cumulative in the sense that it builds on previous work, but revolutionary in the sense that it does not accept all that was done in the past. New theories (paradigms) are accepted and displace older ones. Knowledge based on the older theories may have at best only historical interest (Kuhn, 1970). Science as a body of knowledge is thus dynamic. Policies based on science need to take into account this feature of scientific knowledge. It is certainly a legitimate criticism to point out, as some have done, that policies need to be changed to address new developments.

Science as a body of knowledge is complemented by science as a process, what scientists do and how they do it. Scientists develop theories, make observations, conduct experiments, and so forth. The knowledge they produce, the archive, is what Ziman (1978) calls "public knowledge." It is public in the sense that scientific advances require confirmation and agreement by the community of scientists in a particular field; that is, science as a process operates consensually (Ziman, 1978). Experiments are capable of replication, though replication may be infrequent (Broad and Wade, 1982). Publication of scientific findings, primarily in journals, is subject to peer review. Thus the results become public so that others may evaluate them. The community is governed by a set of informal norms (Barber, 1952; Merton, 1968) as well as by counternorms (Mitroff, 1974) that guide behavior. Those governing norms, such as disinterestedness, universalism, organized skepticism, and communality, ensure that the evaluation is a public process.

Finally, science is not deterministic. All experiments are subject to a certain amount of error; phenomena often behave randomly.[2] Behn and Vaupel (1982, pp. 189–190) describe the importance of the change from a deterministic view of science to a probabilistic one.

> In the seventeenth century, Newton and his laws of motion so dominated scientific thinking that natural law was implicitly defined as one that made deterministic, causal predictions. By the nineteenth century, however, scientific theories that offered probabilistic and statistical predictions were quite acceptable. As Jacob Bronowski has emphasized [in *The Common Sense of Science*], this progress required a revolution in scientific thinking. As a result, in the nineteenth and twentieth centuries natural science made major advances with the discovery of several probabilistic laws: Mendel's laws of heredity; the kinetic theory of gases developed by Maxwell, Calusius, and Boltzmann; and the laws of radioactive decay developed by Rutherford and Soddy, and by von Schweidler.
>
> This shift from a deterministic to a probabilistic paradigm culminated in the formulation of Heisenberg's uncertainty principle, which states the limits to accuracy with which the physical measurements of subatomic particles can be made. No matter how sophisticated the instrumentation, there are inherent uncertainties in the measurements of position and/or momentum. Much of the research now being done in the natural sciences would not be possible without the replacement of deterministic thinking with probabilistic thinking.

The probabilistic nature of science leads to the type of logic endemic to normal science. Ziman (1978) distinguishes between two-valued and three-valued logic. *Two-valued logic* produces "true" or "false" answers. *Three-valued logic* adds the category of the "undecided." This category arises because of various kinds of imprecisions, such as errors in measurement. Physical experiments produce a certain amount of error, and knowledge is gained as error is reduced. In normal sciences, particularly the natural sciences, the undecided category is excluded. As we move from the natural to the social sciences, such as epidemiology, we move from more to less certainty, to more stochastic processes and a greater reliance on statistical reasoning. Determinism is less and less a feature, and idiosyncratic factors play a greater role. For example, if two people smoke and are subject to asbestos exposure, we can say that statistically their chances of getting lung cancer are quite high. Yet one may get it and one may not. (Recall the cholera problem from the previous chapter.) Why? And what does this uncertainty mean for establishing the relationship between smoking, asbestos exposure, and cancer? Can we even tell why someone gets cancer or what the basic mechanisms of cancer are? And if we cannot, do we have "reliable knowledge"? Ziman (1978) would argue that the test of a theory is confirmation of predictions. But if confirmations are statistical only, that is, if we can detect general trends but cannot predict for any individual, is our scientific base valid or invalid? These questions in regard to regulatory science have their source in the nature of normal science.

Regulatory Science

Regulatory science looks and acts much like normal science; the major difference is how it is used. Regulatory science may be defined as science with specific and deliberate public policy implications or with a public policy agenda. For example, under the provisions of the 1976 Toxic Substances Control Act (TSCA), chemicals must be tested and the results submitted to the Environmental Protection Agency (EPA) so that the possible harmful effects of the substance can be determined. Thus, any experiments conducted to meet the requirements of TSCA and its regulations would be part of regulatory science. Regulatory science has also developed its own unique institutions: government, industry, and independent testing laboratories, as well as academic research facilities. For example, the Chemical Industry Institute of Toxicology (CIIT) is an industry-funded but independently operated laboratory established as a result of the passage of TSCA (Wessel, 1980). The features that characterize normal science, such as uncertainty, consensus, and change, also describe regulatory science.

At the same time, regulatory science has its own peculiar features: three-valued logic, direct public policy implications (by definition), new roles for scientists, time pressures, and different standards of proof. Because of time pressures and public policy implications, regulatory science does not have the luxury of discarding the "undecided" category of answers as does normal science. Regulatory science as a guide to action requires considerable interpretation and the making of numerous assumptions (recall the discussion in chapter 1 about facts, consensus, assumptions, and science policy decisions).

As such, regulatory science is an inherent part of what Wessel (1980) calls "socio-technical disputes." Such disputes have the following features:

> First, there is always a deep and abiding public interest in its resolution. Second, the information and understanding required in order to come to a rational judgment are extraordinarily complex and difficult to evaluate. Third, a sound final judgment requires the fine tuning and balancing of a number of "quality-of-life" value concerns, about which different people may have widely varying attitudes and feelings. (Wessel, 1980, pp. 4–5)

Complexity, the second feature mentioned by Wessel, arises because of the three-valued logic and the prevalence of the "undecided" category in socio-technical disputes.

These features change the role of the scientist, whose classic image is the dispassionate observer. Even within pure science, such a characterization overstated the reality (Broad and Wade, 1982; Mitroff, 1974; Watson, 1968). As science played an important role in World War II and the postwar era and as the "scientific state" emerged (Schmandt and Katz, 1981), the roles of scientists expanded. They became advisors or experts, people who understood science and could interpret science for lay policymakers.[3] They also became administrators and policymakers themselves. One other role, and perhaps a key role in regulatory science, is as advocate. In many administrative proceedings or congressional hearings, scientists, representing corporate or environmental interests, interpret science and critique and advocate science policy decisions.

Regulatory science is also conducted or used in a different atmosphere than is normal science. In particular, it operates under considerable time pressure, often in a crisis atmosphere. Normal science progresses slowly; regulatory science is forced to provide at least preliminary answers on an expedited basis. Finally, the standards of proof between the two types of sciences are different. Normal scientific standards of proof are strict. Regulatory science, because it is for a specific purpose, is asked to produce sufficient evidence to justify a decision. Sufficiency of evidence is often less than the normal standards of proof, a fact which makes many scientists uncomfortable as advisors and interpreters.[4]

Elements of Risk Assessment

Risk assessment, defined in chapter 1, is clearly a form of regulatory science. As identified in a number of studies (Lave, 1982; National Research Council, 1983; Office of Technology Assessment, 1981), risk assessment consists of four activities that occur in a roughly sequential order: (1) hazard identification, (2) dose-response assessment, (3) exposure assessment, and (4) risk characterization.

Hazard Identification

Hazard identification has one main regulatory purpose: to determine whether or not a particular substance is a carcinogen. This process is known as "qualitative evaluation" and generally requires a "yes" or "no" answer, though it may also produce the "maybe" answer. The three major techniques of hazard identification are discussed below.

EPIDEMIOLOGY "Epidemiology is generally defined as the study of the distribution and determinants of disease in human populations" (Office of Science and Technology Policy, 1984, p. 21640). As such, it is potentially the most satisfactory method of identifying a hazard because it is the only one that directly studies humans. A well-conducted epidemiological study can provide conclusive evidence that a particular substance is carcinogenic to humans. Epidemiological studies are often classified into two basic types: descriptive and causal (Mack et al. 1977; Office of Science and Technology Policy, 1984; Office of Technology Assessment, 1981). Descriptive studies examine patterns of disease among a given population, whereas causal studies seek to determine the factors behind a disease.

There are two types of causal studies, cohort and case-control (Office of Science and Technology Policy, 1984). Cohort studies look at a sample of the population exposed to a specific substance and follow their experience over time. Case-control studies start with individuals that have a disease and compare them to a similar group without the disease to identify risk factors. Both studies are conducted among a relatively small group of people and after a particular pattern of disease has been identified by descriptive studies.

Epidemiology can provide the best and most direct evidence of the carcinogenicity of a particular substance. To say that, however, is not to say that this outcome frequently occurs. On the contrary, almost all epidemiological studies can be criticized for methodological defects, and some see epidemiological data as so inherently weak that they place little reliance on it (e.g., Occupational Safety and Health Administration, 1980). Indeed, we can see how ideological preferences or values reflect the use to which epidemiology and the other methods of hazard identification are put. Those who prefer prudent, risk-averse cancer policies downgrade the importance of epidemiological studies, though admitting their theoretical potential (see "Special Issue," 1984). Others insist that because epidemiology is the only method of directly assessing human carcinogenicity, it should be the only basis for making cancer decisions (e.g., Doll and Peto, 1981; Efron, 1984). What is even more curious is that advocates of both these positions will criticize the same study.

In 1979 the Environmental Protection Agency issued an emergency ban on many uses of the herbicide 2,4,5-T. While the EPA had considered regulatory action against the herbicide for years, the precipitating factor in the agency's decision to intervene was a study it conducted in rural Oregon. Bonnie Hill, a resident of the Alsea, Oregon, area, had a miscarriage and talked with a number of her neighbors. She found what she believed was a disproportionate number of miscarriages during the same period. All the spontaneous abortions occurred during the spring and shortly after (about two months) the herbicide was sprayed in a nearby forest. The herbicide, Hill believed, spread through the air and infected the pregnant women. (It was sprayed by helicopters and light airplanes.) 2,4,5-T contains small portions of an extremely potent form of dioxin, 2,3,7,8-TCDD, which has been implicated as a teratogen in animals.

Hill's story spread through local, state, and national news media in 1978. EPA then conducted two studies, Alsea I and Alsea II, using the case-control method. EPA confirmed, in the wider Alsea II study, the relationship that Hill had strongly suspected and proceeded to ban the herbicide's use in forested areas (Van Strum, 1983).

Oregon State University, a long-time supporter of the forestry industry and the use of herbicides, published a critique of EPA's Alsea II study. The report concluded:

> This critique shows that EPA reached erroneous conclusions from the Alsea II study because of: (1) failure to account for differences in the characteristics between the Study Area and the Rural and Urban control areas, (2) inaccuracies in the collection of data on spontaneous abortions, (3) failure to account for marked differences in the medical practices among areas, (4) incomplete and inaccurate data on 2,4,5-T use, and (5) failure to recognize that the magnitude of the monthly variations in rates of hospitalized spontaneous abortions (HSAb) in all three areas is not greater than would be expected due to random variations. When corrections for some of these problems are applied, we find the rate of spontaneous abortions in the Study area does not appear to be related to the use of 2,4,5-T.

> Retrospective studies such as the Alsea II study are exceedingly difficult to conduct. The net effect of attempting a comparison among several poorly identified populations is to obscure the potentially significant data by the mass of other data containing no information. When poorly done, these studies confuse rather than clarify issues, in this case the risks from using agricultural chemicals in our country. The original contention of the women from Alsea, Oregon, namely that there is a relationship between herbicide use and miscarriages, is not supported by the data in EPA's Alsea II Report. (Wagner et al., 1979, p. 7)

On the other hand, Bonnie Hill, in her testimony during the 2,4,5-T hearings, criticized the same report for understating miscarriages because many spontaneous abortions are not reported to hospitals or occur in them. Epidemiological studies frequently confront this attack from both sides, an obvious indication that value conflicts are integral to risk assessment.

In the absence of direct experiments on humans, which is not done for obvious ethical reasons, epidemiology suffers from numerous problems that make sole reliance upon it difficult to justify. First, because the incidence of cancer is so great (the estimate is that 25 percent of the population will get cancer), we must be able to distinguish cancer caused by the suspect substance from overall cancer incidence.[5] Unless the cancer is unique, epidemiological methods are unlikely to be sensitive enough to make the distinction. A second problem is the small number of subjects generally used in the study. One would need a rather potent carcinogen to detect effects. Epidemiological studies should be accompanied by a discussion of the "power of the test," the ability of a study to detect an impact if there is one. As the Oregon State University critique of the Alsea II study suggested, it is also difficult to find appropriate control or matching groups. As Arundel and Sterline (1984) put it, epidemiological studies are difficult to design if any of the following occurs: the chemical is common, there are other possible causes of the disease, and there is low relative risk. They conclude:

> We return to the fundamentals of science.
> All scientific evidence is presumptive. It presents a series of observations on which a *prudent* person would judge an association to exist or not to exist. Prudence thus imposes two conditions for judging whether or not epidemiological evidence is meaningful in evaluating a possible association between a disease and exposure to a known toxic contaminant in the environment:
>
> 1) Epidemiological evidence must be considered as only supporting data from properly conducted animal experiments. . . .
>
> 2) It is not the outcome of a single epidemiological study that is important, but the consistency of results from a number

of studies, which control as much as possible for known confounding and biasing factors. (Arundel and Sterling, 1984, p. 5)

Despite these problems, epidemiology has played an important
role in identifying human carcinogens such as tobacco and
asbestos.

BIOASSAYS. While epidemiological studies have been successfully employed to establish a number of human carcinogens,
the problems discussed above suggest that sole reliance on such
studies is problematical. The most common methodology for
determining the qualitative nature of a substance is the classical
controlled animal experiment, referred to here as the "bioassay."
It should be pointed out, however, that most known human carcinogens were first discovered by epidemiological methods and
were later found to be carcinogenic in animals.

In a typical bioassay, an animal model is selected for the
study, typically a rodent bred for this purpose. The animals (usually 100–200) are then divided into control and experimental groups.
The experimental group is administered the test substance; other-
wise the animals are treated the same. Several doses are commonly
employed, including the maximum tolerated dose (MTD). At
various times during the test period (which usually lasts from 18 to
24 months), selected animals are sacrificed and examined. At the
end of the test period, all the animals are sacrificed. Some tests
may be multigenerational. After the animals are examined,
statistical tests are performed to see whether there are differences
in tumor occurrences between the two groups and whether those
differences are significant.

There are a number of considerations in conducting long-term
bioassays, many of which are discussed in the more comprehensive
guidelines (see in particular Interagency Regulatory Liaison
Group, 1979, and Office of Science and Technology Policy, 1984).
These considerations include the proper mode of administrating
the test substance, the number of different species used, protocols
of experimental design and conduct, evaluation of lesions and
tumors, the number and level of doses, and the applicability of test
systems to humans. Many of these problems will be discussed in
subsequent sections on inferences and controversies. The point remains that animal bioassays are the primary method for testing
chemical carcinogenicity.

However, many problems remain in relying on bioassays to identify human carcinogens, including the metabolic differences between humans and test animals and the high experimental doses necessitated by the small number of animals used in the experiments. More risk-averse guidelines rely primarily on bioassays; more risk-tolerent guidelines stress epidemiological studies. Some of these controversies are considered later in this chapter. The larger question of the validity of risk assessments based on bioassays is examined in chapter 7.

SHORT-TERM TESTS. Long-term bioassays, by definition, take a long time to conduct. In addition, these tests are expensive, costing $200,000 or more per test. Thus, they place financial and technical strains on governmental, private, academic, and independent testing facilities. Short-term tests can be used to evaluate substances in as little as two or three days at a small fraction of the cost of bioassays. They are commonly used as screens to provide a quick view of the potential carcinogenicity of a substance.

The first test developed, and the one most frequently employed, is the Ames test. The fundamental premise underlying the Ames and other short-term tests is that many, though not all, carcinogens are also mutagens: that is, they cause some type of damage to the cell's genetic blueprint. The Ames test (Ames, 1979) combines the test substance with salmonella bacteria and rodent liver cells, for two days. Because the Ames test is apparently sensitive to only certain carcinogens and to certain types of mutagenic effects, other short-term tests have been developed. Usually a battery of such tests is administered on a given substance. The 1984 Office of Science and Technology Policy (OSTP) report lists various types of tests and fourteen different endpoints (types of mutagenic damage) that may be sought. Some systems test for mutation, others for chromosome effects, damage to DNA, and transformation of mammalian cells.

If a chemical creates mutagenic effects, it is strongly suspected to be carcinogenic. To substantiate this hypothesis, results of various short-term assays are correlated with results of bioassays. Correlations of 60 to 80 percent predictability are sufficient for screening purposes but not sufficient as a sole or primary indicator for regulatory action.[6] Some known carcinogens, generally those that are promoters rather than initiators, test negative on all short-term tests.

Dose-Response Assessment

The discussion so far has focused on various methodologies for identifying a substance as a potential carcinogen. I now explore a related aspect, the potency of a substance once it has been so identified. In particular, I am concerned with how tumor response relates to dose or exposure to a substance. There are considerable problems here and inferences that need to be made. Usually a mathematical model is fitted to available data and judgments are made on the basis of that model. For example, in long-term bioassays several doses are administered, the maximum tolerated dose (MTD) and one or more doses that are fractions of the MTD. These two to four data points are then used as the basis for fitting a curve. There are numerous models that can be used, including the one-hit model (which assumes that just one exposure can lead to cancer) and various multistage and multitime models. Each model is essentially a theory of how cancer originates and progresses.

> Quantitative theories of carcinogenesis attempt to relate the frequency and time of occurrence of detectable tumors to the concentration and potency of the carcinogen, the age and susceptibility of the host, the duration of exposure to the carcinogen, etc. The theories can be tested by comparing their predictions with observed human cancer incidence and with the results of animal experiments in which cancers are produced by the application of carcinogens. (Whittemore and Keller, 1978, p. 1)

The indication of a dose-response effect is often used by regulatory agencies as confirmation that a substance is indeed a carcinogen.

Quantitative evaluation faces several critical problems. First, the number of data points is quite limited. Second, given the prevalent use of animal bioassays, the data points (doses) commonly used in those tests are considerably higher than those involved in normal human exposure. The most fundamental problem of dose-response assessment, however, is that many of the models fit the data at the observed range but differ dramatically at the lower doses more common to humans (see Lave, 1982, and Office of Technology Assessment, 1981). Table 2.1 from the Office of Technology Assessment (OTA) report (1981) illustrates this problem. At observed doses, the models are essentially identical; at extrapolated doses, the variation in results is great. The model that is selected can have significant regulatory implications. The challenge for researchers is to develop more accurate models.

Table 2.1
Comparing Extrapolation Models

Project percentage of tumor-bearing animals

Dose level	Log-normal model (infralinear)	Log-logistic model (infralinear)	One-hit model (linear at incidence below 10%)
16	98	96	100
4	84	84	94
1	50	50	50
1/4	16	16	16
1/16	2	4	4
1/100	0.05	0.4	0.7
1/1,000	0.00035	0.26	0.07
1/10,000	0.0000001	0.0016	0.007

Source: Office of Technology Assessment (1981), p. 163.

Exposure Assessment

Hazard identification focuses on whether or not a substance is a carcinogen. Dose-response assessment explores the potency of a substance as a carcinogen using the methodologies of hazard identification and the nature of the tumor response to various dose levels. The other important element of risk assessment is estimating the size of the population that has been exposed to the carcinogen. A potent carcinogen to which many are exposed would be subject to regulation. A weak carcinogen to which few are exposed would most likely not be a candidate. Middle situations, such as a weak carcinogen with wide exposure or a strong carcinogen with little exposure, present more troubling problems for regulators.

Exposure assessment seeks different types of data than does hazard identification or dose-response assessment. Air, soil, and land samples and consumer products are surveyed to detect possible exposures to carcinogens. Because data-gathering problems are substantial, analysts must resort to modeling possible exposures.

As an example, in the early 1970s liquid wastes were sprayed in several areas of Missouri to control dust. The wastes contained 2,3,7,8-TCDD, the most potent form of dioxin. The contaminated wastes were removed, but detectable levels of dioxin remained in the soil and became part of the events surrounding Times Beach, Missouri, in 1982. The Carcinogen Assessment Group (CAG) of the Environmental Protection Agency prepared an exposure assessment. Soil samples were collected from various parts of the contaminated area, and estimates were made of exposure to the dioxin contaminant in the soil. CAG had to estimate exposure by three different routes: ingestion, inhalation, and skin absorption. For instance, it estimated how much soil a child ingests in a given day. Various assumptions were used in making these estimates.

All people ingest a certain amount of dust or soil during the course of their lives. The sources of this material range from the food we eat to the dirt from our hands. The behavior of children is such that they generally ingest a proportionately greater amount of soil/dust than do adults. In fact, some children have a particularly strong tendency to ingest this material and are referred to as pick children. The amount of soil ingested by these youngsters ranges from 1-10 g/d.

For the purposes of this exposure/risk assessment the following assumptions are made:

1. The ingester is a 20 kg child.

2. All of the soil ingested by the child is contaminated with 2,3,7,8-TCDD.

3. All of the 2,3,7,8-TCDD on the soil becomes bioavailable upon ingestion.

4. The exposure continues for 7 years. (*PCB and Dioxin Cases*, p. 63)

Note that these are rather risk-averse, or "worst-case", assumptions. The actual likelihood is that some of the soil ingested by a child will not be contaminated and that not all of the dioxin in the soil is absorbed by the body. Yet, for lack of actual data, these may be reasonable premises. On the basis of these assumptions, CAG then calculated probable exposures. The calculations were repeated for adults and for other forms of exposure (inhalation and skin absorption). The result was a range of exposures to the contaminant. Exposure assessment thus involves many assumptions and inferences.

Risk Characterization

The last step in risk assessment is evaluation, or risk characterization. All of the data gathered during the previous steps are combined and a judgment about the substance is made. Table 2.2 lists eighteen substances for which there is sufficient human evidence of carcinogenicity, plus other substances for which the evidence is limited.[7]

Table 2.2
Evaluating the Carcinogenicity of Chemicals

	Degree of evidence	
Chemicals	*Humans*	*Bioassays*
Chemicals judged carcinogenic for humans		
4-aminobiphenyl	sufficient	sufficient
Arsenic and certain arsenic compounds	sufficient	inadequate
Asbestos	sufficient	sufficient
Benzene	sufficient	inadequate
Benzidine	sufficient	sufficient
N,N-bis (2-chlorethyl)-2-napthylamine (chlornaphazine)	sufficient	limited
Bis (chloromethyl) ether and technical grade chloromethyl ether	sufficient	sufficient
Chromium and certain chromium compounds	sufficient	sufficient
Diethylstilboestrol (DES)	sufficient	sufficient
Melphalan	sufficient	sufficient
Mustard gas	sufficient	limited
2-napthylamine	sufficient	sufficient
Soots, tars, and mineral oils	sufficient	sufficient
Vinyl chloride	sufficient	sufficient

Table 2.2 (Cont'd)
Evaluating the Carcinogenicity of Chemicals

| | Degree of evidence | |
Chemicals	Humans	Bioassays
Chemicals judged probably carcinogenic for humans Group A: Chemicals with "higher degrees of evidence"		
Aflatoxins	limited	sufficient
Cadmium and cadmium compounds	limited	sufficient
Chlorambucil	limited	sufficient
Cyclophosphamide	limited	sufficient
Nickel and certain nickel compounds	limited	sufficient
Tris (1-aziridinyl) phosphine sulphide (thiotepa)	limited	sufficient
Group B: Chemicals with "lower degrees of evidence"		
acrylonite	limited	sufficient
amitrole (aminotriazole)	inadequate	sufficient
auramine	limited	limited
beryllium and certain beryllium compounds	limited	sufficient
carbon tetrachloride	inadequate	sufficient
dimethylcarbamoyl chloride	inadequate	sufficient
dimethyl sulphate	inadequate	sufficient
ethylene oxide	limited	inadequate
iron dextran	inadequate	sufficient
oxymetholone	limited	no data
phenacetin	limited	limited
polychlorinated biphenyls	inadequate	sufficient

Source: Office of Technology Assessment (1981), p. 141.

Risk Assessment Policy

Inference Choices

The previous discussion mentioned some of the problems that occur at each of the major steps involved in risk assessment. The

National Research Council (1983) distinguished between two types
of uncertainties, those relating to data and those relating to
theory. Data gaps occur because information may be ambiguous
or missing. Theory problems are due to a lack of accepted explanations as to how two phenomena are related or how something
works. For example, although we know that cancer is really a set
of different diseases with different causes (chemicals, radiation,
viruses, natural bodily processes, etc.) and different impacts
(tumor sites, potency, etc.), there is as yet no underlying theory
that ties the different causes, mechanisms, and impacts together.[8]
Inferences and assumptions must therefore be made to bridge the
gaps.

Appendix B lists the various inference options that scientists
and regulators confront. These inferences and the uncertainties
that necessitate them are the focus of controversies over risk
assessment guidelines and specific risk assessments. It is at this
level, of inference options, that the inevitable mixing of science
and politics occurs. As the National Research Council (NRC)
report states:

> A key premise of the proponents of institutional separation of
> risk assessment is that removal of risk assessment from the
> regulatory agencies will result in a clear demarcation of the
> science and policy aspects of regulatory decision-making.
> However, policy considerations inevitably affect, and perhaps
> determine, some of the choices among inference options. (Na-
> tional Research Council, 1983, p. 33)

In this section I examine some of these issues by focusing on
ten controversies that have marked cancer policy development. I
then compare how nine risk assessment guidelines resolved those
controversies. Table 2.3 is a list of nine guidelines issued by
various agencies from 1976 to 1984. The list is not inclusive; for example, guidelines issued by the Food and Drug Administration
and the Consumer Product Safety Commission during this period
do not appear. They are not essentially different from other
guidelines issued from 1977 to 1980. The list also includes
guidelines issued by nonregulatory bodies, specifically the Interagency Regulatory Liaison Group (IRLG) and the White House

Office of Science and Technology Policy (OSTP). The purpose of both those documents was to provide guidance for agencies in conducting risk assessments and making cancer policy.[9] Finally, not all the guidelines have been adopted, specifically the two 1982 EPA documents and the 1982 OSTP draft. They are included here because they indicate a changed cancer policy.

Table 2.3
Cancer Policy Guidelines

• Environmental Protection Agency (1976), "Interim Procedures and Guidelines for Health Risk and Economic Impact Assessments of Suspected Carcinogens" (EPA76).

• Interagency Regulatory Liaison Group (1979), "Scientific Basis for Identification of Potential Carcinogens and Estimation of Risks" (IRLG79).

• Occupational Safety and Health Administration (1980), "Identification, Classification and Regulation of Toxic Substances Posing a Potential Occupational Carcinogenic Risk" (OSHA80).

• Office of Science and Technology Policy (1980), "Characterization and Control of Potential Human Carcinogens: A Framework for Federal Decision-Making" (OSTP80).

• John A. Todhunter (1982), "Review of Data Available to the Administrator Concerning Formaldehyde and di (2-ethylhexyl) Phthalate (DEHP)" (EPA82A).

• Environmental Protection Agency (1982), "Additional U.S. Environmental Protection Agency Guidance for the Health Assessment of Suspect Carcinogens with Specific Reference to Water Quality Criteria" (EPA82B).

• Office of Science and Technology Policy (1982), "Review of the Mechanisms of Effect and Detection of Chemical Carcinogens" (OSTP82).

• Office of Science and Technology Policy (1984), "Chemical Carcinogens; Review of the Science and its Associated Principles" (OSTP84).

• Environmental Protection Agency (1984), "Proposed Guidelines for Carcinogen Risk Assessment" (EPA84).

What are guidelines, and what is their purpose? Guidelines are documents that guide decisions and inform both those inside and outside the agency how information derived from regulatory science will be treated. Their purposes are to provide uniformity to the decision-making process, to arrive at a generic resolution of risk assessment issues (rather than argue each question in every regulatory proceeding), and, in some cases, to describe the state of the science at a particular time.

Table 2.4 lists ten risk assessment controversies. It is considerably shorter than Appendix B, whch lists the NRC inference choices. The questions presented in table 2.4 are the major sources of controversy and differences among the guidelines. Table 2.5 lists the same controversies and then shows which choices produce a risk-averse cancer policy and which produce a risk-tolerant one. This table, along with the next one, demonstrates the *a priori* nature of many of the options selected by the agencies during the 1976–1984 period. As Light (1985) has shown in another context, the assumptions one chooses have political implications.

Table 2.4
Inference Controversies

What kinds of *evidence* are needed to demonstrate carcinogenicity?

What is the role of *bioassays* in demonstrating carcinogenicity in humans?

What role is given to *positive* versus *negative* studies?

How are *conflicting studies* weighed?

How are *benign* and *malignant* tumors counted?

What are appropriate *dose levels*?

What kinds of *mathematical* extrapolation *models* are used?

How are *thresholds* treated in risk assessments?

Is the distinction between *initiators* and *promoters* used?

Is the distinction between *genotoxic* and *epigenetic* carcinogens used?

Table 2.6 indicates whether the guidelines addressed the ten major controversies and how they did so. Note that not all the

Table 2.5
Patterns of Inferential Choices

| Controversy | *Position* | |
	Risk-averse	Risk-tolerant
Evidence	Bioassays sufficient	Epidemiology only
Bioassays	Indicate human carcinogenicity	May not be accurate
Positive/ negative	Positive more important	Negative may indicate species sensitivity
Conflicting studies	Positive more important	All evidence should be weighed
Benign/ malignant	Benign sufficient	Only malignant significant
Dose levels	High dose provides qualitative evidence	At least three levels should be used; low doses show reversibility; high doses may overwhelm defense mechanisms
Mathematical models	Linear	NOEL for epigenetic carcinogens
Thresholds	Insufficient evidence	May exist for promoters and epigenetic carcinogens
Initiators/ promoters	Cannot demonstrate distinction	Distinction important
Genotoxic/ epigenetic	Cannot demonstrate distinction	Distinction important

guidelines addressed all the questions. Note also that there was considerable consensus in the 1976–1980 period, whereas the 1982 guidelines took considerably different stands on many of the issues. The 1984 OSTP and 1984 EPA drafts were closer to the earlier guidelines (though the 1984 EPA draft contained some of the changes recommended in the 1982 documents). Tables 2.5 and 2.6 clearly demonstrate the mixing of science and politics, facts and values. The 1982 documents reflected different value judgments from those of the preceding period (Ashford et al., 1983a, 1984b).

Table 2.6
Comparing the Guidelines

	Report		
Controversy	*EPA 76*	*IRLG 79*	*OSHA 80*
Evidence	Epidemiology best; bioassays suggestive	Epidemiology or positive in one species acceptable; bioassays suggestive	2 or more short-term tests or bioassay acceptable
Bioassays	Substantial evidence in 1 or more species needed	Role is to demonstrate carcinogenicity	Give evidence of carcinogenicity
Positive/ negative		Positive more important; negative sets upper limits	Negative sets upper limits
Conflicting studies		Positive more important	Positive more important
Benign/ malignant	Count both	Count both	Count either or both
Dose levels		High dose necessary; need >1 dose	High dose provides qualitative evidence of carcinogenicity
Mathematical models	Use variety	Prefers linear nonthreshold; use variety	
Thresholds	No evidence	No method of detection	No evidence
Initiators/ promoters		Cannot distinguish	
Genotoxic/ epigenetic			

Table 2.6 (Cont'd)
Comparing the Guidelines

	Report		
Controversy	*OSTP80*	*EPA82A*	*EPA82B*
Evidence	Positive epidemiology or bioassay needed	Need 2 species, both sexes; >1 dose	Need >1 species; states categories of evidence
Bioassays	Identify potential carcinogen		
Positive/ negative	Positive more important	Negative may indicate species sensitivity	
Conflicting studies	Positive more important	All evidence should be weighed	All evidence should be weighed
Benign/ malignant			Emphasizes malignant
Dose levels	High dose necessary	>1 dose necessary; low levels show reversibility	
Mathematical models			Linear for genotoxic; NOEL for epigenetic
Thresholds		Low exposure may pose little risk	May not exist
Initiators/ promoters	Cannot distinguish	Promoters require repeated exposure	
Genotoxic/ epigenetic	Cannot distinguish	Discusses	Distinguishes

Table 2.6 (Cont'd)
Comparing the Guidelines

Controversy	Report		
	OSTP82	OSTP84	EPA84
Evidence	2 species		Epidemiology best; bioassays acceptable; states categories of evidence
Bioassays	Not always accurate	Identifies suspect human carcinogens	Sufficient if used in multiple strains or multiple experiments
Positive/ negative	Negative sets upper limits	Negative sets upper limits	Negative sets upper limits
Conflicting studies		All evidence should be weighed	All evidence should be weighed
Benign/ malignant	No agreement; count both at site	No agreement; count both at site	Usually count both
Dose levels	3 levels necessary; high doses may overcome defenses	At least 3 levels necessary	>1 level necessary
Mathematical models	Considers NOEL; linear model inappropriate	Discusses variety	Linearized multistage usually recommended
Thresholds	May exist for promoters and epigenetic carcinogens	No evidence	
Initiators/ promoters	Distinguishes	Difficult to separate	
Genotoxic/ epigenetic	Distinguishes	Cannot distinguish	

Controversies and Choices

KIND OF EVIDENCE NEEDED. This is the most fundamental question surrounding cancer policy guidelines. What is acceptable evidence for regulatory decisions? The distinction made earlier between normal and regulatory science is critical. From a normal scientific standpoint, the evidence that a substance is carcinogenic should be clear-cut. By that criterion, few chemicals could be classified as human carcinogens. Even the list of eighteen chemicals given in table 2.2 would probably be pared down. Similarly, if epidemiological evidence is seldom available, what other evidence is acceptable? A decision to regulate a chemical has important economic impacts on affected industries. A decision not to regulate a substance may have important impacts on human health.[10]

A demand that only epidemiological evidence be used would lead to risk-tolerant regulation. A view that epidemiology only rarely provides useful information and that primary reliance should be placed upon bioassays would lead to a more risk-averse policy. Note table 2.2 again; the latter view would add more substances to the list of those that ought to be regulated. The problem is that there is no scientific way to resolve this controversy; political resolutions are made instead.

The EPA76 guidelines stated that epidemiology provides the best evidence and that bioassays are suggestive of human carcinogenicity. EPA84 agreed that epidemiology provides the best evidence but stated that bioassays are acceptable. IRLG79, OSHA80, and OSTP80 accepted bioassays as evidence of human carcinogenicity. OSHA80 went further and accepted positive results in two or more short-term tests as evidence of carcinogenicity. EPA82A, EPA82B, and OSTP82 called for more stringent requirements. All wanted positive results in at least two different test species, EPA82A adding that positive results must occur in both sexes of two species.

ROLE OF BIOASSAYS. Assume that we take the position that biosasays do have a legitimate role in risk assessment. What is the nature of that role? Should bioassays be limited to qualitative determinations of carcinogenicity? Are bioassays reliable enough to provide quantitative evaluations? Again, there is a range of opinions on this issue.

The International Agency for Research on Cancer (IARC), which has issued monographs for years reviewing the evidence on carcinogens, takes the position that only human studies provide sufficient evidence for human carcinogenicity. This is the same position that Doll and Peto (1981) took in their study of the causes of cancer, which was sponsored by the Office of Technology Assessment. Those who prefer risk-tolerant positions also take this position. Given the limitations of epidemiology discussed above, few substances would be given status as human carcinogens.

Others believe that bioassays are sufficient by themselves, given the limitations of epidemiological studies, to justify regulatory action. One of the arguments is that epidemiology studies people who already have cancer, whereas bioassays are used to predict substances that might be cancerous. Nearly all biomedical research and advances have used animals, from cancer research to the development of antibiotics. Therefore, bioassays are seen as an acceptable basis for regulation.

> When grappling with evidentiary problems, scientists acknowledge with an extraordinary degree of consensus that, despite problems of interpretation, animal and other short-term tests are helpful, valid tools for assessing whether chemicals induce cancer, birth defects, neurological and other problems in people. Through these tests, scientists can discover and characterize problems under relatively simple, controlled conditions. By contrast, human exposures are very complex, and human genetic and behavioral variability are enormous. Furthermore, synthetic chemicals add to and interact with naturally-occurring ones. It may therefore be difficult, or sometimes even impossible, to identify the harmful effects of low doses of problem chemicals by directly studying people's exposures and long-term adverse outcomes. (Bauman, 1984, p. 2)

With one exception (arsenic), all substances that have been proven to be human carcinogens in epidemiological studies have also been shown to be animal carcinogens. It does not follow, however, and here is the difficulty, that animal carcinogens are invariably human ones. Again, one chooses a position on an *a priori* basis. The middle position, and the scientifically most neutral one, is that bioassays demonstrate that a substance is a mammalian carcinogen and may be used to label that substance as a suspect human carcinogen.

The problem is that rodents differ from humans in metabolism, size, life-span, and reaction to chemicals. Rodents used in bioassays are specifically bred for that purpose; they are genetically homogeneous. Humans are genetically diverse. The animals are tested under controlled conditions, where exposure is limited to the test substance. Humans are exposed to a variety of real and potential carcinogens under uncontrolled conditions. Finally, the rodents are generally healthy, whereas exposure in humans is to the healthy, the ill, and the highly susceptible (young, old). One additional problem has been raised. Certain strains of mice have high spontaneous incidences of tumors, especially in the liver. To what extent should such test animals be used as the basis for regulatory judgment? Despite all these problems, bioassays are still used and are considered appropriate for regulatory purposes. In 1977 the National Research Council stated the following position:

> Effects in animals, properly qualified, are applicable to man. This premise underlies all of experimental biology and medicine, but because it is continually questioned in regard to human cancer, it is desirable to point out that *cancer in men and animals is strikingly similar.* Virtually every form of human cancer has an experimental counterpart, and every form of multicellular organism is subject to cancer, including insects, fish,and plants. Although there are differences in susceptibility between individuals of the same strain, carcinogenic chemicals will affect most test species, and there are large bodies of experimental data that indicate that exposures that are carcinogenic to animals are likely to be carcinogenic to man, and vice versa. (cited in Office of Technology Assessment, 1981, p. 122; emphasis in original)

The 1976–1980 guidelines and OSTP84 viewed bioassays as demonstrating either that a substance is a carcinogen or that it is a potential one. The OSTP82 report stressed that bioassays are not always accurate. EPA84, employing a categorization scheme, stated that bioassays are sufficient evidence of carcinogenicity if used in multiple strains or in multiple experiments, or if there is some unusual response.

POSITIVE VERSUS NEGATIVE STUDIES. Positive studies are those showing a statistically significant higher tumor incidence in experimental than in control groups. Negative studies show no such statistically significant results. The issue of positive versus negative studies asks the following question: does a negative study mean that a substance is not a carcinogen?[11] The answer is maybe; again it depends on who is answering the question. Those promoting risk-averse policies say that it does not, those promoting risk-tolerant policies say that it does. Complicating matters is that some substances may be simultaneously carcinogens (increasing the incidence of some cancers) *and* anticarcinogens (decreasing the incidence of other cancers). As Weinberg and Storer (1985) point out, the existence of these "ambiguous" carcinogens means that regulations and recommendations that would ban or restrict such substances should be approached cautiously.

Negative studies may be less than convincing for several reasons. Both epidemiological and bioassay tests look for significant differences between experimental and control groups (those exposed and those not exposed to the test substance, respectively). Significance hopefully means biological significance, but more commonly it means statistical significance, the likelihood that a particular set of results will be as different or more different as the null hypothesis of no difference.[12] Negative epidemiological and bioassay studies are susceptible to what statisticians call Type II errors: accepting the null hypothesis when, in fact, it is false (e.g., the hypothesis that a substance is a carcinogen is correct, but the study shows no significant difference).

Random factors are most evident in human studies, where doses are typically low, where there is exposure to other carcinogens (both natural and man-made), and where there is a high background level of cancer incidence. A negative study is usually accompanied by a discussion of the power of the test, the ability to detect an effect if there is one. Given the problems of epidemiology, negative studies are quite common and thus supply evidence for those who prefer risk-tolerant positions and insist on human evidence. Bioassays suffer from the problem of small numbers, as discussed above. Since the typical experiment involves 25 to 50 animals in each of four groups (taking into consideration sex and control and experimental groups), the power of such a test to detect an effect may only be 1 out of 100 (1×10^2), or one cancer out of one hundred experimental subjects. If the true effect is 1 out of 1,000 (1×10^3), that effect may not be seen. But 1×10^3 is well within boundaries used by agencies to regulate a substance.

If a number of tests show negative results, or if no test shows positive results, then one may confidently state that the substance is not a carcinogen. If there are some negative and positive results, then the most common use of negative tests is to set the upper limits for exposure; that is, to say that it is unlikely that there is an effect beyond a certain range.[13]

IRLG79, OSHA80, and OSTP80 all said that positive evidence is more important than negative evidence; IRLG79 and OSHA80 also stated that negative evidence sets the upper limits. OSTP82, OSTP84, and EPA84 concurred on that role for negative evidence. EPA82A stated that negative evidence may indicate that a species is sensitive to a substance.

CONFLICTING STUDIES. What if the epidemiological studies are negative and the bioassays positive, or vice versa? What if, with bioassays, some studies with one strain of rodent or different rodents are positive while others are negative? These are different versions of the same problem. In general, because of the difficulties with negative studies, the positive is given greater weight. Negative studies, again, are used primarily to set upper limits. The Interagency Regulatory Liaison Group (IRLG) guidelines state the issue as follows (1979, p. 203):

> The response to carcinogens in different animal species and even strains is known to vary greatly because of genetic, metabolic, nutritional, and other factors that affect susceptibility in a given test animal. Present knowledge indicates that a substance that is clearly carcinogenic in one test species is likely to be carcinogenic in other species, that it may take extensive tests in several species to demonstrate this correlation, and that the responsive target tissues or organs and the types of tumors induced in different species may vary greatly. Therefore, although concordance of positive results (even if different tumor types are involved) adds support to an evaluation of carcinogenicity, the findings of negative results in some other species generally does not detract from the validity of a positive result as evidence of carcinogenicity for the test substance.

In this respect, positive results supersede negative ones.[14]

IRLG79, OSHA80, and OSTP80 all agreed that positive results are more important and supersede conflicting studies. EPA82A, EPA82B, OSTP84, and EPA84 suggested that all the evidence should be weighed in making determinations.

BENIGN AND MALIGNANT TUMORS. The issue of benign versus malignant tumors concerns the evaluation of test results from bioassays. A strict view suggests that only malignant tumors should be counted for statistical purposes. By definition, a benign tumor is one that does not spread or metastasize. However, the usual practice is to consider the strong possibility that benign tumors foreshadow a malignant effect at a latter stage of carcinogenesis. For regulatory purposes, the issue is that if both types of tumors are counted, the chances of obtaining a statistically significant result are enhanced. That possibility, in turn, increases the likelihood that an agency would consider some type of regulatory action against the substance. Again, as with many of the other issues, the particular outcome may depend upon prior policy decisions. The IRLG report consistently used the term *prudent* in characterizing its decisions on these issues.

EPA76, IRLG79, OSHA80, and EPA84 were willing to count both tumor types, with OSHA80 taking the extreme position of accepting benign tumors alone, that is, OSHA80 accepts the presence of benign tumors as an indication of potential carcinogenicity. EPA82B emphasized malignancy (the other extreme from OSHA80), and OSTP84 stated that there is no agreement on this issue and that both kinds of tumors should be counted at the site (the organ where the tumors are found).

DOSE LEVELS. The next three issues are also related. The problem of dose levels is perhaps the most disputatious and misunderstood of the controversies. For various reasons, high doses of test substances are typically administered in bioassays. If the results of the test are positive, media and opponents of the regulation will depict the ridiculousness of the implication—for example, that drinking twenty glasses per day of a soft drink with saccharin increases the risk of cancer. Clearly, the doses administered to test animals greatly exceed the doses common to human exposures. Why?

The answer, a standard one in toxicology, is that because so few animals are used in the experiments (as few as 100 animals), the effects, if any, are generally small; therefore the highest dose short of lethality, or the maximum tolerated dose (MTD), is used to maximize the possibility of obtaining a response. Other doses, fractions of the MTD, are employed to obtain dose-response curves. Critics of this approach say that high doses, "megadoses," overwhelm the animal's metabolism and defense mechanisms and thus produce a cancer effect (see Gehring et al., 1977, and chapter 5). Relying on megadoses is therefore unwarranted.

IRLG79, OSHA80, and OSTP80 all stated that high doses are necessary to qualitatively demonstrate that a substance is a carcinogen. IRLG79 and EPA84 also stated that more than one dose should be used. EPA82A agreed with this last statement but added that low dose levels show reversibility of effects. OSTP82 and OSTP84 both said that at least three dose levels should be used. OSTP82 also stated that high doses may overcome the animal's defensive mechanisms.

MATHEMATICAL MODELS. If few doses are administered in bioassays, and those at high levels, how does one extrapolate to lower doses more common to human exposure? At lower levels, as we saw earlier, models differ by orders of magnitude.[15] It is difficult, at present, to verify any of the models. The one most frequently used is the linear model, which suggests that there is a directly proportional relationship between dose and response. The Environmental Protection Agency (1984C, p. 46298), in its recently completed risk assessment guidelines, defended the linearized model.

> No single mathematical procedure is recognized as the most appropriate for low-dose extrapolation in carcinogenesis. When relevant biological evidence on mechanism of action exists, the models or procedures employed should be consistent with the evidence. However, when data and information are limited, as is the usual case given the high degree of uncertainty associated with the selection of a low-dose extrapolation model, specific guidance on model selection is necessary to provide a desirable degree of consistency in risk assessments. The choice of low-dose extrapolation models should be consistent with current understanding of the mechanisms of carcinogenesis and not solely on goodness of fit to the observed tumor data. Although mechanisms of the carcinogenesis process are largely unknown,

at least some of the elements of the process have been
elucidated, e.g., linearity of tumor initiation. In further support
of a linear model, it has been shown that, if a carcinogenic agent
acts by accelerating the same stages of the carcinogenic process
that lead to the background occurrence of cancer, the added effect of the carcinogen at low doses is virtually linear. Thus, a
model that is linear at low doses is plausible.

There have been attempts to develop models that more accurately
portray cancer progression (see Cornfield, 1977; Gehring et al.,
1977; Hattis, 1982; and chapter 5). Possibly the best way to treat
the problem, given all the attended uncertainties characteristic of
risk assessment, is to extrapolate with several models and then indicate a range of possible effects.

EPA76, IRLG79, and OSTP84 all discussed a variety of
models and suggested that no one model be preferred. IRLG79
recommended the linear, nonthreshold version, and EPA84, as
noted, suggested the linearized model unless additional information implied an alternative one. EPA82B stated that the linear
model is appropriate for genotoxic carcinogens (carcinogens that
act directly on DNA) and that the no-observable-effects (NOEL)
model (which tests animals and finds a level at which no effects are
observed) be employed for epigenetic carcinogens (those that do
not act directly on DNA). OSTP82 considered the NOEL model
and viewed the linear model as inappropriate.

THRESHOLDS. The question of dose-response effects and
mathematical models leads directly to the question of thresholds.
As Cornfield (1977) pointed out, two types of models have been
employed. The no-observable-effects model (NOEL) is used to test
for acute health problems in food safety studies. A safety factor is
then applied on the presumption that humans are more sensitive
than test animals. For carcinogens, the linear nonthreshold model
is generally used. The basic premise of this model is that any exposure to a carcinogen, no matter how small, increases the probability of incurring cancer. Although there may be no observed effects at low doses, for reasons discussed above, extrapolations may
be made below the levels of observable effects. The nonthreshold
thesis or assumption leads to greater regulation. Others see that a
threshold assumption or model may be appropriate, at least in certain circumstances.

EPA76, IRLG79, OSHA80, and OSTP84 all agreed that there is no evidence for the existence of a threshold, or at least no available methods for detecting one. EPA82A stated that low exposure to a potential carcinogen may pose little risk. OSTP82 said that there may be a threshold for promoters and epigenetic carcinogens. EPA82B observed that there may not be thresholds.

INITIATORS AND PROMOTERS. The last two issues address cancer mechanisms. The process of carcinogenesis consists of at least two stages, initiation and promotion. Initiation occurs when a normal cell is transformed into a potentially cancerous one. Promotion is then the expression of that transformation (Berenblum, 1978). The distinction between the two phases was known as early as the 1940s (Berenblum, 1941). Some carcinogens are initiators, some are promoters, and still others, known as "complete carcinogens," act as both. Initiation may require but a single exposure, even a small one. Promotion, on the other hand, requires prolonged exposures. The latency in cancer development is due, presumably, to the lengthy promotion phase. From a regulatory standpoint, the significance of the distinction is that more exposure would be permissible to promoters than to initiators. From the standpoint of the threshold controversy, initiators would not have a threshold but promoters might. A major difficulty in resolving these issues is that most bioassays cannot distinguish between the two phases. Only in the case of skin and liver cancer has promotion been clearly identified (Office of Science and Technology Policy, 1984). A final complicating factor is that people are not exposed to a single carcinogen (whether promoter or initiator) as are experimental animals, but to a variety of carcinogens. This exposure to a number of initiators might have an accelerating effect.[16]

IRLG79, OSTP80, and OSTP84 all affirmed that the distinction cannot be demonstrated. OSTP82 distinguished between the two mechanisms. EPA82A made the distinction and added that promoters require repeated exposure, thus permitting more risk-tolerant regulation.

GENOTOXIC AND EPIGENETIC. A genotoxic carcinogen is one that operates directly on a cell's DNA. An epigenetic carcinogen is one that acts through some other mechanism, for example, as a substance that modifies hormones, as an immunosuppressor (a substance that inhibits the body's immunization system from counteracting the carcinogen), or as a promoter (Williams, 1983). A genotoxic carcinogen may not require long-term testing, given the strong relationship between mutagenesis and carcinogenesis. An epigenetic substance would require further testing. From a regulatory perspective, repeated exposures to an epigenetic substance might be permissible, whereas strict regulation might be appropriate for genotoxic compounds. Again, genotoxic substances would not have a threshold, whereas epigenetic ones might. Some state that there is no basis for such distinctions (e.g., Perara, 1984).

Because this is a relatively recent controversy, the earlier guidelines did not address this question. EPA82A, EPA82B, and OSTP82 all discussed the two mechanisms, with the latter two guidelines clearly distinguishing between them. OSTP84 stated that experiments cannot differentiate between genotoxic and epigenetic compounds.

Evaluating the Guidelines

In its 1983 report, the National Research Council suggested four criteria for evaluating cancer guidelines: (1) comprehensiveness, (2) extent of detail, (3) flexibility, and (4) format. Table 2.7 evaluates the guidelines by those standards.

Comprehensiveness reflects the extent to which guidelines consider all the steps of risk assessment and the number of inference options that are discussed. By that standard, the most comprehensive guidelines were the nonagency ones: IRLG79, OSTP82, and OSTP84. EPA82A and EPA82B addressed only a small portion of possible considerations. Indeed, EPA82A clearly showed up as something different, a document created to evaluate a specific substance (formaldehyde). The other documents were somewhere in between.

Extent of detail reflects the thoroughness by which cancer policy guidelines discuss risk assessment and inference options. While a guideline may touch upon an issue, it may do so in only a cursory fashion. EPA76 was a perfect example. It was the first and shortest of the guidelines, comprising only four pages in the *Federal Register*, including comments by EPA administrator Russell Train. As an initial effort, it sought to alleviate some fears

Table 2.7
Evaluating the Guidelines

Guideline	Comprehensiveness	Extent of detail	Flexibility	Form
		Criterion		
EPA76	Medium	Low	High	Established procedures
IRLG79	High	High	Medium	Recommendations
OSHA80	Medium	Medium-high	Low	Regulations
OSTP80	Medium	Low	High	Recommendations
EPA82A	Low	Medium	Medium	Established procedures
EPA82B	Low	Medium	Medium	Established procedures
OSTP82	High	High	Medium	Recommendations
OSTP84	High	High	High	Recommendations
EPA84	Medium	Medium	High	Established procedures

related to pesticide regulation (see chapter 3) but provided little guidance. By contrast, the most detailed of the guidelines was OSTP84. It presented a "state of the science," including principles and a consensus. IRLG79 was also comparatively detailed. By contrast, OSTP80 seemed to be a preliminary effort with little detail. The OSHA80 guidelines by themselves were somewhere in the middle. However, the guidelines were prefaced by an extensive discussion of virtually every risk assessment issue and how and why OSHA made its inference policy decisions.

The third criterion is *flexibility*. Do guidelines lock an agency into one position? Do guidelines allow the agency to consider a variety of options on any inference point? Do guidelines consider changes in regulatory science? In one sense, we can place the various guidelines into two simple categories: OSHA80 and all the others. A major criticism of the OSHA guidelines was that having decided the answers to recurring questions, they were virtually set in stone (see chapter 4). The guidelines do allow for consideration of discrepant evidence, particularly in the 1981 and 1982 amendments, but on the whole, OSHA seems to have firmly stated its conclusions. The other extreme is EPA76, which had the most general of guidelines, the least amount of detail, and the greatest flexibility.

Finally, the *form* of the guidelines reflects the extent to which they are binding on the agency. The National Research Council (1983) distinguishes among three forms: (1) regulations, (2) established procedures, and (3) recommendations. The OSHA guidelines are clearly adopted as regulations, another reason why they were so controversial. The nonagency guidelines—IRLG79, OSTP80, OSTP82, and OSTP84—are recommendations to regulatory agencies. The four EPA guidelines can be classified as established procedures.

A Final Assessment

The various guidelines, finally, can be classified by their overall approach to resolving uncertainties (see table 2.8). The approaches are presumption-rebuttal, weight-of-the-evidence, and leave-it-to-the-scientists (McGarity, 1983).

The *presumption-rebuttal* approach, characteristic of OSHA80, states certain premises or makes certain inference choices and then allows deviation from those choices only under specified and rigid conditions. OSHA80 permitted consideration of arguments in certain cases, but the standards were so strict that they were unlikely to be met. For example, the OSHA guidelines, as already pointed out, permitted consideration of benign tumors alone as sufficient evidence of potential carcinogenicity and allowed other evidence to be considered if it conformed to the folowing criteria:

> Criteria. (i) Data are available from at least two well-conducted bioassays in each of two species of mammals (or from equivalent evidence in more than two species);

Table 2.8
Overall Approaches Taken by the Guidelines

	Approach		
Guideline	*Presumption-rebuttal*	*Weight of the evidence*	*Leave-it-to-the-scientists*
EPA76		X	
IRLG79		X	
OSHA80	X		
OSTP80			X
EPA82A		X	
EPA82B		X	
OSTP82		X	
OSTP84		X	
EPA84		X	

(ii) Each of the bioassays to be considered has been conducted for the full lifetime of the experimental animals;

(iii) The relevant tissue slides are made available to OSHA or its designee and the diagnoses of the tumors as benign are made by at least one qualified pathologist who has personally examined each of the slides and who provides specific diagnostic criteria and descriptions; and

(iv) All of the induced tumors must be shown to belong to a type which is known not to progress to malignancy or to be at a benign stage when observed. In the latter case, data must be presented to show that multiple sections of the affected organ(s) were adequately examined to search for invasion of the tumor cells into adjacent tissue, and that multiple sections of other organs were adequately examined to search for tumor metastases. (Occupational Safety and Health Administration, 1980, p. 5287)

This is a substantially higher standard of proof than what OSHA required for positive studies; it is clearly a risk-averse policy position. One can argue that OSHA's mission was to protect the health of workers, but it was a prior policy decision that was reflected in these (and other) criteria.

The *weight-of-the-evidence* approach was taken by most of the guidelines; EPA84 is a good example. Essentially, this approach said that regulators and their advisers will consider the entire body of scientific evidence in any specific case. All the post-1980 documents took this approach, as did EPA76.

OSTP80 adopted a different course, *leave-it-to-the-scientists*. In particular, OSTP80 recommended that an independent body or board of scientists be given the responsibility for making risk assessment judgments. This is a position advocated by industry and is based on the two-stage model examined in the previous chapter. Risk assessment is seen as an objective (e.g., scientific) process, and locating risk assessments in an independent body would, according to OSTP, remove that part of the risk control process from politics.[17]

I began this chapter by emphasizing the foundations of risk assessment. The documents discussed throughout the book are presumably based on regulatory science. The generic cancer risk assessment guidelines, or cancer policies, are not really scientific documents (McGarity, 1983). Normal science does not produce a consensus statement about a given subject (though textbooks may reflect such a consensus) because it is unnecessary to do so. The consensus in normal science arises from publications, peer review, communications, etc. Cancer risk assessment guidelines, on the other hand, are at best only partially scientific documents and are at least equally as political. They are political because governmental agencies issue them, though scientists may be responsible for much of their content, especially with the nonagency guidelines. But even nonagency guidelines have a political or policy purpose. It is clear that the IRLG79 and OSTP84 documents were designed to guide regulatory agencies in setting their internal policies. Because of this dualistic nature, controversies over the science are, in essence, controversies over the policies. Politics explains why the guidelines were necessary in the first place and to a considerable extent explains changes in the content of those policies. I address these concerns, the role of policy and politics, next.

3

Origins of Cancer Policy

Like those in the last century who tilled a plot of land to exhaustion and then moved on to another, we in this century have too casually and too long abused our natural environment. The time has come when we can wait no longer to repair the damage already done, and to establish new criteria to guide us in the future.

The fight against pollution, however, is not a search for villains. For the most part, the damage done to our environment has not been the work of evil men, nor has it been the inevitable by-product either of advancing technology or of growing population. It results not so much from choices made, as from choices neglected; not from malign intention, but from failure to take into account the full consequences of our actions.

. . .

The tasks that need doing . . . call for fundamentally new philosophies of land, air and water use, for stricter regulation, for expanded government action, for greater citizen involvement, and for new programs to ensure that government, industry and individuals all are called on to do their share of the job to pay their share of the cost.

--Richard Nixon, 1970 p. 22-A

The presence of toxic chemicals in our environment is one of the grimmest discoveries of the industrial era. Rather than coping with these hazards after they have escaped into our environment, our primary objective must be to prevent them from entering the environment at all.

At least a dozen major federal statutes, implemented by seven different agencies, address this problem in various ways. With the enactment last year of the Toxic Substances Control

Act, no further comprehensive federal legislation should be necessary. Now we must inaugurate a coordinated federal effort to exclude these chemicals from our environment.

--Jimmy Carter, 1977, p. 31-E

These two excerpts from presidential messages, just seven years apart, indicate how dramatically environmental politics has changed. Nixon's message was the first presidential one devoted to the environment and came amidst a national mobilization to tackle pollution problems. Carter's statement indicated, in some respects, how far we had gone. First, he addressed a subject, toxic substances, that was not explicitly considered in 1970. The focus of environmental problems has shifted over the years from an original concern with the impact of man's activities on the environment and the more obvious pollution problems to a newer, less visible, and more difficult concern with human health ("Administrator's Job," 1984; Davis, 1984; Rosenbaum, 1985; Ruckelshaus, 1985). Second, by 1977 legislation was in place that focused on toxic substances; the problem was now one of implementation. Finally, it was during the Carter administration (1977–1980) that the federal government began to develop policies designed to tackle a specific disease from a specific cause: cancer due to toxic substances.

Public policy does not develop instantaneously, as if by spontaneous generation. Rather, the need for action in a given area usually develops gradually over a period of years. In this chapter, I begin my examination of cancer policy development by exploring its origins in the pre-1977 period. In doing so, I employ two models, one of agenda building (Kingdon, 1984) and a second of the political actors (Hamlett, 1984).

Agenda Building and Policy Formulation

To date, the impact of cancer policy guidelines has been largely symbolic because few guidelines have been implemented.

Rather, the need for such a policy has been articulated and various agencies have adopted them. Therefore, we need be concerned primarily with the early portions of the policy process—specifically problem recognition, agenda building, and policy formulation.[1]

Kingdon (1984; see also Elder and Cobb, 1984) provides a useful model for this portion of the policy process. He writes (p. 92):

> The federal government is seen as an organized anarchy. . . . the properties of problematic preferences, unclear technology, and fluid participation are in evidence. Separate streams run through the organization each with a life of its own. These streams are coupled at critical junctures and that coupling produces the greatest agenda change.

Kingdon sees three streams or "families of processes" interacting in agenda setting. The first is problem recognition, the *problem stream*. Problems, as Lindblom (1980) has pointed out, are not out there waiting to be solved. Someone has to recognize that a problem exists and to interpret it as such. Problem definition and interpretation are critical, if not *the* critical, parts of policy making. If a problem can be defined out of existence, then it does not have to be dealt with. It makes considerable difference who is doing the defining and interpreting. This stage structures the rest of the policy process, determining what, if any, kinds of solutions will be considered appropriate (Jones, 1984; Rushefsky, 1984a). Kingdon points out, for example, that indicators such as crime rates and inflation rates do not by themselves set the agenda. For example, the question of whether there is a cancer epidemic (discussed in chapter 7) becomes problematic in light of the following quote by Kingdon (1984, p. 99):

> Indicators are not simply a straightforward recognition of the facts. Precisely because indicators have such powerful implications, the methodology by which facts are gathered and the interpretations that are placed on these facts become prominent items for heated debate.

The second stream is the *policy stream*, which involves formulating and developing proposals. Kingdon states that there are, in each issue area, policy communities made up of specialists, each with their own set of proposals (see also Heclo, 1978). The specialists may be members of interest groups, agencies, universities, think tanks, etc. For example, Umberto Saffiotti, a prominent cancer researcher, has been advocating a vigorous cancer policy since at least 1970. Similarly, Bruce Ames has recently reconsidered data on carcinogens and has been actively articulating a changed view.[2]

The third of Kingdon's streams is the *political stream*, which consists of elections, changes in administration, national mood, partisan or ideological changes in Congress, and interest group activity. This and the other streams flow separately from one another: "the streams . . . are largely separate from one another, largely governed by different forces, different considerations, and different styles" (Kingdon, 1984, p. 93).

At critical points or junctures, these three separately flowing streams merge, creating "windows of opportunity" for change.

> Basically, a window opens because of a change in the political stream (i.e., a change in administration, a shift in the partisan or ideological distribution of seats in Congress, or a shift in national mood); or it opens because a new problem captures the attention of governmental officials and those close to them. (Kingdon, 1984, p. 176)

The history of cancer policy development suggests that first we see the recognition of a new problem, and then a policy development that is affected by changes in administration.

Given this model of agenda building, we can identify four critical periods in cancer policy. The first is the pre-1977 period. During this time, there was recognition first of general environmental problems (leading to an outburst of legislation) and later of a possible cancer problem (both of cancer incidence and of mortality) and of toxic substances as an important cause of the problem. In addition, dissatisfaction with the War on Cancer and gaps in environmental legislation laid the foundation for considering cancer policy. This period, labelled the "precursor period", is the focus of this chapter. The second critical period is 1977-1980, the tenure of the Carter administration. During this time, numerous cancer risk assessment guidelines were issued, and a vigorous attempt was made to coordinate the various policies. These events are described and analyzed in chapter 4. The third critical period begins with the 1980 presidential election and the inauguration of the Reagan administration. That administration was concerned with regulatory relief and reducing the burdens of environmental programs. Chapter 5 discusses this challenge and reaction to Carter administration cancer policy developments. The fourth, and, so far final, period began in late 1982 with scandals in the Environmental Protection Agency and turnovers among high-level agency personnel. This is the concern of chapter 6.

Political Perspective: The Clash of Estates

Within the policy model just described are the political actors that make policy decisions and attempt to influence decision-makers. Hamlett (1984) has developed a model of political actors, modifying Price's (1965) concept of estates. Rather than *estates*, Hamlett uses the term *arena*. However, because 'arena' has been used elsewhere in a different context,[3] we will continue the use of 'estate' as a cluster of participants.

Hamlett (1984, pp. 35–37) describes an 'arena' in the following manner:

> The concept of an arena [estate] of technological decision making is an attempt to characterize the general environments in which individual decisionmakers must operate, and to gather together into identifiable clusters those decisionmakers who share common environments.
>
> Each technological decisionmaking [estate] possesses its own characteristic incentives, influences, pressures, constraints, and goals, and individuals within an [estate] must make their decisions within that general environment. . . . there does exist a general tendency for participants who are similarly situated to perceive their circumstances and opportunities in corresponding ways, and to share certain general outlooks and motivations, especially when compared with participants in other [estates].

As Hamlett descries the 'arenas' (or 'estates'), we have essentially a corporatist[4] rather than a pluralist model of politics. A pluralist model sees a wide variety of interest groups participating in policy making and politics. For example, the environmental interest groups that are active in cancer policy include the Environmental Defense Fund and the Natural Resources Defense Council. The corporatist model instead views the scene from a higher level, as aggregations of interests. The seven 'estates' in this model are the corporate-managerial, executive, congressional, regulatory, academic-professional, consumerist-environmentalist, and organized labor 'estates'.[5] From the perspective of cancer policy making, we should expect the corporate-managerial 'estate' to oppose a rigorous cancer policy and the consumerist-environmentalist and organized labor[6] 'estates' to advocate a strong cancer policy. The executive 'estate', or administration, sets the agenda for cancer policy (Kingdon, 1984), depending upon the administration in power. The political perspective thus can be seen as a clash of 'estates', each with its own interests and operating in predictable ways. For example, the congressional 'estate' generally plays a balancing role *vis-a-vis* the executive 'estate', questioning risk-averse cancer policies during the Carter administration and challenging risk-tolerant ones during the Reagan administration. It plays this role in the environmental area as a whole and also appears to play it in other policy areas (Pastor, 1984).

Perhaps the most intriguing of the 'estates' is the academic-professional one, corresponding to Price's (1965) scientific 'estate'. Here we can see a conflict of roles. On the one hand, scientists are supposed to be impartial, engaged in a dispassionate, objective activity. On the other hand, regulatory science, because it supports regulatory policies, has an inherently political character. Scientists as experts are prominent players in cancer policy making and are employed in many of the 'estates'. A number of scientists have been advocates of cancer policy; other scientists working within the corporate-managerial 'estate' are supportive of positions emanating from that 'estate'. To a large extent, scientists are used by these other 'estates' to forward policy positions, one of the reasons why there exists "disputes among experts" (Mazur, 1973).

Birth of the Modern Environmental Movement

The birth of the modern environmental movement was precipitated by the publication of Rachel Carson's *Silent Spring* in

1962.[7] Carson, a marine biologist and well-acclaimed author, dramatically pointed to potential problems with this country's manner of controlling agricultural pests. *Silent Spring* was immediately controversial. It attacked the basis for the pesticide practices of farmers, the agribusiness industry, and the U.S. Department of Agriculture. Most observers agreed with her evidence; it was the inferences and conclusions that she drew that so ignited the scientific, political, and industrial communities (Graham, 1970). The major effect of Carson's book was to focus attention on man's impacts on the physical environment.

Other incidents reinforced this awareness of environmental problems. The long-running dispute over the Cross-Florida Barge Canal captured the attention of Floridians and led to the creation of environmental organizations such as the Florida Defenders of the Environment (Carter, 1974). The new environmental organizations became important as articulators of environmental concerns and pressed for public action. An important precipitating national event came in January 1969, when a Union Oil Company drilling platform blew up off the coast of California, spilling millions of gallons of oil on the shores near Santa Barbara. The spill, the cleanup, and the aftermath made headlines in the newspapers and dramatic pictures on television. Incidents such as these reinforced a growing concern for the environment.[8]

Other explanations have been offered for the flowering of this second environmental movement. The United States in the 1960s was experiencing one of the country's longest sustained and most rapid periods of economic expansion. Because of this expansion, the econonmy was not a problem and the country could afford to look at such things as the environment (at least it appeared to be able to afford it).[9] In addition, it had an activist upper-middle class that could devote time to such concerns. Advocacy journalism and the various news media brought environmental problems to the fore. The press, as Whitaker (1976) put it, was a "pollinator." There was also the absence of any other great challenge; the space program might have provided one, but funding for that project peaked in 1965. Moreover, in a period of unrest—civil rights, the Vietnam War, draft resistance, women's movement—the environment provided a unique focus for criticizing society. It was bad enough that we were doing all these other things, but now we were threatening our own health, those of our children, and our survival. Science also played a role.

> Science has contributed another—and unique-dimension to the national agitation. To the obvious signs of pollution that people could see, feel, and smell, science added a whole panoply of invisible threats: radiation, heavy metal poisons, chlorinated hydrocarbons in the water, acidic radicals in the atmosphere—all potentially more insidious, more pervasive, and more dangerous than the familiar nuisances. This could happen only in a country able to support a large, advanced scientific community. (Whitaker, 1976, pp. 24-25)

One final factor was the criticism of federal environmental legislation passed in the 1960s. In particular, reports issued by Ralph Nader's organizations on air and water pollution legislation harshly attacked both the implementation of the laws and their inherent weaknesses. Senator Edmund Muskie (D.-ME.) was singled out as the major architect of the legislation. The criticisms stung, and when new legislation was considered beginning in 1969, Muskie ensured that he would have a distinct impact. This conflict led to a bidding war between Congress and the president (Jones, 1974; Rosenbaum, 1977; Whitaker, 1976).

All of these events created a public that was ever more concerned about environmental problems.[10] Whitaker and others have charted this growth in public awareness. For example, polls by the Opinion Research Corporation showed an increase in concern about air pollution from 28 percent of the sample in 1965 to 69 percent of the sample in 1970 (Whitaker, 1976). During the 1968 presidential electon, neither Richard Nixon nor Humbert Humphre had much to say about the environment or pollution (Whitaker, 1976). By January 1970, President Nixon had signed the National Environmental Protection Act.

Environmental Legislation

The result of the events just described was a burst of environmental legislation in the late 1960s and early 1970s.[11] Table 3.1 lists the major statutes passed during this period. The legislation covered a wide gamut of environmental concerns: air, water, pesticides, consumer protection, and occupational safety and health. A major problem with these acts is that they treated risk

Table 3.1
Major Environmental Legislation

Year	Law
1969	National Environmental Policy Act
1970	Occupational Safety and Health Act
1970	Clean Air Act
1970	Federal Water Pollution Control Act
1972	Federal Insecticide, Fungicide, and Rodenticide Act
1972	Consumer Product Safety Act
1972	Noise Control Act
1973	Endangered Species Act
1974	Safe Drinking Water Act
1975	Hazardous Materials Transportation Act
1976	Toxic Substances Control Act
1976	Solid Waste Disposal Act
1976	Resource Conservation and Recovery Act
1977	Surface Mining Control and Reclamation Act
1977	Clean Air Act Amendments
1977	Federal Water Pollution Control Act Amendments
1980	Comprehensive Environmental Response, Compensation, and Liability Act
1984	Resource Conservation and Recovery Act Amendments

Source: Dodge and Civiak (1981); Mosher (1980).

differently, thus creating coordination problems. Table 3.2 lists the risk framework or basis for some of the laws that were passed and also indicates the degree of protection given by each law.[12]

Note first that table 3.2 employs three risk frameworks. A risk-based law is one "that provides for regulations to reduce risks to zero without considering other factors" (Office of Technology Assessment, 1981, p. 177). Balancing laws are those that imply some degree of risk above zero and the consideration of other factors. Finally, technology-based laws are those that either set standards so high as to require the development of new technologies (technology-forcing) or that require the use of a given technology (e.g., the "best-available technology").

Sometimes the same law had more than one risk basis. The best example is the Clean Air Act, the most complex and controversial environmental law. The section (110) that dealt with stationary sources (e.g., power plants) was risk based, the section

Table 3.2
Public Laws Providing for the Regulation of
Exposures to Carcinogens

Legislation (agency)	Basis of the legislaton	Degree of protection
Federal Food, Drug and Cosmetic Act (FDA)		
Food	Risk (additives)	No risk permitted; additives banned
	Balancing (contaminants)	"Necessary to the protection of public health"
Drugs	Balancing	Risks and benefits of drugs are balanced
Cosmetics	Risk	Action taken on the basis that cosmetic is adulterated
Occupational Safety and Health Act (OSHA)	Technology (or balancing)	"Adequately assures to the extent feasible that no employee will suffer material impairment of health or functional capacity . . ."
Clean Air Act (EPA)		
Sec. 112 (stationary sources)	Risk	"An ample margin of safety to protect the public health"
Sec. 202 (vehicles)	Technology (includes a risk-risk test for deciding between pollutants that might result in control attempts)	"Standards which reflect the greatest degree of emission reduction achievable through . . . technology . . . available"
Sec. 211 (fuel	Balancing (technology-based with	"Standards which reflect the greatest degree

Table 3.2 (Cont'd)
Public Laws Providing for the Regulation of
Exposures to Carcinogens

Legislation (agency)	Basis of the legislaton	Degree of protection
	consideration of costs, but health-based in requirement that standards provide ample margin of safety	of emission reduction achievable through . . . technology . . . available
Clean Water Act (EPA) Sec. 307	Technology	Defined by applying BAT[1]; economically achievable but effluent levels are to "provide(s) an ample margin of safety"
Federal Insecticide, Fungicide, and Rodenticide Act and the Federal Environmental Pesticide Act (EPA)	Balancing "unreasonable adverse effects"	Not specified
Resource Conservation and Recovery Act (EPA)	Risk	"That necessary to protect human health and the environment"
Safe Drinking Water Act (EPA)	Balancing	"To the extent feasible . . . (taking costs into consideration) . . .
Toxic Substances Control Act (EPA) Sec. 4 (to require) testing)	Balancing "unreasonable risk"	Not specified
Sec. 6	Balancing; protect	"To protect adequately

Table 3.2 (Cont'd)
Public Laws Providing for the Regulation of
Exposures to Carcinogens

Legislation (agency)	Basis of the legislaton	Degree of protection
(to regulate)	against "unreasonable risk"	against such risk using the least burdensome requirement"
Sec. 7 (to commence civil action against imminent hazards)		Based on degree of protection of sec. 6
Federal Hazardous Substances Act (CPSC)	Risk	"Establish such reasonable variations or additional label requirements . . . necessary for the protection of public health and safety"
Consumer Product Safety Act (CPSC)	Balancing "unreasonable"	"Standard shall be reasonably necessary to prevent or reduce an unreasonable risk of injury"

Source: Office of Technology Assessment (1981).
[1]BAT—best available technology.

(202) that dealt with vehicles was technology-based, and the section (211) that dealt with fuel additives used a balancing framework.

There was also wide variation among the laws in definitions of toxics, degrees of protection, and agents that are regulated. It is as if each piece of legislation had been considered separately with no thought given to a coherent strategy for accomplishing an important objective. The same lack of focus existed in the implementation of the various laws, which never met the expectations of the lawmakers and also varied among the agencies. These problems were addressed by the Carter administration and by William Ruckelshaus in his second tenure as EPA administrator.

By 1977, as President Carter pointed out, the legislative framework was in place. But the focus on cancer originated elsewhere.

The War on Cancer

Paralleling the passage of environmental legislation was a specific and differently driven concern with cancer. The National Cancer Institute (NCI) was created in 1937 to fund biomedical research in two directions: fundamental research directed toward a better understanding of underlying biological mechanisms, and more applied and clinical research directed toward seeking out the etiology and cures for cancer (Rettig, 1977). The National Cancer Act of 1971 explicitly stated that the goal of the NCI was to conduct research and experiments "relating to the cause, prevention, and methods of diagnosis and treatment of cancer" (quoted in Rettig, 1977, p. 12). The two strategies (basic and applied research) have frequently been in conflict, particularly over allocation of funds.

The driving force behind the applied-clinical strategy (and of increased funding for biomedical research in general) was a well-organized group of lobbyists centered around Mary Lasker. Lasker, motivated by great compassion and a personal commitment that stemmed from childhood illness, helped move the federal government into large-scale support of medical research after 1944. Lasker brought to the lobbying effort commitment, contacts, and craft. Strickland (1972, p. 33) describes her skills as "problem analysis, political persuasion, and public opinion molding—of comprehensive, purposeful strategy building." She and her allies used popular media (such as *Reader's Digest*) to build public support, succeeded in raising millions of dollars in private funds for cancer research, and was instrumental in reorganizing the American Cancer Society (Strickland, 1972).

Despite the success of the medical research lobby, dissatisfaction remained because of the continued failure to develop a cure for cancer. Lasker, in the face of declining research support, wanted a national goal focused on cancer that would revitalize the effort and generate public support. A 1968 book by Solomon Gant, *Cure for Cancer: A National Goal*, suggested that this cure should be a national goal in the same way that President Kennedy made landing a man on the moon by 1970 a national goal ("if we can land a man on the moon, why can't we . . .?") (Rettig, 1977). Lasker bought the idea, and a citizens panel she organized made such a recommendation.

The result of this agenda setting, combined with presidential politics (President Nixon would run for reelection in 1972) and legislative activity, was the National Cancer Act of 1971. The fiscal year (FY) appropriation for 1971 was $233 million; by FY 1977, the appropriation had increased by 255 percent to $815 million (Rettig, 1977). The overall goal was to find a cure for cancer through research into fundamental mechanisms and causes and clinical trials with experimental treatments (e.g., chemotherapy). From our perspective, the important points are the setting of a national goal and the enhanced effort. The payoffs from the program were by no means immediate, nor could they be. The early theory was that since cancer had primarily a viral origin, treatments could be developed to attack the virus. Since then, we have learned that cancer is much more complex, really a set of different diseases with different causes. The failure of the immediate effort to cure cancer led to a greater emphasis on prevention.

History of Cancer Research

Related to the new effort were changes in the scientific basis of cancer policy: cancer research. Cancer research originated several centuries ago in classic epidemiologic studies. Those early studies suggested a link between the incidence of cancer and occupation and lifestyle. In the eighteenth century, various observers noted the high frequency of breast cancer among nuns (presumably due to a celibate lifestyle) and the relationship of tobacco snuff users and cancer of the nasal passages. The most famous of these early descriptive studies was by Percival Pott. Pott observed a rare occurrence of cancer of the scrotum and discovered the one factor that the victims had in common: they were all chimney sweeps and exposed to soot. Pott's observation was apparently the first to link cancer with occupation. In the nineteenth century, other studies showed a relationship between bladder cancer and exposure to aromatic amines, as well as between sunlight and skin cancer (Office of Science and Technology Policy, 1984).

More systematic studies began in the early 1900s. The first successful attempt to induce cancer in animals came in 1910, when X-rays were used to produce skin cancers in rats. The first successful chemical carcinogenic test was in 1915 with the production of cancers by painting coal tars on the ears of rabbits. The skin-painting technique was widely used and

> served not only to identify causative agents for cancer and as a guide for their extraction and purification, but also to study modifying factors of carcinogenesis and the mechanisms of the carcinogenic process. (Homburger, 1983a, p. 2).

These studies were used, for example, to demonstrate as early as the 1940s that the carcinogenic process consists of at least two states, initiation and promotion (Berenblum, 1941). The classical animal feeding studies, now the foundation for long-term bioassays, began in the 1940s and eventually superseded in importance the skin-painting experiments (Homburger, 1983b; Wiesburger, 1983).

The original research emphasis was on understanding the causes of cancer and the mechanisms by which cancer progresses. By the early 1960s that emphasis began to shift. In September 1966 the National Advisory Cancer Council requested that the NCI conduct a survey of research opportunities, knowledge gaps, resources, and training needs; the report was delivered in March 1968. In October 1968 the council approved the "Program Plan on Chemical Carcinogenesis and Prevention of Cancer, 1968," which became the basis for NCI's carcinogenesis program (Saffiotti, 1977; Weisburger, 1983).

Bioassays were now being adapted for regulatory purposes; that is, regulatory agencies such as the Food and Drug Administration (FDA) were using the results of bioassays as a principal basis for deciding whether to restrict the use of a substance. The 1958 Delaney amendment to the Pure Food, Drug, and Cosmetic Act required that any substance added to the food supply be banned if it were shown to cause cancer in man or animals. The amendment allowed no discretion, and action could be taken even if only one bioassay were positive. This use of regulatory science raised the question of whether animal experiments developed for one purpose were being used appropriately for another (Gori, 1980). By 1971 the research enterprise was in place. The question, as Gori suggested, was how that research would be used.

Reports

During the same period in which the War on Cancer was being launched and environmental legislation was passed, three reports were issued by federal agencies that concentrated, wholly or in part, on carcinogens, chemical substances implicated as cancer agents. These reports played an important role in agenda building by pointing out a culprit that caused cancer and suggesting that efforts be directed toward limiting its effects. In addition, two of the studies, the Mrak Commission and the Ad Hoc Committee reports, asserted some fundamental premises that would form the basis for later cancer policies.

The first report was issued when Health, Education, and Welfare (HEW) Secretary Robert Finch appointed a commission in 1969 to examine the relationship between pesticides and the environment (Turner, 1971). The study, *Report of the Secretary's Commission on Pesticides and their Relationship to Environmental Health* (1969), known as the "Mrak Commission Report" after chairman Emil Mrak, reached the following conclusions (p. 464; emphasis in original):

> 1. The presence of carcinogenic substances (of both synthetic and natural origin) in food might be a significant factor in the occurrence of what is commonly referred to as "spontaneous" cancer in man and animals. Thus, an important objective in cancer prevention is the elimination, or reduction to a minimum achievable level, of all substances in the diet of man proven to be carcinogenic in either man or animal.

> 2. Since the effects of carcinogens on target tissues leading to tumor formation appear irreversible, with accumulation of effects over extended periods of exposure, *the reduction of exposure to carcinogenic substances to the lowest practicable level may be one of the most effective measures towards cancer prevention.*

3. Many different factors may influence dose-response in carcinogenesis in man and animals. Their complexity is such that no assuredly safe level for carcinogens in human food can be determined from experimental findings at the present time.

The Mrak Commission acknowledged the problems in the quality of studies, problems of extrapolation from animals to humans, and the complexity of the environment. In addition, it took a balancing view toward pesticides, recommending their use if no proven noncarcinogenic alternative were available and if banning a substance would be detrimental to human health. Complete testing of pesticides was recommended, as was new legislation that would take into account the public interest, advancing technology (e.g., the ability to detect smaller amounts of a substance), and problems in safety evaluation. It is important to note that the commission stated that no thresholds can be shown to exist and that carcinogenic effects seem irreversible, assumptions that underlie a risk-averse cancer policy and that were challenged during the Reagan administration (see chapter 5).

A second report was issued by the Council on Environmental Quality (CEQ) (1971). The council began looking at the question of toxic substances (such as metals, metalic compounds, and synthetic organic compounds) that entered the environment and that were in consumer products but were not covered by existing legislation. CEQ pointed out that these substances occurred in minute quantities, were present in many different media (land, air, and water), and were potentially toxic at those low levels. Legislation in force at that time (early 1971) focused on one medium at a time, on substances that occurred in large quantities, and on substances that were readily identifiable through measurement techniques. No legislation covered the total impact or total dispersion of toxic substances. CEQ recommended passage of a toxic substances control act that would give the Environmental Protection Agency authority to regulate such substances and to issue standards for testing potentially toxic chemicals. Just before the report was issued, the Nixon administration proposed such a bill (developed by CEQ) in February 1971. Five years later the Toxic Substances Control Act was passed.

The final report more specifically addressed the question of cancer risk assessment. In October 1969 the surgeon general of the

United States established an ad hoc committee, made up of prominent scientists, "to review the problems relating to the evaluation of low levels of environmental carcinogens, to consider the scientific bases on which such evaluations can be made, and to advise the Department of HEW [Health, Education, and Welfare] on the implications of such evaluations" ("Evaluation of Environmental Carcinogens," 1970, p. 180). The report was apparently a reaction to an earlier paper issued by the Food Protection Committee of the National Academy of Sciences/National Research Council. That report, "Guidelines for Estimating Toxicologically Insignificant Levels of Chemicals in Food," suggested that under certain conditions, potentially harmful substances could be considered safe in the food supply (see "Evaluation of Environmental Carcinogens," 1970, and McGarity, 1983).

The Ad Hoc Committee made a number of recommendations. Of significance is how they addressed some of the inference controversies discussed in chapter 2 and how their recommendations resembled many of the risk-averse cancer guidelines issued later, especially the 1980 OSHA cancer policy.

> 1. a. Any substance which is shown conclusively to cause tumors in animals should be considered carcinogenic and therefore a potential cancer hazard for man. . . .
>
> b. Data on carcinogenic effects in man are only acceptable when they represent critically evaluated results of adequately conducted epidemiologic studies.
>
> 2. No level of exposure to a chemical carcinogen should be considered toxicologically insignificant for man. . . .
>
> 4. No chemical substance should be assumed safe for human consumption without proper negative lifetime biological assays of adequate size. . . .
>
> 5. Evidence of negative results, under conditions of the test used, should be considered superseded by positive findings in other tests. . . .
>
> 6. The implication of potential carcinogenicity should be drawn both from tests resulting in the induction of benign tumors and those resulting in tumors which are obviously malignant. . . .

7. The principle of zero tolerance for carcinogenic exposures should be retained in all areas of legislation presently covered by it and should be extended to cover other exposures as well . . . ("Evaluation of Environmental Carcinogens," 1970, p. 181)

The report also contained an intriguing appendix by one of the committee members, Marvin Schneiderman. The appendix demonstrated "a method for determining the dose compatible with some 'acceptable' level of risk." Schneiderman wrote that because extrapolations of dose levels were only for the species tested, a conservative dose-response model was used to produce conservative estimates of an acceptable risk dose ("Evaluation of Environmental Carcinogens," 1970). We can see in this early paper grounds for later complaints that some agencies were mixing science and politics—in this case, by making a prior selection of a conservative (risk-averse) model to produce a conservative result.

The Ad Hoc Committee report was submitted for publication to the *Journal of the National Cancer Institute* but was not published; it did appear in two Senate hearings in 1971. Its importance was that it was one of the first statements of the *principles approach*: that there was an agreed-upon set of principles that should guide risk assessments. This approach became a mainstay of many of the cancer policy documents issued from 1976 to 1984; the latest and most sophisticated version of this approach appears in the 1984 draft of the Office of Science and Technology Policy (see appendix A). Equally important was that members of the committee, such as chairman Umberto Saffiotti and Marvin Schneiderman, both prominent cancer scientists, continued to push those principles.

I have examined, to this point, four simultaneous sets of trends that helped create an environment for considering and setting cancer policy. The events can be placed on a continuum from most general to most specific. The environmental movement and the legislation that resulted considered environmental problems as a whole with little concern, as the Council on Environmental Quality (1971) report pointed out, for low levels of toxic substances in the environment. In the middle of the continuum is the War on Cancer, embodied in the National Cancer Act of 1971.

Arising from a completely different set of causes from the environmental movement, the act focused on the disease cancer, but from a variety of perspectives: causes, mechanisms, treatments, cures, and prevention. The carcinogenesis program within the National Cancer Institute, which would provide some of the scientific basis for cancer policy, was just beginning to emerge and was not an explicit focus of those advocating an enhanced research effort. Finally, the three reports focused specifically on toxic substances as a major cause of cancer, with attention centered on prevention. Prevention implies some kind of risk assessment and, following the reasoning of the CEQ report, some coherent policy. The Ad Hoc Committee report came close to advocating a cancer policy. As we shall see in the next section, dissatisfaction with environmental statues and the War on Cancer led to new legislation and the view that an explicit cancer policy was necessary. Saffiotti and others such as Schneiderman played an important role in this change.

Mid-1970s

In 1971 President Nixon sent a bill to Congress to regulate toxic substances. There was a large gap in environmental legislation, as CEQ had stated, that the bill was designed to rectify. In 1976, during the Ford administration, Congress passed the Toxic Substances Control Act (TSCA). What distinguished TSCA from other legislation was its emphasis on prevention; that is, it was designed to anticipate problems such as the carcinogenicity of a chemical and either ban or restrict the use of that chemical.[13]

TSCA is important to our story for several reasons. First, as the most comprehensive and focused statute dealing with potentially toxic substances, it virtually required risk assessments, though the statutory language was typically vague. EPA could take action if a substance posed an "unreasonable risk." What "unreasonable risk" meant was not clear and was subject to differing interpretations.[14] The presence of ambiguous language forced the agency to develop new and different criteria for deciding whether and how to act.

As important as the TSCA requirements was the legislative history of the act. As we shall see below with the War on Cancer, Congress increasingly identified the cancer problem as largely due to environmental causes. It is clear that Congress wanted to attack those causes, and TSCA was one method of doing so. Typical of this sentiment was the following statement by Andrew Maguire (D.-N.J.):

> The subcommittee is deeply concerned about the high incidence of cancer due to manmade carcinogens in the environment and in the workplace. A consensus has emerged in the scientific and medical community which holds that the great majority of all cancers results from environmental factors.
>
> We are finding that most cancers may well be deadly byproducts of our modern industrialized society. Scientists are continually identifying new and old substances as carcinogenic. These are added to the already long list of carcinogens in our air, water, and food, as well as those in the workplace.
>
> Congress has a responsibility to the Nation to investigate these causes of cancer. In particular, Congress must assess the efficacy of present laws designed to reduce the sickness and death associated with substances in the environment. Are these laws being effectively implemented? Are these laws sufficient? Are new laws necessary?
>
> These questions are quite relevant at a time when Congress is considering new legislation to control toxic chemical substances and mixtures. (*Environmental Causes of Cancer,* 1976, p. 1)[15]

The War on Cancer also came under scrutiny. Five years after the passage of the National Cancer Act, it was clear that finding a cure for cancer was considerably more complicated than had been anticipated (Rettig, 1977). Moreover, there was a general concern that the "cancer crusade" was focusing too much on cure and not enough on prevention. If the curative orientation was controversial, the smaller carcinogenesis program was even more so. Yet as Rettig (1977) points out, many believed that much could be accomplished by preventing cancer, even if the underlying mechanisms were poorly understood. This belief was explicitly mentioned in the report accompanying the fiscal year 1977 appropriations bill. The report stated that insufficient emphasis had been given to the carcinogenesis program, only 6 percent of total National Cancer Institute funding, with equally small staffing.

The committee provided for substantial staffing increases (*Report on Departments of Labor, and Health, Education, and Welfare*, 1976).

Echoing this dissatisfaction with the War on Cancer in particular, and on federal regulatory efforts toward carcinogens in general, was a 1976 report by the General Accounting Office (GAO) (1976). The GAO study pointed to fragmentation and overlap among federal agencies, with no one agency assuming a leadership role. The report also pointed to a number of unresolved technical issues that hampered public protection, including the difficulty of accepting animal data as the basis for regulation and the lack of scientific principles to guide risk assessments, issues that still plague cancer policy. The report called for a "uniform policy for identifying and regulating carcinogens" (General Accounting Office, 1976, p. 11).

All these reports, studies, and acts recommended that the environmental carcinogenic problem be explicitly addressed; they also emphasized the need for a coherent cancer policy.

EPA 1976 Interim Guidelines

The first cancer risk assessment guidelines were proposed by the Environmental Protection Agency. While the events just described created the atmosphere for developing a generic cancer policy, the specific precipitating events were EPA's decisions to cancel registrations for the pesticides aldrin and dieldrin in 1974 and for chlordane and heptachlor in 1975. The latter decision was especially controversial because it reversed the ruling of the administrative hearing judge.

As part of the summaries of the two cases, EPA attorneys abstracted a number of principles that presumably guided their decisions.[16] The principles aroused great fear in the agricultural chemical community (McGarity, 1983). McGarity reports that the EPA associate general counsel for pesticides (Anson Keller) asked Umberto Saffiotti to summarize the principles, that then might be used in a subsequent case against the pesticide mirex. The results are reprinted below. There is a marked resemblance between these principles, the principles enunciated in the 1970 Ad Hoc Committee report discussed above, and the cancer policies issued during the Carter administration (chapter 4):

(1) A carcinogen is any agent which increases tumor induction in man or animals.[17]

(2) Well-established criteria exist for distinguishing between benign and malignant tumors; however, even the induction of benign tumors is sufficient to characterize a chemical as a carcinogen.

(3) The majority of human cancers are caused by avoidable exposure to carcinogens.

(4) While chemicals can be carcinogenic agents, only a small percentage are.

(5) Carcinogenesis is characterized by its irreversibility and long latency period following initial exposure to a carcinogenic agent.

(6) Individual susceptibility to carcinogens varies greatly.

(7) The concept of a "threshold" exposure level for a carcinogenic agent has no practical significance because no valid method of establishing such a level exists.

(8) A carcinogenic agent may be identified through analysis of tumor induction results with laboratory animals exposed to the agent, or on a post hoc basis by properly conducted epidemiological studies.

(9) Any substance which produces tumors in animals must be considered a carcinogenic hazard to man if the results were produced in a valid carcinogenesis test. ("EPA Wrongfully used Definitions of Cancer," 1976, p. 1954)

These are particularly prudent risk assessment assumptions (see table 2.5) if one presumes, despite the fourth principle, that many chemicals will be shown to be carcinogenic. The motion to include these principles in the mirex hearing produced several months of protest, and the principles were reduced to the following "three basic facts" (McGarity, 1983, p. 89):

(1) There is presently no scientific basis for concluding that there is a "no effect" level for chemical carcinogens.

(2) Experimental data derived from mouse and rat studies can be used to evaluate whether there is a cancer risk to man.

(3) All tumorigens must be regarded as potential carcinogens. For purposes of evaluating carcinogenicity hazard, no

distinction should be made between the induction of tumors diagnosed as benign and the induction of tumors diagnosed as malignant.

A scientist for EPA requested a review of those principles by the National Cancer Advisory Board (NCAB). Though the request was withdrawn, NCAB reviewed the principles anyway. The board implicitly rejected them, though the June 1976 EPA guidelines were similar to Saffiotti's summary draft. NCAB would issue its own set of guidelines the next year (McGarity, 1983).

EPA began work on its cancer policy in 1975. Alvin Alm, assistant administrator for planning and management, sent a memo to EPA Administrator Russell Train outlining an approach to cancer policy. The memo recommended three departures from present practices: establishing procedures for assessing risks and benefits from carcinogens, designating a carcinogen assessment group to review the health aspects of agency decisions, and requiring external scientific reviews of agency procedures and specific risk assessments (Alm, 1975). The result, some five months later, was the EPA Interim Guidelines.

The guidelines were issued to reassure the public (especially the agricultural chemical industry) that EPA policy had not changed. EPA Administrator Train stated, in the preamble to the guidelines, that a two-step decision-making process would be employed. The first step would be to assess the carcinogenicity of a substance; the second would be to determine what, if any, regulatory action should be taken.[18] Train pointed out the difficulties of conclusively proving that a substance was a human carcinogen; therefore, he stated, a statistically significant increase in either benign or malignant tumors would establish a presumption of risk. He contnued: "However, the decision that a cancer risk may exist does not mean that the EPA will automatically take regulatory action" (Environmental Protection Aency, 1976, p. 21403). Any such regulatory decision would have to be based on detailed assessments of risks and benefits (economic), costs, and availability of controls and substitutes. The reassurances continued:

> In considering the risks, it will be necessary to view the evidence for carcinogenicity in terms of a warning signal, the

strength of which is a function of many factors including those relating to the quality and scope of the data, the character of the toxicological response, and the possible impact on public health. It is understood that qualifications relating to the strength of the evidence for carcinogenicity may be relevant to this consideration because of the uncertainties in our knowledge of the qualitative and quantitative similarities of human and animal responses. In all events, it is essential in making decisions about suspect carcinogens that all relevant information be taken into consideration. (Environmental Protection Agency, 1976, p. 21403)

The guidelines were extremely flexible and employed a weight-of-the-evidence approach. According to the guidelines, the best evidence is epidemiological with confirmatory animal studies. Substantial evidence comes from bioassays. Suggestive evidence derives from studies showing a benign tumor response that is not life threatening (Environmental Protection Agency, 1976). The format for both the risk assessment and the economic impact analyses was spelled out. The guidelines were quite general and avoided committing the agency to a particular stance, for example, in the use of dose-response models. Its major purpose, as stated above, appeared to be one of reassurance, and it implicitly rejected the principles approach advocated by Saffiotti. That approach would be incorporated in the OSHA guidelines during the Carter administration.

National Cancer Advisory Board

At the same time that the EPA guidelines were published in the *Federal Register*, the National Cancer Advisory Board (NCAB) issued its own criteria for assessing carcinogenicity (National Cancer Advisory Board, 1976). The board affirmed that the "criteria adopted are based upon those generally used in the application of the scientific method to any question" (National Cancer Advisory Board, 1976, p. 543). As with the EPA cancer policy, the NCAB guidelines were general and stated that each case must be considered by itself. The document stated that compounds shown to be carcinogenic in humans have also been shown (with a few exceptions) to be carcinogenic in animals, thereby affirming the validity of bioassays. It also maintained that differences between initiators, promoters, and other modifying agents cannot be made in either bioassays or epidemiological studies. The document distinguished between malignant and benign tumors but noted that benign tumors might themselves be life threatening and might also be an early stage in the transition to malignancy. Finally, NCAB said that negative studies do not prove that a suspect substance is safe; they may be used to indicate upper limits of exposure (see chapter 2 for an explanation of upper limits).

Conclusion

Cancer policy development had reached a new stage by the end of 1976. The various streams were coming together to create a momentum for significant change in government's approach to cancer risk assessment. The new emphasis would be on more detailed guidance and coordination. This early period, which may be labelled the "precursor" period, was necessary to set the stage for later evolution. The flurry of activity during the years of the Carter administration was defined by the actions taken during this pre-1977 period. Three problems were joined together: the problem of cancer incidence and mortality, the identification of the cause of that problem with environmental substances, and the need to address those problems. Solutions, the policy stream, were advocated by policy entrepreneurs such as the scientist Saffiotti and the lawyer Keller. They pushed for a vigorous cancer policy based on a set of principles presumably grounded in the underlying science. What was needed was a meeting with the third stream, the political stream, to create the "window of opportunity" that would lead to the maturation of cancer policy. That third stream was the 1976 presidential election.

4

Maturation of Cancer Policy

Underlying regulatory decisions and agency policies on carcinogens are certain principles and technical considerations. These principles, on which there is wide agreement, form the basis of federal efforts to identify potential human carcinogens. Although they have been the subject of considerable public misunderstanding, these principles are widely supported in the scientific community and in the deliberations of rulemaking and adjudicatory bodies, the courts, expert committees, and international agencies

--Toxic Substances Strategy Committee, 1980 p. 125

The "window of opportunity" for the full-scale ripening of cancer policy was completed with the November 1976 election of Jimmy Carter as president. Carter brought to the presidency two emphases that shaped the course of cancer policy development. One was a genuine commitment to environmental protection; the other was an equally strong espousal of regulatory reform. The legislative output during the 1977–1980 period was modest (see table 3.1), consisting largely of adjustments to the Clean Air Act and Clean Water Act, and new initiatives in strip mining and abandoned wastes. Much of the focus was on implementation, including that of the new Toxic Substances Control Act.

Carter's twin commitments can be seen in his May 1977 environmental message to Congress. He called for a "coordinated federal effort to exclude [toxic chemicals] from our environment."

I am therefore instructing the Council on Environmental Quality to develop an interagency program (1) to eliminate

85

overlaps and fill gaps in the collection of data on toxic chemicals, and (2) to coordinate federal research and regulatory activities affecting them. (Carter, 1977, p. 31-E)

In addition, the president called for an increased emphasis on toxic chemicals under the Toxic Substances Control Act, the Federal Water Pollution Control Act, the Safe Drinking Water Act, and the Occupational Safety and Health Act. Thus, the president's plan had two themes: attack the problem of toxic substances as a genuinely serious one, but coordinate federal activities and eliminate overlap.

Regulatory Reform

In March 1978 President Carter issued Executive Order 12044.[1] The order required agencies to perform regulatory impact analyses and to set the criteria for those analyses. The analyses should include a statement of the problem, a description of alternative ways of alleviating the problem, the economic costs of each of the alternatives, and the reason for selecting one of the alternatives. Agencies were also to issue a calendar of regulatory actions every six months. While the executive order had no direct impact on cancer policy development, it did require that the economic consequences of proposed regulations be considered.[2]

The second part of Carter's regulatory reform package was the establishment in January 1978 of the Regulatory Analysis Review Group (RARG). RARG was to review some ten to twenty regulations a year for their inflationary impact. It was composed of most of the cabinet departments, the White House Office of Science and Technology Policy, the Environmental Protection Agency (EPA), the Council of Economic Advisers, and the Office of Management and Budget. RARG became involved in negotiations over many environmental, as well as other, regulations (White, 1981).

The final element also came in 1978 with the establishment of the Regulatory Council, composed of representatives of all the executive branch and independent regulatory agencies. The council's major impact was the publication of a calendar of major rules to be considered by the agencies. From our standpoint, the council was important because it adopted a federal cancer policy in 1979 (Gottron, 1982).

The Drive Toward a Coherent, Governmentwide Cancer Policy

The president, in his 1977 environmental message, called for a coordinated policy on toxic substances. To this end, two other groups were established. The first, by direct order from the president to the Council on Environmental Quality (CEQ), was the Toxic Substances Strategy Committee (TSSC). The committee was chaired by CEQ and included representatives from federal agencies that had regulatory or research responsibility over toxic substance.[3] The major product of their effort was a report issued in May 1980 (Toxic Substances Strategy Committee, 1980). One other important result was the centralizing of federal research in toxic substances under the auspices of the National Toxicology Program (NTP) within the Department of Health, Education, and Welfare.

Another group played a more direct and important role in coordinating federal policy toward toxic substances. This was the Interagency Regulatory Liaison Group (IRLG), brought together in August 1977 by agreement of the heads of the Environmental Protection Agency (EPA), the Occupational Safety and Health Administration (OSHA), the Consumer Product Safety Commission (CPSC), and the Food and Drug Administration (FDA), later joined by the Food Safety and Quality Service of the U.S. Department of Agriculture. IRLG formed working groups on issues, such as formaldehyde, that cut across agency jurisdiction (Rushefsky, 1984a). Its most important product came in 1979 with the issuance of generic cancer risk assessment guidelines. Those guidelines, as we shall see later, were adopted by the Regulatory Council to guide individual agencies in making specific decisions and issuing their own cancer policies.

The problem of legislative and bureaucratic overlap, addressed by these Carter administration initiatives, is captured nicely in the following quote from a 1977 *National Journal* article. Note that the quote is referring to overlap of coordinating bodies.

A recent CEQ memorandum identified eight such interagency groups—although EPA's deputy administrator Barbara Blum insists she has at least a dozen organizations on her list. One of the groups on the CEQ list, the Ad Hoc Interagency Toxic Substance Data Committee, is described as having participating members from no less than 32 federal agencies. . . . There is the Committee to Coordinate Toxicology and Related Problems (nine agencies from within the Department of Health, Education and Welfare) and its subcommittee, the Toxicology Information Program (observers from eight agencies outside HEW). At least seven agencies are represented either as members or observers on the Policy Board of the National Center for Toxicological Research.

And then too, there is the Interagency Collaborative Group on Environmental Carcinogenesis (ICGEC), which should not be confused with the NCI's Clearinghouse on Environmental Carcinogenesis, a group of mostly nongovernmental types that failed even to make the CEQ list. (Kirschten, 1977, pp. 1222-1223)

The plethora of coordinating bodies (in cancer policy as well as in the regulatory reform program in general was replaced by the Office of Management and Budget during the Reagan administration.

OSHA's Cancer Regulations

While EPA was issuing its interim guidelines in 1976 and the Carter administration was beginning its attempt to coordinate cancer policy, the Occupational Safety and Health Administration (OSHA) was moving on its own. By 1977 OSHA had issued standards for only four substances: asbestos, 14 carcinogens, vinyl chloride, and coke oven emissions (Clark, 1978).[4] Each of these standards took time to develop, was subject to extended regulatory proceedings, and was challenged by industry as too stringent and by labor as too lenient. During the four sets of hearings, similar questions were raised about the scientific validity of the regulations, questions about the meaningfulness of bioassays and the existence of thresholds. Each issue was considered separately in the four hearings.

One source that led to the generic cancer regulations, according to the *National Journal*, was a series of television programs on cancer aired by CBS News in 1976. The OSHA administrator at

orton Corn, was asked what the agency's cancer
'orn then asked Grover C. Wrenn, OSHA's health
'gram director, the same question before the inter-
replied that there was no coherent policy, though the
agency was giving the same answers in all four hearings.

"That question from CBS really got us started on developing a cancer policy," said Wrenn. "We saw that with different
chemicals and different situations, the agency had come to the
same general policy conclusions. So we decided to try to answer
some questions conclusively. It doesn't make sense to
revisit—and re-litigate—the same questions over and over again.
It appeared there was an ultimate truth, that we could deal with
some questions in a generic conceptual way.

"What is the role of animal evidence in identifying a carcinogen? Is there a safe level of exposure? If not, what is the
basis for deciding how to regulate?" (Clark, 1978, p. 2058)

There were other factors that made OSHA a logical ground
for proposing a strong generic cancer policy.[5] OSHA was sym-
pathetic to the approach of the 1970 Ad Hoc Committee report
OSHA also felt, on the basis of its record and court decisions, that it
could not weigh risks and benefits in setting standards. Another
contributing factor was that Anson Keller, formerly associate
general counsel for pesticides (see chapter 3), left EPA and became
a special assistant to the OSHA administrator. Keller circulated a
draft cancer policy in late 1976, and OSHA published its draft proposal in the *Federal Register* in October 1977.

The proposed regulations were exceptionally controversial.
Within a year, they generated a quarter of a million written comments as well as hearings on the regulations during 1978–1979;
they also spawned a new interest group, the American Industrial
Health Council (AIHC). Why the controversy?

The obvious first answer is the impact that the generic cancer
regulations would have on affected parties, especially on industry.
The approach taken by OSHA reinforced the cancer policy controversy. At the end of chapter 2, a distinction was made between
three general approaches: regulation, established procedures, and
recommendations. The nonregulatory guidelines (by IRLG and

OSTP [Office of Science and Technology Policy]) were recommendations to regulatory agencies; all the other policies were general procedures (see table 2.7). Only OSHA adopted cancer policy as a regulation, which, of course, has the force of law. The regulatory nature of the policy was compounded by the rigidity of its policy determinations. Again, recalling the discussion from chapter 2, OSHA was the only agency to adopt a presumption-rebuttal posture, as opposed to a leave-it-to-the-scientists or the more common weight-of-the-evidence approaches. Grover Wrenn stated that there "appeared to be some ultimate truth," presumably embodied in the Ad Hoc Committee's report, that could be questioned only under unusual circumstances.

Finally, OSHA's early implementation of its statutory mandate did not endear it to industry. OSHA originally focused on safety standards (which were easier to assess than health standards) and, to ease its administrative burden, adopted voluntary, industrywide standards. Having done so, it then vigorously tried to enforce them; thus were born the horror stories about OSHA, from which it never recovered (McNeil, 1981).

OSHA's final policy, adopted in 1980, was essentially that proposed in 1977. The policy itself was fairly short, only 14 pages in the *Federal Register*. The accompanying preamble, however, was quite illuminating, some 280 pages. The preamble summarized the two years of hearings and the overwhelming amount of written comments; it also presented OSHA's rationalizations for the positions it took.

The regulations incorporated the principles approach to cancer policy. Its three basic propositions were that it is appropriate to extrapolate from animal bioassays, that positive results are generally superior to negative results, and that there is no evidence for the existence of a threshold (Pelham, 1978). OSHA also took extreme positions on other issues, such as willingness to rely solely on benign tumors in its consideration of carcinogenicity. On the basis of those principles OSHA then divided substances into one of two categories. The agency defined a *potential occupational carcinogen as:*

> any substance, or combination or mixture of substances, which causes an increased incidence of benign and/or malignant

neoplasms, or a substantial decrease in the latency period between exposure and onset of neoplasms in humans or in one or
more experimental mammalian species as the result of any oral,
respiratory or dermal exposure, or any other exposure which
results in the induction of tumors at a site other than the site of
administration. This definition also includes any substance
which is metabolized into one or more potential occupational
carcinogens by mammals. (Occupational Safety and Health Administration, 1980, p. 5283)

Category I substances are those that meet the above definition
in humans or in a single bioassay where the results are in concordance with other evidence, or in a single bioassay without concordance if the secretary of labor decides the requirement is unnecessary. Category II substances are those that meet the criteria;
however, the evidence may be only suggestive, or there may be no
concordance with the single mammalian bioassay. Category I
substances will be either banned or regulated to lowest feasible
levels; Category II substances will have exposure appropriately
reduced (Occupational Safety and Health Administration, 1980).
The regulations also call for setting priorities among chemicals and
set some conditions for examining exceptions to OSHA's policy
positions.

One other significant part of the OSHA cancer regulations
was its view of quantitative evaluation (quantitative risk assessment). OSHA's position was that quantitative analysis rested on
too uncertain a basis for regulatory purposes and that, of the other
regulatory agencies, only the Environmental Protection Agency
made regular use of it (see Occupational Safety and Health Administration, 1980, pp. 5178–5201).

The OSHA policy was subject to criticism both inside and
outside the administration. Most of those criticisms may be found
in the preamble to the cancer regulations. We will provide just a
few examples. It is important to note that most of the people testifying at the hearing were scientists, an illustration of how scientists
may serve the interests of other 'estates'.

One of the results of the Carter administration's focus on
regulatory reform was the attempt of various White House agencies to modify proposed regulations.[6] One of these groups was the
Regulatory Analysis Review Group (RARG), headed by the chair-

man of the Council of Economic Advisors, Charles Schultze. RARG pointed out that the OSHA proposal considered only qualitative evaluation for classification purposes. Other factors that lent themselves to quantitative evaluation, such as potency and entry, RARG stated, ought to be considered to keep the OSHA standards flexible (Occupational Safety and Health Administration, 1980).

Regulatory agencies were generally supportive of OSHA's proposal. The same could not be said for industry, which would be directly affected by the cancer policy. Industry scientists consistently opposed OSHA's positions over the entire range of issues. Perhaps the most interesting of the critiques was that of the American Industrial Health Council (AIHC). AIHC was formed in the fall of 1977 as a reaction to OSHA's draft proposal. Its membership consists of individual firms and trade associations. Its purpose is to produce a "socially responsible" position on the issue of chemical safety. AIHC not only critiques the OSHA policy but also recommended an alternative. As we shall see below, AIHC did the same thing for the IRLG cancer policy.[7]

AIHC accepted the general goals of OSHA's generic cancer policy: to reduce cancer deaths from chemical substances, to have a generic policy, and to classify substances for regulatory purposes. It differed considerably on the details. For example, the critique began by examining two propositions of OSHA's policy: that there is a cancer epidemic and that industrial chemicals are an important cause of cancer. It also objected to the rigidity of the proposed regulation, stating that it would "freeze" science. Further, it asserted that OSHA attempted to achieve the unachievable, a "no-risk" society (American Industrial Health Council, 1978).

The AIHC critique examined at length the principles underlying OSHA's approach. It concluded (American Industrial Health Council, 1978, p. A-1): "OSHA identifies principles alleging to represent the relationship of chemicals to cancer. OSHA's principles taken collectively present an erroneous concept for sound regulatory policy decisions." It then offered six points, or "scientific principles," to OSHA as a guide for its policy decisions. For example, the AIHC principles stated that absolute safety (no- or zero-risk) is impossible; "socially acceptable risk" should be the standard, based on relative risk (a comparison of risks) and risks above background levels. Other parts of the principles stated that the threshold concept has strong scientific support, that high doses are only suggestive of human carcinogenicity, that negative studies are much more important than OSHA acknowledged, and that metabolic similarity between animal test models and humans should be demonstrated before findings from bioassays are applied to humans (American Industrial Health Council, 1978). The report concluded:

> The state of knowledge of carcinogenicity is dynamic. Regulatory decisions should be based on careful evaluation of data judged according to accepted scientific principles. OSHA should not foreclose reconsideration of procedures, identification and classification criteria; such foreclosure negates the likely possibility that scientific progress will be made in understanding the cause of cancer and preventing it. It should not be necessary to set standards for thousands of chemicals at lowest feasible levels. Such levels do not necessarily better insure greater employee health protection. Further, they may not be achievable at a reasonable enough cost to permit continued manufacture and/or use of many chemicals of great value to man and his environment. (American Industrial Health Council, 1978, p. A-11).

Two phrases of the quote are especially interesting. First, note that it refers to the "cause of cancer and preventing it." The implication is that there is only one cause of cancer (and certainly not chemicals) and that as soon as we find it we can prevent cancer. Second, note the reference to setting standards for "thousands" of chemicals. While there is a debatable point here, this is basically the argument of "does everything cause cancer?" OSHA (1980) and others (e.g., Epstein, 1978) said that only a relatively few substances cause cancer. Efron (1984), on the other hand, argued that the methods recommended by regulatory agencies (and here she specifically had OSHA in mind, the major example of her book) would implicate thousands of chemicals.

AIHC's recommended alternative was based on the principle that determining carcinogenicity is a scientific rather than a regulatory question, the view underlying the two-stage model discussed in chapter 1. Therefore, that determination should be made by an independent science panel outside of OSHA (or any other regulatory agency) composed of qualified scientists objectively evaluating all the data. The panel's determinations would be subject to judicial but not agency review. The report then offered detailed criteria (based on valid human data) for classifying a substance into one of three categories, each one, as with the OSHA proposal, with its own regulatory response. For example, category I substances would be known human carcinogens and would be further categorized by level of potency (high, intermediate, or low). The detailed proposal also suggested that risks and benefits be analyzed in setting standards.

Despite such critiques, OSHA adopted its generic cancer policy in essentially the same form as its 1977 draft. Further changes to the cancer policy came as a result of U.S. Supreme Court decisions in 1980 (benzene) and 1981 (cotton dust).[8]

Interagency Regulatory Liaison Group

The other especially controversial cancer policy document of this period was that of the Interagency Regulatory Liaison Group (IRLG) in 1979. The document, a product of an interagency group of scientists, was intended to provide guidance to agencies that were responsible for making risk control regulations. To recall, IRLG was formed in the summer of 1977 by agreement of the four major regulatory agencies (CPSC, FDA, EPA, and OSHA) as part of the Carter administration's effort to coordinate policy actions. The head of the Risk Assessment Group was Eula Bingham, assistant secretary of labor (administrator of OSHA); seven others from the various agencies were part of the work group, including Anson Keller of OSHA, a principal mover behind the principles approach to cancer policy. The working group was assisted by other scientists and reads as a list of prominent cancer researchers and advocates of risk-averse cancer policy: Roy Albert, head of the Carcinogen Assessment Group within EPA; Richard Bates of the National Institute of Environmental Health Sciences (NIEHS); David G. Hoel, also of NIEHS; Umberto Saffiotti; and Marvin Schneiderman of the National Cancer Institute (NCI). The work group also acknowledged the assistance of others, including Arthur C. Upton, Director of NCI, and David P. Rall, Director of NIEHS.

The report, entitled "Scientific Bases for Identification of Potential Carcinogens and Estimation of Risks," was published in the *Federal Register* for comment and later in *JCNI* (formerly the *Journal of the National Cancer Institute*). A major complaint about the report was that it did not undergo peer review (one of the principal characteristics of science; see chapter 2) before its publication in the *Federal Register*. In the *JCNI* article, IRLG stated that its publication there constituted peer review. However, because the article was accepted two weeks after submission, it is unlikely that the peer review, if any, was especially strong. This remained one of the major arguments against the IRLG report: that it was not a good model for how peer reviews should be conducted. Even those who supported the report agreed with this point (see *Control of Carcinogens*, 1983).

The IRLG report differed from the OSHA cancer policy in several important respects. First, it was not a regulation, but a recommendation to agencies about what to consider and how. Second, the approach of the IRLG report was a weight-of-the-evidence one, as opposed to OSHA's presumption-rebuttal approach. OSHA was satisfied with qualitative evaluation, that is, with whether or not a substance was a carcinogen, in making its regulatory determinations. IRLG went further and looked at potency and other factors. Quantitative evaluation was an integral part of IRLG's recommendations. The IRLG guidelines were also the most comprehensive of all the cancer policy documents issued during the Carter administration. For example, the report considered population exposure at length.

In addition to its rather weak peer review procedures, the IRLG report was criticized because of its explicit risk-averse approach to cancer policy. In several places, IRLG made "conservative" or "prudent" assumptions that could lead to rigorous regulation. These assumptions are the clearest example of how facts and values in cancer policies were mixed during the Carter administration. The problem, at least for some (see the AIHC discussion of the IRLG report below), is that it appeared as though IRLG had made prior decisions to be risk-averse through inferences and assumptions, and then used the results of the risk-averse science policy decisions to produce evidence that would justify stiff regulatory decisions. For example, note the language of the following quote from the IRLG report:

> Despite the uncertainties, risk estimates can be and are being made, not only by some regulator agencies but by other scientific bodies. Because of the uncertainties, however, and because of the serious public health consequences if the estimated risk were understated, it has become common practice to make *cautious and prudent assumptions* wherever they are needed to conduct a risk assessment. This approach has a precedent in other areas of public health protection where similar problems arise because of gaps in knowledge. . . . Thus, current methodologies, which permit only crude estimates of human risk, *are designed to avoid understatement of the risk.* . . . The linear nonthreshold dose-response model is most commonly used at the present time. Of the various models, it appears to have the soundest scientific basis and is *less likely to understate risk than other plausible models.* (Interagency Regulatory Liaison Group, 1979, p. 209; emphasis added)

The IRLG report was originally published in the *Federal Register* in 1978. In September 1979 the Regulatory Council, chaired by EPA administrator Douglas Costle, issued a statement on regulating chemical carcinogens (Regulatory Council, 1979). The council's purpose was to consider the issues stated in the IRLG document—as well as efforts by other agencies (such as the White House Office of Science and Technology Policy, discussed below), comments on OSHA's proposed cancer policy, and the National Cancer Advisory Board statement—and to produce a "government-wide policy which reflected this Administration's actions to promote more effectively the public health without imposing unnecessary burdens upon the economy, and to eliminate potential inconsistencies and inefficiencies in the government's regulatory program" (Regulatory Council, 1979, p. 9). The council accepted the IRLG document and further announced precepts for risk assessment, priority setting, and regulatory considerations. The council suggested, under the risk assessment category, that any exposure to a carcinogenic substance may cause cancer (the nonthreshold concept), that agencies making quantitative risk assessments should follow IRLG procedures, and that sources of uncertainty should accompany all risk assessments. For priority setting, the council recommended that higher priorities be assigned where the substance is likely to present a risk of human cancer, where the level of exposure or risk is high, and where the exposed population is either large or special (e.g., children). For regulatory action, agencies should consider the following factors: risk, technical and economic feasibility, and comparisons of costs and benefits. The council also stated that zero-risk (e.g., zero-exposure) should not be routinely considered by agencies (Regulatory Council, 1979, pp. 12–13).

The IRLG document was the object of many of the same criticisms, by many of the same critics, as the OSHA regulations. We again examine the AIHC critique. The AIHC report began by stating that much of the IRLG policy was sound and generally accepted. It welcomed publication of the report because it was "a significant step toward the formulation of a national cancer policy," and it clearly recognized that "the identification and estimation of the carcinogenic risk that may be posed to humans is a scientific function involving scientific judgment and evaluation of all the data" (American Industrial Health Council, 1979, p. 2). However, it felt that the close publication of two other reports, especially the one by the White House Office of Science and Technology Policy (OSTP, discussed below) pointed to weaknesses in the IRLG report.

The most fundamental criticism of the IRLG report was that it mixed scientific and regulatory considerations. Compare the following quote with the previous one from the IRLG report.

> Thus, when the IRLG report speaks of the importance of using conservative methods or assumptions so as not to underestimate human risk, the Report is mixing regulatory considerations into the scientific function. The scientific determination should be made separately from the regulatory determinations. . . .

> We urge that the IRLG take special care to separate the scientific functions and judgments from the administration functions and judgments. The scientific judgments should be based on the best science and should select methodologies based

on all the facts. The scientific judgment should be unbiased and not encumbered by administrative constraints or conservative models of assumptions. (American Industrial Health Council, 1979, p. I-6)

As with its OSHA critique, AIHC recommended an alternative framework for identifying and regulating carcinogens based on the separation of scientific and policy decisions, the interplay between regulatory agencies and independent science panels, and the use of risk estimation to assign priorities and to select among regulatory approaches. AIHC's other complaints included IRLG's discounting of human data and the over reliance on yet unvalidated short-term tests.

The IRLG report had a curious history. The initial draft was published for comment in the *Federal Register* and in *JCNI* (which constituted its sole peer review), and was essentially adopted as governmentwide policy by the Regulatory Council. But a final draft was neither published nor accepted by any of the regulatory agencies. However, those agencies did take it into consideration, and it remained the major statement of federal cancer policy until the advent of the Reagan administration.

Office of Science and Technology Policy

The AIHC critique praised another set of guidelines that appeared at about the same time as the IRLG report, this one by the White House Office of Science and Technology Policy (OSTP). The OSTP report recommended a two-stage decision-making process and a "consistent approach for deciding what chemicals pose a carcinogenic risk to humans, for characterizing the nature and extent of that risk, and for evaluating Federal (agency) actions" (Calkins et al., 1980, p. 169). OSTP's approach was the archetype of the two-stage model of risk control. The first stage was research and evaluation of cancer risks from chemicals. This stage would be coordinated and managed by the National Toxicology Program (NTP), in essence a centralized science panel. The OSTP report viewed these stage I activities as "dependent primarily on scientific activity and scientific judgments" (Calkins et al., 1980, p. 175), a perspective that makes this a leave-it-to-the-scientists approach.

Stage II, choosing among regulatory options, required more coordination within and across agencies and should be overseen by the Regulatory Council and the Regulatory Analysis Review Group. The OSTP report also recommended that the final decisions be reviewed by an "independent, scientifically qualified group to ensure consistency of the decision with the scientific basis" (Calkins et al., 1980, p. 175).

The report also considered several risk assessment issues. For example, OSTP stated that a consensus was emerging on three (among other) issues related to bioassays: extrapolation to humans (that it is prudent to view positive results as indicating potential human carcinogenicity and that high doses are necessary); conflicting data (positive results supersede negative results, all data should be considered); and assessment of promoters (cannot distinguish between promoters and initiators in the laboratory). In their discussion of combining risk factors, OSTP made the following statement, which was applauded by the AIHC:

> In evaluating overall human cancer risk from a particular chemical, one could construct an equation describing the relative impact of each factor described above (potency, exposure, and susceptibility). Risk could be expressed in terms of increased cancer cases or cancer deaths expected as a result of exposure to that chemical. As noted above, current data do not often allow a precise estimate of potency, exposure, or susceptibility. What value should be entered into the equation for each of these factors to obtain an accurate characterization of overall risk? A commonly used approach is to select a risk estimate from the high end of the range for each term in the equation. This practice results in an extreme estimate of human risk. Another approach is to use the most likely value for each term, including confidence intervals that express the precision of each estimate; this approach generates a risk estimate that has a greater probability of being accurate and seems to us to be more logical. (Calkins et al., 1980, p. 174)[9]

This statement, with its emphasis on the most likely value and with its strict separation of scientific and regulatory functions, made the OSTP report the closest to industry positions of all the guidelines that appeared during the Carter administration (McGarity, 1983). One other feature endeared the OSTP report to industry: unlike the IRLG report, it was distributed for peer review before publication.

Toxics in Air and Water

EPA's 1976 Interim Guidelines specifically addressed pesticides (the pesticide issue was part of the background leading to their issuance), but they were used as guidelines for all the agency's programs until 1984 (see chapter 6). However, both Section 112 of the Clean Air Act (CAA) and Section 307(a) of the Water Pollution Control Act (WPCA) contained provisions, though vague ones, that covered toxic substances. EPA issued air and water toxic guidelines as a result of out-of-court settlements of suits brought by the Environmental Defense Fund and the 1977 amendments. Both documents differed considerably from the EPA 1976 Interim Guidelines in their greater specificity on many of the issues, and were closer to the IRLG approach than to EPA's overall approach.

The water guidelines, entitled "Water Quality Criteria Documents. Availability (Final)," were notable for one action in particular. Until that time—late November 1980—EPA had employed the one-hit model as its major dose-response model on the grounds that it was the least likely to understate the true risk. In the water quality criteria document, the agency adopted instead a linearized, multistage model which it felt was more accurate (Environmental Protection Agency, 1980; Anderson et al., 1983).[10]

The airborne carcinogen policy took the standard approach of agencies in the Carter administration and used the 1976 Interim Guidelines and the IRLG report for guidance. While there is no need to go into detail on these two sets of guidelines because they duplicate much of what was said before,[11] they are mentioned here because they both became subject to reexamination during the Reagan administration. In particular, that administration prepared a replacement for the water toxic guidelines that differed dramatically from the 1979 version. The airborne carcinogen policy is of interest for two reasons. First, we shall see how that policy has developed, and is still developing, over several drafts during the 1980s. Second, during this same period, attempts were made to estimate how much, if any, cancer was due to the presence of airborne carcinogens (see chapter 6).

Toxic Substances Strategy Committee

The report on toxic substances ordered by President Carter in his 1977 environmental message was delivered in May 1980. The Council on Environmental Quality's (CEQ) charge from the president was "to develop an interagency program to eliminate overlaps and fill gaps in the collection of data on toxic chemicals and to coordinate federal research and regulatory activities affecting them" (Toxic Substances Strategy Committee, 1980, p. iv). In its report the Toxic Substances Strategy Committee (TSSC) suggested that there is a relationship between the growth of the chemical industry and the increased incidence of cancer. It preferred a preventive approach through the regulation of carcinogens. Perhaps the most important part of the TSSC report was its vigorous advocacy of the principles approach to risk assessment. The report cited a long list of advisory committee reports (see table 4.1) that agreed, TSSC wrote, on the following principles:

Table 4.1
Reports by Expert Advisory Committees
on Carcinogenicity Principles

Date	Organization	Title
1956	IUCC	Report of a Symposium on Potential Cancer Hazards from Chemical Additives and Contaminants to Foodstuffs
1959	NAS/NRC	Problems in the Evaluation of Carcinogenic Hazards from the Use of Food Additives
1961	WHO	Evaluation of the Carcinogenic Hazards of Food Additives
1964	WHO	Prevention of Cancer
1969	HEW	Report of the Secretary's Commission on Pesticides and Their Relationship to Environmental Health

Table 4.1 (Cont'd)
Reports by Expert Advisory Committees
on Carcinogenicity Principles

Date	Organi- zation	Title
1969	WHO	Principles of Testing and Evaluation of Drugs for Carcinogenicity
1969	IUCC	Carcinogenicity Testing
1970	NAS/NRC	Evaluating the Safety of Food Chemicals
1971	FDA	Report on Cancer Testing in the Safety Evaluation of Food Additives and Pesticides
1974	WHO	Assessment of the Carcinogenicity and Mutagenicity of Chemicals
1975	Canada H&W	The Testing of Chemicals for Carcinogenicity, Mutagenicity and Teratogenicity
1975	NAS/NRC	Pest Control: An Assessment of Present and Alternative Technologies
1977	NCI/NCAB	General Criteria for Assessing the Evidence of Carcinogenicity of Chemical Substances
1977	NAS/NRC	Principles and Procedures for Evaluating the Toxicity of Household Substances
1977	NAS/NRC	An Evaluation of the Carcinogenicity of Chlordane and Heptachlor
1977	NAS/NRC	Drinking Water and Health
1977	OTA	Cancer Testing Technology and Saccharin
1978	NAS/NRC	Saccharin: Technical Assessment of Risks and Benefits
1979	NAS/NRC	Food and Safety Policy: Scientific and Societal Considerations
1979	IRLG	Scientific Bases for Identification of Potential Carcinogens and Estimation of Risks
1979	RC	Regulation of Chemical Carcinogens

Table 4.1 (Cont'd)
Reports by Expert Advisory Committees
on Carcinogenicity Principles

Date	Organi-zation	Title
1979	OSTP	Identification, Characterization, and Control of Potential Human Carcinogens: A Framework for Federal Decision-Making

Note: Canada H&W—Health and Welfare Ministry of Canada.
  FDA—Food and Drug Administration.
  HEW—Department of Health, Education, and Welfare.
  IRLG—Interagency Regulatory Liaison Group.
  IUCC—International Union Against Cancer.
  NAS/NRC—National Academy of Sciences/National Research Council.
  NCI—National Cancer Institute.
  OSTP—Office of Science and Technology Policy.
  OTA—Office of Technology Assessment.
  RC—Regulatory Council.
  WHO—World Health Organization.

Source: Toxic Substances Strategy Committee (1980).

Carcinogenesis is a biological phenomenon; most substances do not cause cancer, even at high doses.

Properly designed and conducted tests using appropriate animal species (e.g., rats and mice) are accepted valid ways to identify chemical substances that may cause cancer in humans.

Established test protocols, which include administration of high test doses, sometimes by a route different than the expected human exposure route, are appropriate and scientifically valid test methods for identifying carcinogens.

Induction of benign tumors is accepted as an indication of the carcinogenic potential of a substance unless definitive evidence shows the substance incapable of inducing malignant tumors.

Methods do not now exist for determining a "safe" threshold level of exposure to carcinogens.

Methods now available for quantifying the estimated human risks from a given exposure to a potential carcinogen can provide only rough approximations of the actual risk. (Toxic Substances Strategy Committee, 1980, pp. 125–134)

Again, these principles can be directly traced to the Ad Hoc Committee report (see chapter 3) and earlier reports; in essence, they had not changed much, if at all, during the decade of the 1970s. TSSC made the following recommendations: (1) adopt generic cancer policies to clarify the basis for regulation and expedite decisions and adopt interim regulatory procedures; (2) increase the coordination of carcinogen regulation; and (3) explain the scientifically based principles to the public.

Other Efforts During the Carter Administration

The other two regulatory agencies with major risk responsibility, the Consumer Product Safety Commission (CPSC) and the Food and Drug Administration (FDA), also issued agency cancer risk assessment documents. In general, they agreed with those of the other agencies. CPSC, however, had some legal problems with its effort. The commission attempted to imitate OSHA but through informal rather than formal rule making. CPSC was sued on the grounds that the cancer policy was essentially a rule rather than an established procedure. After several court cases and attempts by CPSC to rectify the situation, the guidelines were withdrawn (McGarity, 1983).

Conclusion

Cancer policy development was affected, as we have seen, by the three streams described in the Kingdon model of agenda building: the problems stream (an awareness of cancer incidence and mortality as well as of environmental causes, particularly chemicals); the policy stream (characterized by the presence of policy entrepreneurs such as Umberto Saffiotti and Anson Keller and agency chiefs and members with strong environmental leanings); and the political stream (the election of the Carter administration). The result was an intense four-year period of policy making.

The Carter administration, building on the foundation of the Nixon-Ford years, brought to cancer policy development two equally emphasized concerns: strong environmental protection, and regulatory reform based on consistency and coordination (which tempered the first concern). While each of the major regulatory agencies (CPSC, FDA, EPA, and OSHA) issued its own cancer policy guidelines, there were strong attempts to produce a governmentwide cancer policy. That effort had two major results.

First, the coordination or regulatory reform effort itself appeared uncoordinated. There were many committees and interagency groups doing virtually the same things. In addition, the agenda for cancer policy and regulatory reform was an extremely ambitious one and threatened to overload the capacity of the political system to address issues. This problem is illustrated by the numerous comprehensive proposals submitted to Congress by the Carter administration. As we shall see in the next chapter, the Reagan administration had fewer legislative priorities and attempted to carry out many of its changes through an administrative strategy.

Second, most of the policies were consistent in their approaches (though there were a few exceptions, such as the OSHA and OSTP proposals). For example, all the guidelines, including the OSTP report, opted for a risk-averse cancer policy. Given all the uncertainties of the various steps of risk assessment, the agencies adopted "prudent" approaches to public health. But those approaches, as critics repeatedly charged, involved value judgments, judgments to protect human health that were incorporated in the risk assessments themselves (the stage I activities of the OSTP report) that would then provide the basis for risk-averse regulatory decisions. Those critics pointed out that the scientific foundations of risk assessment had changed but that agency policies did not reflect the change; science was "frozen" at a single point in time. In addition, it was alleged that by adopting policies without a sound scientific basis, cancer policies were contributing to the economic problems of the 1970s. Government, as the successful candidate for the presidency in 1980 put it, was the problem. Thus a new set of streams, a new "window of opportunity," coalesced in the Reagan administration to change the course of cancer policy and to (hopefully) incorporate better science and different value judgments. The science and value judgments were used, as we shall see next, to reinforce each other.

5

The Reagan Administration: Challenge and Change

America must get to work producing more energy. The Republican program for solving economic problems is based on growth and productivity. . . . [Energy development] must not be thwarted by a tiny minority opposed to economic growth which often finds friendly ears in regulatory agencies for its obstructionist campaigns.

Make no mistake. We will not permit the safety of our people or our environmental heritage to be jeopardized, but we are going to reaffirm that the economic prosperity of our people is a fundamental part of our environment.
    --Ronald Reagan, 1980, quoted in Kraft, 1984, p. 35

At a time when a new generation of environmental problems demands attention, the search for solutions has been lost in a storm of attacks and counterattacks. The bipartisan consensus that supported federal protection of the environment for more than a decade has been broken by an administration that has given priority to deregulation, defederalization, and defunding domestic programs. . . .

Without question, the Reagan administration has introduced a fundamental discontinuity into national resource and environmental policy. It has pursued its domestic goals with such single-mindedness, so aggressively, as to allow conservationists no alternative but to protest.
    --Conservation Foundation, 1982, p. 1

107

By the end of 1980, there was a consensus among federal regulatory agencies about the shape of cancer policy. Most of the guidelines agreed on a set of guiding principles and, at least on paper, it could be said that the federal government did indeed have a cancer policy. That policy, as we shall see in this chapter, was challenged both by some scientists and by a new administration. The "new" scientific developments and new administration reinforced each other and attempted to produce a dramatically different cancer policy.

In this chapter I will explore these changes, again calling upon the Kingdon model to help explain the events that took place. The chapter is divided into three parts. In the first part, I will examine the scientific literature, developed largely after 1977, that was critical, implicitly if not explicitly, of the course of cancer policy development. This body of literature provides part of the rationale for the Reagan administration's proposed risk assessment changes. In the second part, I will examine how the new agenda was implemented through an "administrative strategy." In the third part, I will focus specifically on changes in cancer policy.

Scientific Challenge

While there was much in the scientific literature that supported the thrust of cancer policy,[1] there was also a sizable literature that suggested, either implicitly or explicitly, that the principles of cancer policy rested on a shaky foundation. In general, the scientific challenge can be divided into two groups, with some overlap. The first group pointed to new developments in the science, such as new views on cancer mechanisms, that had not been considered by previous risk assessments policies. The second group relied on these new developments to suggest changes in cancer policies. We look first at the literature on new developments and then at suggested changes.

In a relatively early piece (for cancer policy), Gehring et al., (1977) asserted that while the normal procedure of using maximum tolerated doses to establish carcinogenic potential and then extrapolating downward to lower doses was adequate for screening chemicals for further evaluation, such a procedure tended to overstate potential risk and was too simple. Basically, the authors stated that chemicals are, first of all, metabolized in different ways and, more importantly, that high doses may overwhelm the body's defensive mechanisms. Gehring et al., also pointed out that rats administered a small dose of vinyl chloride showed no tumors, though extrapolations from the higher doses administered predicted a 9 percent incidence. They concluded:

> As an overall conclusion, the dose-dependent alterations in the fate of chemicals must be considered when using tox-icological data, including carcinogenesis, obtained at high doses to assess the hazard of low doses. For many chemicals, large doses exceed metabolic and physiological thresholds, leading to prolonged retention in the body, formation of different metabolites, and in some cases disproportionate increases in reactions between reactive electrophilic metabolites and macromolecules, and, consequently, there is a disproportionate increase in toxicity, including carcinogenesis. Other compounds for which there is evidence indicating that their fate may be dose-dependent include styrene, ethylene glycol, aniline, carbon disulfide, 2-naphthylamine, benzopyrene, bis-hydroxycoumarin, salicylamide, amphetamine, and sulfobromophthalein. It is likely that as more compounds are evaluated, dose-dependent fate will be found to be the rule rather than the exception. (Gehring et al., p. 201)[2]

The implication is clear. The body reacts in a qualitatively different manner when exposed to high doses (as opposed to low doses), and therefore the results of high-dose testing do not predict low-dose effects. Because humans are normally exposed to low doses, animal bioassays are not reliable indicators of human carcinogens.

Williams' (1983) explored the distinction in the mechanisms of carcinogenesis. The process of carcinogenesis involved, he wrote, at least two states: initiation (conversion of a normal cell to a neoplasm) and promotion (conversion of the neoplasm to a tumor). Initiators react with DNA, and promoters facilitate the transformation from neoplasm to tumor. Thus, as Williams pointed out, chemicals may be carcinogens through different mechanisms. Williams had previously suggested that carcinogens be classified into genotoxic carcinogens (which react with and damage DNA) and epigenetic carcinogens (which produce other biological effects, including, but not limited to, promotion). Since then, he stated, the categorization scheme has been recognized by others.

Williams then described how the two different types of carcinogens are identified.[3] Genotoxic carcinogens can be identified either by demonstrating through biochemical techniques that the substance damages DNA or through short-term tests for mutagenicity.[4] For epigenetic carcinogens, the identification process is more complicated. First, short-term tests would show that the substance is not genotoxic. Further testing would then be necessary to demonstrate the type of effect the carcinogen might have. For our purposes, the importance of Williams's work is that he saw epigenetic carcinogens as posing a different and less serious risk than genotoxic carcinogens.

Williams's distinctions were supported by Rubin (1980), who argued that the somatic mutation hypothesis (that carcinogens operate on DNA) is not the only and perhaps not the major mechanism of carcinogenesis (but see Hattis, 1982). In particular, Rubin objected to relying primarily on short-term tests.

> In his book "Cancer: Science and Society" . . . John Cairns points out that explanations for the malignant transformation of normal animal cells into cancer cells are very much influenced by the scientific fashions of the times and that the current fashion is molecular genetics. Not surprisingly, therefore, it has become increasingly popular to accept somatic mutation as the causal event in the transformation of cells to the malignant state, and, indeed, Cairns himself gives much credence to this view. Proponents of the somatic mutation hypothesis agree that some observations about cancer cells would be difficult to explain by the somatic mutation hypothesis . . . and grant that there are probably other routes to the same end, but they generally hold to the view that damage to DNA is the primary event in chemical carcinogenesis. This hypothesis has now become a critical issue from the public policy point of view because a belief in the somatic mutation theory of carcinogenesis underlies the increasingly widespread use of bacterial mutation tests as screens for potential chemical carcinogens in our environment. (Rubin, 1980, p. 995)

Thus, Rubin points to overreliance on one set of technologies (short-term tests) on the basis of a hypothesis that may be fashionable but not entirely accurate. The problem with this view is that short-term tests are used only as screens; agencies examine other evidence as well, particularly those (the majority) that employ a weight-of-the-evidence framework.

Cornfield (1977), bridging the gap between the two groups of scientific literature, took advantage of these distinctions among cancer mechanisms and asserted that there was no basis for distinguishing between carcinogenic and noncarcinogenic toxicity; the dose-response curves for the two types of toxicity differ only in quantity rather than quality. He then developed models incorporating these ideas and showed that even with the most conservative or risk-averse assumptions (i.e., with the one-hit model), thresholds may exist. Thus Cornfield advocated the use of the no-observable-effects-level (NOEL) model more common to food safety studies (for a critique of Cornfield, see the letters and Cornfield's reply in *Science*, vol. 202, Dec. 8, 1978, pp. 1105–1108).

Perhaps the most important of the critiques of the scientific foundations of cancer policy was that of Gori (1980), a deputy director of the National Cancer Institute. He noted that the need to regulate carcinogens was undisputed but that the premises and practices of carcinogenic regulation were indeed in dispute. In particular, Gori questioned the premise tht "animal tests can provide meaningful data for extrapolation of human risk" (Gori, 1980, p. 257). He pointed out that the origin of animal tests was in basic research in understanding carcinogenesis. Because negative result were useless, larger doses were administered to obtain some effect. He also argued that guidelines often introduced bias into experimental designs; an example would be the use of sensitive strains. Other biases stemmed from the route of administration, the use of maximally tolerated doses, and diet. Gori wrote:

> In general, one can only conclude that current guidelines for the testing of carcinogens frequently introduce deliberate bias in order to enhance the probability of a positive response and that they ignore a number of sources of variability that cannot be controlled or are difficult to control with available technology. Under current testing a carcinogen may go

undetected in a particular test, but just as likely a positive result may be valid only for the particular species and test conditions utilized; current science cannot predict or explain the outcome. (Gori, 1980, p. 258)

On the basis of his judgments about the adequacy of risk assessment methodologies, he recommended an alternative regulatory approach based on the inevitabliity of risk, the utility of substances, and relative risk (the risk of using one substance versus the risk of using a replacement). Regulatory science, Gori contended, "should be limited to those instances where nearly certain assessment of human risk is feasible and legitimate" (p. 260). Gori also recommended the use of an independent court outside the agencies (a centralized science panel?) that would impartially and fairly resolve uncertainties.

Thus, Gori combined several contentions that would lead to a more relaxed, risk-tolerant cancer policy. Of course, he did not argue for such a policy, but rather against biased procedures that deliberately produce a risk-averse policy. First, he demanded near certainty of evidence. Given all the problems associated with risk assessment, such a demand effectively means no regulation. Second, and a related point, is that the evidence must relate directly to humans; bioassays were developed for a different purpose and are inappropriately used to detect or predict human cancers. Again, the effect of such a demand would mean little or no regulation. Finally, the call for some kind of independent science panel (see also the discussion of the American Industrial Health Association above) also leads to more risk-tolerant policies. It is an attempt to move regulatory science with its three-valued logic back to normal science with its two-valued logic. Normal science can afford to ignore ambiguity.

Weisburger and Williams (1981) continued the assault on cancer policy. They also pointed to the problems with animal testing, and they added the genotoxic/epigenetic distinction. They then offered a decision point approach to regulating carcinogens. This approach relies on a sequence of tests to determine what type of carcinogen a substance might be. The first stage would be to compare the structure of the chemical with the structure of known carcinogens, and to then conduct a series of short-term tests for genotoxicity. The first decision point would follow: if a substance shows genotoxicity in more than one test, it should be highly suspect; if in only one test, results should be treated cautiously because not all mutagens are carcinogens. The next stage would be limited *in vivo* bioassays[5] and would be followed by the second decision point: a substance with positive results in two or more short-term tests plus positive results in the limited bioassays would be highly suspect (especially if at moderate doses), while a substance showing indications of promotion with no indication of gentoxicity would be subject to long-term bioassays. The third decision point would be as follows: if a substance shows evidence of carcinogenicity but no evidence of genotoxicity, then it is probably an epigenetic agent. Weisburger and Williams (1981), p. 406) pointed out the implications of the epigenetic category.

> Most epigenetically acting agents are active only at high, sustained doses and, up to a certain point, the effects they induce are reversible. Thus, these types of agents may represent only quantitative hazards to humans, and it may be possible to formulate safe levels of exposure after appropriate toxicologic dose-response studies are conducted.

Squire (1981) also suggested changes in regulating proposed carcinogens. He noted that although epidemiological evidence was the most persuasive and least controversial (a debatable point), bioassays were the primary basis for regulation. However, recent advances in scientific knowledge permitted a more sophisticated approach than the "all or nothing" one that agencies were taking.[6] He criticized other approaches (such as the genotoxic/epigenetic one) as being overly rigid and conservative dose-response models for assuming low-dose linearity.

As a resolution to these problems, Squire proposed a regulatory classification scheme based on six factors: the number of different species affected, the number of different types of neoplasms in one or more species, spontaneous incidence of neoplasms, dose-response relationships, the malignancy of induced neoplasms, and the genotoxicity of the substance (see table 5.1). On the basis of total factor scores, carcinogens would be ranked in different classes. Each class would have its own regulatory response, ranging from class I carcinogens (which would be ranked 86 or higher and be restricted or banned) to class V carcinogens (which might be subject to a variety of options, from doing nothing to educating the public). As an example of how this approach might be used, Squire classified ten carcinogens according to his ranking scheme (see table 5.2). He noted that the options "would be influenced by the nature of the intended use of a chemical, the estimated types and levels of human exposure, the number of people exposed, and by considerations of health and economic benefits" (Squire, 1981, p. 225). Some of the cancer policies to be considered below directly refer to Squire's proposal (see below and chapter 6).

The most direct attack on the principles approach to cancer policy was that of Salsburg and Heath (1981). Their basic point was that, as the article title suggests, science had progressed but that federal research and regulatory agencies had not taken that progress into account. Salsburg and Heath stated that the National Cancer Institute, in its evaluation of chemical carcinogenicity, made one fundamental assumption and several subsidiary ones. The basic assumption was that there is a unique and specific way of causing cancer. The subsidiary assumptions were that only a few chemicals cause cancer, that lifetime bioassays are needed, that high doses are necessary to capture the effects of weak carcinogens, and that virtually all human carcinogens are also animal carcinogens. Salsburg and Heath pointed out that until recently the normal pathology of test animals was unknown and that some substances are anticarcinogens for some types of cancers (see also Weinberg and Storer, 1985). Two scientists (Gori and Gehring) were praised for trying to change the "philosophical framework on which carcinogenicity testing rests" (Salsburg and Heath, 1981, p. 37). Unfortunately, they were part of a small minority. Salsburg and Heath's challenge was to change our concept of cancer because of new research.

> A new scientific and philosophical framework is obviously needed. The concept of carcinogenesis proposed in 1954 is in need of modification, or at least refinement. . . .
>
> By allowing its old "truths" to set into a rigid matrix, the regulatory authorities run the danger of being unable to adjust even when a new framework is defined. . . .

Table 5.1
Proposed System for Ranking Animal Carcinogens

Factor	Score
A. Number of different species affected	
Two or more	15
One	5
B. Number of histogenetically different types of neoplasms in one or more species	
Three or more	15
Two	10
One	5
C. Spontaneous incidence in appropriate control groups of neoplasms induced in treated groups	
Less than 1 percent	15
1 to 10 percent	10
10 to 20 percent	5
More than 20 percent	1
D. Dose-response relationships (cumulative oral dose equivalents per kilogram of body weight per day for 2 years)	
Less than 1 microgram	15
1 microgram to 1 milligram	10
1 milligram to 1 gram	5
More than 1 gram	1
E. Malignancy of induced neoplasms	
More than 50 percent	15
25 to 50 percent	10
Less than 25 percent	5
No malignancy	1
F. Genotoxicity, measured in an appropriate battery of tests	
Positive	25
Incompletely positive	10
Negative	0

Source: Squire (1981).

Our only hope is that the bureaucracies of the government might have the courage and honesty to admit that they can be wrong in their fundamental assumptions. Progress in scientific knowledge has always depended upon the ability of scientists to realize when they have made mistakes. A good scientist knows that he will make mistakes because he is exploring the unknown.

Table 5.2
Approximate Rank of Ten Animal Carcinogens
Based on the Proposed System

Carcinogen	Score	Ranking
Aflatoxin	100	I
Dimethylnitrosamine	95	I
Vinyl chloride	90	I
Tris (2,3-dibromopropyl)-		
phosphate (Tris)	90	I
2-Napthylamine	81	II
Chloroform	65	III
NTA	51	IV
Chlordane	40	V
Saccharin	36	V
DDT	31	V

Source: Squire (1981).

> If government bureaucracies are going to explore the unknown, they also must be prepared to acknowledge their mistakes. (Salsburg and Heath, 1981, pp. 38–39)

The significance of these writings is twofold. First, they demonstrated that at least some scientists saw the need for change in basic principles and regulatory policy. Some of them—Squire, Weisburger and Williams, and Gori—suggested alternatives. Second, this body of literature was used by the Reagan admnistration. Coming to office on a platform that supported a less active role by government, both the critiques and the alternatives provided a basis for justifying changes the administration wanted to make. A number of the suggested changes appeared in the new administration's cancer policy documents, such as the existence of thresholds, the epigenetic/genotoxic and promoter/initiator distinctions, and categorization schemes.

Change of Administrations

Ronald Reagan's victory in the 1980 presidential elections was due to several factors, perhaps the major one being the rejection of the Carter administration.[7] In the period between the election and the inauguration, three transition reports were submitted to the president-elect. One by Michigan congressman David Stockman (and supported by New York congressman Jack Kemp), entitled "Avoiding a GOP Economic Dunkirk," asserted that the financial picture that the President-elect had painted during the campaign was much worse than was originally thought (Stockman, 1980). Stockman emphasized what he called a "ticking regulatory time bomb." Unless action was taken immediately to stop the "time bomb," there would be an enormous increase in the "regulatory burden" that the President-elect had decried during the campaign and indeed during much of his political life.

> Similarly, a cradle-to-grave hazardous waste control system will take effect in 1981 at an annual cost of up to $2 billion. Multi-billion overkill has bloomed in the regulatory embellishment of the Toxic Substances Control Act. Three thousand pages of appliance efficiency standards scheduled for implementation in 1981 threaten to create multi-billion-dollar havoc in the appliance industry. All told, there are easily in excess of $100 billion in new environmental safety and energy compliance costs scheduled for the early 1980s. (Stockman, 1980, pp C-5)

Stockman recommended a three-part program of "regulatory ventilation": (1) the administrative deferral, revision, or rescinding of existing and pending regulations where possible; (2) temporary and permanent revisions in statutes; and (3) a legislative regulatory reform package inserting "mandatory cost-benefit, cost-effectiveness and comparative risk analysis into the basic enabling acts" (Stockman, 1980). The new administration followed the first recommendation and a modified, administrative version of the third.

A second report was made by the official Reagan transition task force, headed by Daniel Lufkin and including William Ruckelshaus as one of the members (as well as Russell Train, the second EPA administrator). According to Kraft (1984), the task force called for moderate reforms and a reexamination of environmental laws, but not the wholesale cutting of environmental programs. The report also advocated economic reforms (the use of economic incentives) such as pollution taxes.[8] As Kraft notes, the task force report was ignored: only three copies were made.

A much more influential report was that of the Heritage Foundation (1980), a relatively new conservative think tank. The report's purpose was to provide an agenda for the new conservative administration. In Kraft's words, it referred to EPA as a " 'morass of regulatory controls' and argued that it needed 'proper administrative direction and not legislative remedy' " (Kraft, 1984, p. 39). Much of the advice offered in the report was used by top Reagan administration appointees, particularly by James Watt as Secretary of the Interior and by Anne Burford as EPA administrator.[9]

Administrative Strategy

The Reagan administration sought to achieve its agenda of regulatory reform and a reduced role for government through an admnistrative strategy. Richard Nathan (1983), in *The Administrative Presidency*, noted that the Nixon administration had attempted legislative change, but faced with a hostile Democratic congress, largely failed. Learning that lesson from his first administration, Nixon began making administrative changes that required no statutory alterations (see also Randall, 1979). Only the Watergate scandals and the president's subsequent resignation prevented him from succeeding. The Reagan administration eschewed legislative changes from the start and resorted to administrative measures. A key example of this tactic was the handling of the Clean Air Act. It was due for reauthorization in 1981 and thus provided a perfect opportunity for the administration to realize many of its environmental goals. However, rather than crowd its legislative agenda, the administration settled for offering merely a set of guiding principles for changes to the act (see "Spectrum," 1981). As of this writing (early 1986), the Clean Air Act has still not been reauthorized.

The administrative strategy consisted of several parts: budget changes, personnel cuts, and regulatory reform. The budget cuts were part of the massive Omnibus Reconciliation Act of 1981. The fiscal year 1981 budget for EPA was $1,351.1 million. It was cut by almost 20 percent in current dollars to $1,086 million, and by even more in constant dollars (adjusting for inflation). The fiscal year 1984 proposal was for $948.2 million, a 30 percent reduction in current dollars from the 1981 level. Personnel cuts were of a similar magnitude. Personnel peaked at 12,700 employees in fiscal 1981 and dropped to a proposed 10,400 for fiscal 1984, lower than the level existing in fiscal 1980. The load imposed by the budget and personnel cuts was compounded by the increased responsibilities that EPA was facing, especially the hazardous waste superfund legislation that was passed in the last few days of 1980 (Rosenbaum, 1985).

Even more significant was the emphasis on regulatory relief. The president appointed a task force on regulatory change chaired by Vice-President George Bush. In addition, increased responsibility over agencies was given to the Office of Management and Budget (OMB). In early 1981, OMB identified thirty-six regulations that were being reviewed for either deferral (delay) or recision (withdrawal); among those rules were the airborne carcinogen guidelines (Mosher, 1981, p. 258).

The most important of the regulatory changes, and a key part of the administrative strategy, was Executive Order #12291, issued February 17, 1981. That order modified the Administrative Procedures Act of 1946 by interposing OMB in the regulatory process and centralizing regulatory authority within the White House. The executive order provided that proposed, major regulations must be accompanied by a formal benefit-cost analysis and must maximize public benefits (benefits exceeding costs). The benefit-cost process was overseen by OMB, which could order additional analyses. This new part of the process would occur before regulations were published in the *Federal Register*. The actual effect, and undoubtedly its intended one, was to delay the issuance of regulations.[10] In early 1985 this centralization was strengthened when the president permitted OMB to review regulations at the writing stage (Burnham, 1985).[11]

The impact of the executive order can be seen in the response by EPA in its draft guidelines for performing the benefit-cost analyses (Environmental Protection Agency, 1982a). Two sections of the draft guidelines are of interest, on quantifying health effects and on carcinogens. Under health effects, the guidelines stated that each potentially adverse effect will be evaluated on a case-by-case basis for each substance[12] and that the evaluation will include a discussion of the likelihood that the substance has been incorrectly classified as harmful to humans (a typical administrative technique to shrink a program) and evidence about dose-response functions and no-observable-effect levels. In addition, it must present information about the possible reversibility of effects and whether effects require repeated exposures. For carcinogens, risk assessment should be on a case-by-case basis (because carcinogens work differently). The determination that a substance is a human carcinogen will be based on a weight-of-the-evidence judgment. Quantitative risk assessment will be used to estimate the impact on the population. The agency may use a variety of models and should use the maximum likelihood estimates as well as upper and lower estimates. Finally, estimates of duration and the nature of disabilities produced from cancer will be made where data permit.

The draft guidelines, while not focusing specifically on cancer policy, showed the beginning of a change and some reliance on the critical scientific literature discussed in the previous section: the notion that there are different types of cancers with different causes, the possibility of thresholds and reversibility of effects,and the possibility that for some carcinogens, at least, repeated exposures might be necessary to produce cancer.

Cancer Policies in the Reagan Administration: Early Period

Todhunter Memorandum

In the Spring of 1981, the new Reagan EPA leadership was confronted with its first major cancer risk decision. The industry-sponsored Chemical Industry Institute of Toxicology (CIIT) had developed evidence that formaldehyde was a carcinogen. The results, later confirmed by EPA staffers, were disturbing on several grounds. First, the test animals were exposed to relatively low doses of the substance through inhalation. Second, the cancers produced were rare nasal cancers. Finally, since formaldehyde is used in a wide variety of products, the impact of a restriction or ban would be serious. The problem for EPA was whether the results of the CIIT test were sufficient to activate section 4(f) of the Toxic Substances Control Act (TSCA). Section 4(f) requires EPA to decide within a six-month period whether to regulate a substance (if evidence of carcinogencity is developed) under other sections of TSCA. The holdover Carter administration staffers decided that such action was called for and recommended as much to the head of the Office of Toxic Substances. That recommendation arrived the day EPA administrator Anne Burford and deputy administrator John Hernandez took office. Burford ordered Hernandez to work something out with industry, and a series of meetings were held.[13] Hernandez and John Todhunter, assistant administrator for pesticides and toxic substances, decided that section 4(f) action was unnecessary, and Todhunter wrote a memorandum to Burford to that effect. It is that memorandum that we discuss here.[14]

The memorandum was not a guideline per se, as were the others discussed in this and other chapters; it was specific to one chemical, formaldehyde. However, it is included here for several reasons. First, it was one of the first actions related to carcinogens taken by the Reagan administration EPA. Second, it indicated the direction that cancer policy should take in that administration. Finally, it addressed many of the same risk assessment issues as the other guidelines.

The memorandum began by defining the section 4(f) issues, for example, the meaning of ill-defined statutory language such as "significant", "serious", and "widespread". A finding that a chemical is serious would require, according to Todhunter, positive results in bioassays in both sexes of at least two species, with multiple doses and at doses close to human exposure. In a footnote, Todhunter wrote that the weight-of-the-evidence considerations are generally in line with criteria set forth by the International Agency for Research on Cancer, Weisburger and Williams, and Squire.

Todhunter noted that most of the formaldehyde studies were negative and that the effects of the CIIT study seem to be strongly species specific (that is, the rat is an "obligatory nose breather") (Todhunter, 1982, p. 256). Further, effects at low levels appear to be reversible. "This suggests that a higher exposure level or longer exposure time may produce a qualitatively different outcome with respect to carcinogenesis than would result from low level or short term exposure" (p. 257). Moreover, formaldehyde, while a mutagen and therefore genotoxic, may work primarily as a promoter. Therefore, the memorandum concluded, low-level exposures would probably not pose a significant risk.

The document then considered epidemiological data. It pointed out that formaldehyde has been in use for a long time and that there had been few if any reports of the rare nasal cancer found in the CIIT rat studies. It stated further that human exposure is at a much lower level than in those studies, even though the dose levels in the CIIT study were relatively low.

Next, the report looked at the risk assessment done in the original document sent to Todhunter's office. That risk assessment employed the Crump dose-response model based on high exposure estimates.[15] The estimated risk in the original document was 1 x 10^{-6} to 1 x 10^{-4}, a range, the memorandum states, "in which priority action is often not considered" (Todhunter, 1982, p. 265).[16] The memorandum also noted that the 5.6 ppm (parts per million) dose level showed no effects and was essentially a zero-risk or threshold level. The risk estimates did not, the memorandum continued, take into consideration that "tumor formation in rats appears to require a long term, high level exposure and that the human exposures are likely to be relatively short" (Todhunter, 1982, p. 265).[17]

In sum, although the Todhunter memorandum was not a cancer policy risk assessment guideline per se, nor did it cover all the issues that guidelines might address, it did indicate the course that EPA was willing to take at that time and did consider several risk assessment inference options. For example, the memorandum distinguished between promoters and initiators and strongly implied the existence of a threshold. Its criteria for determining carcinogenicity from bioassays were among the most stringent of all the documents. Perhaps most interesting is the claim that risks in a particular range, noted above, are not worthy of priority action.

Water Quality Guidelines

Appearing the same year as the Todhunter memorandum was the draft water quality guidelines (Environmental Protection Agency, 1982a), an addendum to EPA's 1976 interim guidelines and the 1980 water quality guidelines. This document had two purposes: to adopt a formal approach for stratifying weight-of-the-evidence judgments, and to distinguish between mutagenic (genotoxic) and nonmutagenic (epigenetic) carcinogens in quantitative risk assessment. The classification system employed in the guidelines was based on a system developed by the International Agency for Research on Cancer (IARC). The guidelines distinguished among three classes of evidence for carcinogenicity of the test substance: sufficient, limited, and inadequate. For example, sufficient evidence of carcinogenicity from bioassays includes increased incidence of malignant tumors in multiple species or strains, in multiple experiments, or to an unusual degree. On the basis of this classification, the guidelines then offered the following scheme for evaluation of human cancer risk. Group 1 includes those substances that are carcinogenic for humans. This category consists solely of substances proved carcinogenic by sufficient evidence from epidemiological studies. Group 2 chemicals are probably carcinogenic for humans. This category consists of chemicals for which the epidemiological evidence is almost sufficient and those for which it is suggestive. Bioassays are important in this category, though in an unexplained manner. Group 3 chemicals are those that are possible human carcinogens. The classification scheme was later adopted in EPA's 1984 cancer risk assessment guidelines (see chapter 6).

The quantitative risk assessment section was based on the distinction between genotoxic and epigenetic carcinogens, though it does not employ those terms. For genotoxic or mutagenic carcinogens, the "linear non-threshold dose-response extrapolation model" was considered plausible, on the basis that there is a correlation between mutagenicity and carcinogenicity. However, for nonmutagenic carcinogens such a model may not be accurate.

> In the absence of gene mutation, the use of the linear non-threshold dose-response model becomes less plausible. Many mathematical extrapolation models fit most tumor data in the range of experimentally observed responses but give widely divergent estimates of risk at the low doses generally encountered with environmental exposure, where it is not possible to obtain direct experimental or epidemiological dose-response relationships. The selection of a particular mathematical extrapolation model requires some acceptance of a mechanism of carcinogenic action. The plausibility of the linear non-threshold extrapolation model depends heavily on acceptance of the somatic-mutation theory of cancer. We currently do not know enough about the mechanism of action of non-mutagenic carcinogens to plausibly extrapolate dose-response relationships for

such agents to low levels of exposure. (Environmental Protection Agency, 1982a, p. 112)

The document then proposed to use what it called the "conventional toxicological" approach based on the no-observable-effect level (NOEL) typically used in food safety studies and recommended by Cornfield (1977). It suggested that since evidence of mutagenicity may not be decisive, in practice both the linear and the NOEL models should be used with appropriate weights. The conventional approach was modified by using a multistage extrapolation model corresponding to a 10 percent response.[18] The guidelines also recommended the use of the maximum likelihood estimate and a dose conversion from animals to humans based on body weight rather than on surface.[19] Again, the guidelines stratified, or classified, the mutagenicity of a chemical. Of the four categories, only one (variously labelled "sufficient" and "adequate") would permit classification of a substance as mutagenic, and then only gene mutations would count, not chromosome mutations or other DNA damage (which would provide only supportive evidence). Dunkel (1983) and the Office of Science and Technology Policy (1984) both point out, however, that there are a variety of endpoints that could be tested. By restricting the results to direct gene mutation, the number of genotoxic compounds is reduced.

The final section of the guidelines considered water criteria and updated the 1980 water criteria guidelines. Those criteria, according to the authors of the more recent document, were based on the 1976 interim recommendations and used the linear model regardless of mutagenicity. Again, a classification scheme was proposed. For substances where there is sufficient evidence of mutagenicity and of carcinogenicity, the linear model would be employed. Where there is sufficient evidence of carcinogenicity but negative evidence of mutagenicity, the conventional NOEL model would be used. For those substances where the evidence of carcinogenicity and of mutagenicity is mixed (for example, where there is sufficient carcinogenic but inconclusive mutagenic evidence), a midrange between the two models would be used. The guidelines illustrated with several examples that the NOEL approach would allow concentrations of substances from 10 to 369 times greater than those allowed by the linear method. Finally, the guidelines examined alternatives in formulating the water quality criteria. These alternatives included using a 95 percent confidence level instead of a maximum likelihood estimate, using the surface area rather than weight conversion, and using an arithmetic rather than a geometric mean for midrange guidance. The options were assessed for their risk aversiveness; in general, the guidelines opted for the more risk-tolerant approaches.

What did these guidelines do? First, they were based on the distinction between genotoxic and epigenetic carcinogens, though they did not use those terms. Where the carcinogen was considered epigenetic (essentially a residual category because the test is for mutation, the absence of which indicates that the substance is not a mutagen), then a more risk-tolerant model, the "conventional" NOEL model, was employed. Even here, the guidelines accepted only one of a possible number of endpoints that short-term tests assess. Second, the guidelines placed more reliance on epidemiological data than did previous ones (an emphasis retained in the 1984 EPA guidelines). Note that only human data could provide sufficient evidence of human carcinogenicity; with limited exceptions, bioassays could not provide the best data for determining human carcinogenicity. Finally, there were judgments about conversion factors, appropriate statistics, and other factors that tended to make the guidelines risk tolerant. The applications section of the document is as clear a statement of this bias as can be found. If the OSHA regulations were at one extreme (highly risk averse), then the water quality document was at the other extreme (highly risk tolerant).

Office of Science and Technology Policy

In 1982 the White House Office of Science and Technology Policy (OSTP)circulated a rough draft of a cancer policy document within the scientific community. OSTP had previously published such a document in 1980, though it was sketchy. The newer document was an attempt to produce a more thorough statement of risk assessment principles and to assess the "state of the science" in this field. The OSTP members consisted of scientists from seven different agencies with either research or regulatory responsibility in this area.[20]

The OSTP draft (Office of Science and Technology Policy, 1982), entitled "Potential Human Carcinogens: Methods for Identification and Characterization, Part I," began by noting the concern with cancer but stated that there is considerable hope in fighting the disease. It then observed that public concern remained high, especially about the suggestion that many cancers are environmentally induced and presumably preventable rather than due to genetic factors. It said that Congress had responded with numerous laws aimed at those environmental causes.

> Each of the legislative acts . . . contains elements which are products of the thinking which existed at the time of enactment. Because of developments in the scientific understanding of cancer, such thinking has evolved over the years. Consequently, these acts are not uniform in their view of the disease, the role chemical substances might play in its incidence, and what ought to be done about such potential carcinogens. (Office of Science and Technology Policy, 1982, p. 3)

For example, the draft pointed out that the (1958) Delaney amendment to the Food, Drug and Cosmetics Act attempted to remove all carcinogens on the grounds that any exposure would be risky; the Toxic Substances Control Act (almost twenty years later) balanced risks and benefits. In addition, the draft pointed to advances in analytical chemistry that permitted detection of ever smaller amounts of substances, to the parts per trillion level. It further stated that the importance of lifestyle as part of the environmental causation of cancer had complicated the situation.

The purpose of the document was to articulate or generate a consensus of the scientific principles or science underlying cancer policy.

> The present report, the latest in the continuing series of such statements, is promoted at this time by what the agencies believe to be the significant advances in science which should affect the manner in which the regulatory bodies deal with suspected carcinogens. The purpose of this document, then, is to articulate a view of chemicals and cancer that the agencies hold in common today and that can serve as the basis for separate, but consistent, regulatory cancer policies which these agencies can tailor to meet the requirements of the legislative acts they are charged to implement. (Office of Science and Technology Policy, 1982, p. 5)

The draft then presented "current views" of the whole range of risk assessment: carcinogenesis mechanisms, epidemiology, short-term tests, bioassays, exposure assessment, and risk assessment. The document is summarized below.

Chapter II, on cancer mechanisms, began with a statement of current beliefs.[21] These beliefs included the following: that there are different types of cancer-causing agents (physical, chemical, and biological); that estimates of the potency of carcinogens may be inexact and may vary considerably; that the development of tumors is a multistage process "involving both genetic and epigenetic events" (p. 2); that this process may be modified by bodily functions (e.g., metabolic processes); that various factors may alter the frequency of tumor induction at various stages in the process; that tumors originate with the alteration of genes and subsequently the expression of those changes; that there is still an incomplete understanding of mechanisms and stages; and, finally, that only by completely understanding this process will the potential of chemical substances and lifestyle factors be discovered. The chapter then discussed cancer mechanisms, reviewing the literature on DNA repair, detoxificaton, and other factors that might modify the effects of carcinogens.

Section III of this chapter considered promoters at length (almost five pages). Promotion, discussed above, is that stage which permits the expression of the genetic damage caused during the initiation stage. The document pointed out that promotion requires a lengthy period of exposure (probably the reason for the delay in the appearance of tumors) and that "low-level exposure to carcinogens may only become significant after subsequent exposure to promoters" (p. 25). Further, at early stages of promotion, removal of the promoting substance produces either the regression or nonappearance of tumors. In other words, the process is reversible. There are also a number of "antipromoters" which inhibit promotion. Finally, there may be compounds naturally occurring in the body that are promoters.[22]

The chapter concluded by briefly examining the role of science in regulation (to provide information necessary for "scientifically sound and reasonable judgments" [p. 31]) and then looked at emerging and needed research areas tht might affect regulation. The document noted that "what we do not know, but need to know is equally as important a question as what we already know and are currently learning about" (p. 35). To summarize the important points of this chapter, the document distinguished between genotoxic and epigenetic carcinogens and the related initiation and promotion stages of carcinogenesis. Promotion is a long-term, potentially reversible stage, and the existence of thresholds, at least for promoters, is implied.

The next three chapters (III–V) reviewed methods of identifying carcinogenic substances, epidemiology, short-term tests, and bioassays. Most of the discussion consisted of critiques of those methods and a consideration of their regulatory impact. For instance, it examined the rationale for high-dose levels, a discussion which certainly places it within the critical scientific literature such as Gehring et al., (1977) discussed above.

> The principal reason for the controversy is the fact that, in general, the higher the dose the greater the likelihood of a substance proving to be positive in the carcinogen bioassay. It might be questioned, in light of the inherent insensitivity of the carcinogen bioassay, why anyone should object to providing maximum sensitivity irrespective of the dosage level required. The answer offered has been that extreme dosage may generate a variety of events that potentially occur that are qualitatively different from that which occurs at far lower dosages. The argument has been presented that when normal physiology, homeostasis, detoxificaitons and repair mechanisms are overwhelmed, cancer, which otherwise would not occur, is produced or promoted. There is even recent evidence . . . which suggests that critical cellular macromolecules are attacked and damaged by enzymes which are normal cellular components when cells and tissues are exposed to excessive and toxic levels of chemicals. (Office of Science and Technology Policy, 1982, p. 9)

The final chapter discussed risk assessment issues, for example, the use of dose-response extrapolation models. Echoing some of the literature cited above (for example, the Cornfield 1977 article and the 1982 draft water quality guidelines), the OSTP draft suggested that a modified NOEL or conventional toxicological approach be used, perhaps by itself or in combination with extrapolation models.

Much of the OSTP first draft appeared to be a critique of existing methods interspersed with suggestions for considering new scientific developments, such as the use of pharmacokinetic data (how the body metabolizes carcinogens) as suggested by Gehring et al. (1977) and others and the use of alternative risk assessment models (e.g., NOEL). As such, the guidance provided by the OSTP emphasized a changing view of carcinogenesis and research needs. In terms of cancer policy, it clearly pointed regulatory and research agencies in a different direction.

Airborne Carcinogens

As was briefly discussed in the last chapter, in 1979 EPA issued a draft cancer policy document concerning airborne carcinogens, under authority of section 112 of the Clean Air Act and prodded by a petition by the Environmental Defense Fund. The concern was that by 1976 only four substances had been listed as hazardous (asbestos, berylium, benzene, and vinyl chloride); by 1983, three more chemicals had been added to the list (arsenic, mercury, and radionuclides). Progress obviously had been slow, but as the draft document noted, the scientific foundation is full of uncertainties. The 1979 draft took the same approach as the other cancer policy guidelines issued during the Carter administration: the linear, nonthreshold model, the prudent approach to protecting public health, and so forth. That document was based on the statement of the Regulatory Council and the 1976 Interim Guidelines.

The proposed airborne policy was controversial, and the slowness with which section 112 was implemented became the subject of congressional concern (see *Clean Air Act, Part 2*, 1981).[23] Congressional prodding led to attempts by EPA beginning in 1982 (and continuing into 1985) to devise a toxic air pollutant strategy (see Conservation Foundation, 1985; and Environmental Protection Agency, 1982b, 1983a, 1983b, and 1985).

The first of the drafts noted that the contribution of air pollution to the incidence of cancer is less than that of smoking, occupational exposure, and diet. However, it is higher than for other media and is more direct than for those other media.[24] The first draft, but not the other two, added concerns that did not appear in the 1979 draft guidelines.

Progress in controlling toxic pollutants under section 112 has been slow with relatively few pollutants identified and fewer ac-

tually controlled compared to the known inventory of potentially hazardous emissions. Several factors have contributed to this.
First, we have been unable to establish acceptable substantive
criteria for dealing with potential hazardous pollutants in the
face of considerable scientific uncertainty. We also have been
reluctant to implement actions under the relatively restrictive
section 112 without a clear indication that the cost of control is
not grossly disproportionate to the health benefits. (Environmental Protection Agency, 1982b, p. 1184)

The second draft described three general principles underlying
EPA's approach to risk assessment of air toxins: reliance on
bioassays as well as epidemiological data; use of quantitative risk
assessment to compare pollutants and alternative control levels
and to establish priorities (but not as a major factor in regulatory
decisions); and consideration of residual risk after the application
of the best available technology (BAT) to meet the "ample margin
of safety" language of section 112. The third draft reviewed a
variety of statutes that might be applicable to toxic air pollutants.
It noted, for example, that one of the implementation problems of
section 112 was that it lacked an economic or balancing test: "a
literal interpretation of section 112 would not preclude zero emissions requirements for non-threshold pollutants" (Environmental
Protection Agency, 1983b, p. 2283). The draft also described its
proposed process for evaluating and controlling air toxics, a process that would take 4 to 7 years for each substance.

   To summarize, the cancer policy documents issued during the
early Reagan administration (1981–1983) relied upon a body of
scientific literature that was critical of the consensus developed
during the Carter administration. That consensus implied a risk-
averse cancer policy. The changes suggested in the literature and
adopted by the Reagan administration implied a more risk-tolerant
posture toward potential carcinogens. This attitude can be seen in
discussions of promotion and epigenetic carcinogens, the possibility of reversibility, the possible existence of thresholds for carcinogens, the use of the no-observable-effects-level model, and, as
seen in the airborne cancer drafts, the inclusion of some kind of
benefit-cost analysis. Those changes, grounded in some of the
scientific literature, blended well with the Reagan administration's

emphasis on regulatory relief. They were partially thwarted when scandals erupted within the Environmental Protection Agency, creating a new "window of opportunity" for policy change. We consider those developments next.

6

Critique, Scandal, and Consensus

Risk assessment at EPA must be based only on scientific evidence and scientific consensus. Nothing will erode public confidence faster than the suspicion that policy considerations have been allowed to influence the assessment of risk.

--William Ruckelshaus, 1983, pp. 1027-1028

Critique and Scandal

The Reagan administration's attempt to change the course of cancer policy was denounced by those who supported the policies of the Carter administration; more importantly, it was thwarted by scandals that erupted over EPA in 1982 and 1983 and that led to the wholesale replacement of the top leadership at the agency (Wines, 1983). In this section, we consider first the critiques and then the scandals.

Critique

The Reagan administration's cancer policies (both the guidelines and the individual decisions such as those on formaldehyde and permithron) were the subject of congressional hearings in the democratically controlled House of Representatives in 1982 and 1983 (*Control of Carcinogens*, 1983; *Formaldehyde*, 1982). Many of the prominent scientists who supported the older policies testified at those hearings; the new policies were defended by scientists and leadership within EPA.[1]

133

One set of hearings focused specifically on cancer policy (*Control of Carcinogens*, 1983). The hearings began with a panel discussion by prestigious cancer researchers. This discussion commenced with a statement by Weinstein, who reiterated "basic scientific principles of environmental carcinogenesis" (p. 3): (1) cancer is the second leading cause of death; (2) the majority of cancers are due to environmental causes and are in principle preventable; (3) there has been an increase in human exposure to synthetic chemicals; (4) cancer has a long latency period between exposure and the appearance of tumors; (5) carcinogenesis is dose dependent; (6) the carcinogenic process is a multistage one; (7) tumor initiators act by producing highly reactive metabolites; and (8) other factors may act as cocarcinogens (*Control of Carcinogens*, 1983, pp. 7-10). Weinstein then turned to four sets of risk assessment issues. The third issue typifies the approach of the defenders of the displaced cancer policy.

> *The third issue is the general question of the existence of a threshold level for certain carcinogens in humans.* As stressed above, although the response to various types of carcinogens is likely to be dose dependent, I know of no evidence that clearly establishes a threshold level for any carcinogen. Furthermore, even if this were established in a given experimental system, it would be dificult to predict with confidence the threshold level in a heterogeneous human population. It is prudent, therefore, not to assume the existence of a threshold dose for any carcinogen. Obviously, it will not be possible to completely remove all carcinogens from our environment. Nevertheless, we should attempt to reduce human exposure to the lowest feasible levels. (*Control of Carcinogens*, 1983, p. 16; emphasis in original).[2]

Nelson, another participant, distinguished between principles of cancer testing and principles of cancer policy. He accused the administration of trying to change that policy in a covert manner and suggested that we stay with the previous cancer policy until better ones are produced. Nelson criticized the Todhunter memorandum ("It is the sort of a document that one would not expect an objective scientist to produce nor to be produced by a responsible public agency" [p. 71]) and the forum of the OSTP review of science policy, preferring a review by the National Academy of

Sciences. The Interagency Regulatory Liaison Group (IRLG) document, he concluded, was a "perfectly good statement of many of the policies for cancer control" (p. 73).

Perera, testifying for the Natural Resources Defense Council (NRDC), identified three ways in which EPA had shifted cancer policy: (1) by discounting positive bioassay results as presumptive evidence of human carcinogenicity; (2) by its "reliance on theories concerning mechanism of action and the assumption of probable threshold to justify low concern for human risk of cancer" (p. 105); and (3) by EPA's acceptance "of a higher tolerable level of cancer risks for the U.S. population (100x or higher) than was sanctioned under previous administrations" (p. 109).

Silbergeld, of the Environmental Defense Fund, employed perhaps the starkest language in characterizing policy changes. She referred to those changes as "the unraveling of a scientifically based federal policy" and its replacement with a "revisionist" one (p. 164). She connected the "revisionist" cancer policy (for example, the use of acceptable daily intake [ADI] based on NOEL) to the administration of superfund, thus linking the change in cancer policy to scandal. She also documented similar efforts at changing cancer policy at the Food and Drug Administration and the Occupational Safety and Health Administration. (see pp. 167–186).

The Reagan administration was not without its defenders. Browning, representing the American Industrial Health Council (AIHC), made several points in his prepared statement to the House subcommittee. First, he argued that the models currently in use severely overestimated risk and did not include all relevant biological data, only tumor incidence. Therefore, the models did *"not provide an actual estimate of human risk"* (p. 295). Second, Browning argued that while a national policy on cancer assessment is a reasonable goal, generic cancer regulations are not because they dictate "the outcome of scientific evaluations" (p. 295).[3] For that reason, AIHC rejected the Interagency Regulatory Liaison Group (IRLG) guidelines. Browning also noted the IRLG report's lack of peer review. The OSTP working group, on the other hand, operated on a much sounder basis. He pointed out how the OSTP report (first draft) did make use of new scientific developments.

I am certain the Committee appreciates the great strides being made in the science of carcinogenesis. Many new
developments have impacted scientific evaluations in the immediate past and will continue to do so in the near future. Recent discoveries include the development of monoclonal an-
tibodies, the discovery of *oncogenes*, the disclosures about the
role of vitamins in inhibition of cancer—and indeed in the rever-
sal of the oncogenic process, the role of oxygen in the form of
free radicals in the oncogenic process and other information on
the mechanism by which carcinogens operate.

Part I of the OSTP document is an attempt to set out these
new developments, which provide information on the
characterization of risk, information which we would be remiss
not to consider. On the other hand, to rely on yesterday's
"sophistication" when it has been supplemented or modified by
new scientific developments, raises serious social questions.
(*Control of Carcinogens*, 1983, p. 300)[4]

The administration's policies were also defended by George
Keyworth, director of the Office of Science and Technology
Policy, and by Christopher DeMuth, administrator for information and regulatory affairs in the Office of Management and
Budget and executive director of the President's Task Force on
Regulatory Relief. Both officials placed the cancer policy in the
context of the regulatory relief effort. DeMuth pointed to three
problems in past cancer policy documents that needed to be addressed: the use of "conservative assumptions," the exclusion of
"negative evidence," and the limitations of scientific thinking until 1977. The OSTP working group was designed to consider these
three criticisms.[5]

Others outside the hearings criticized the changed cancer
policy. For example, Ashford et al. in two articles (1983a, 1983b)
looked at how three agencies (EPA, OSHA, and CPSC) handled
the evidence of the carcinogenicity of formaldehyde. The authors
found fault with EPA's and OSHA's handling of the case and
stated, concerning the Todhunter memorandum, that the "most
troublesome procedural problem lies in Todhunter's failure to
acknowledge his departure from prior agency positions on many
of the science policy issues involved. Where an agency has changed
a previously articulated policy or departed from a relevant agency

precedent, the courts have required the agency to provide a detailed rationale" (Ashford et al., 1983b, p. 897).

Perera (1984), already discussed above in connection with the congressional hearings, addressed the genotoxic/epigenetic distinction. Such a distinction was based, she wrote, on the assumption that short-term tests provide adequate information about carcinogenic mechanisms, that the information produced by those tests would allow regulators to categorize risk to humans, and that human exposure guidelines could be written to take this risk into account. She noted that a number of carcinogens classified as epigenetic show genotoxic effects. She also made the point that the linear model is appropriate "if the assumption is made that carcinogenesis by an external agent acts additively with any ongoing or 'background' carcinogenic process" (Perera, 1984, p. 186).[6]

Scandal

While there were strident attacks on Reagan administration cancer policy among scientists, environmental interest groups, and House Democratic members (and an equally vigorous defense of those policies), what eventually stalled the changes was a set of scandals that erupted in EPA in 1982 and 1983 (and, to a much lesser extent, in OSHA). Those scandals led to the replacement of EPA leadership and a partial return to the previous consensus on cancer policy.

Of the various scandals, the major one concerned the operation of the emergency superfund hazardous waste cleanup program. In December 1980, Congress passed the Comprehensive Environmental Response, Compensation, and Liability Act (Superfund). Prodded by the events of Love Canal (Levine, 1982), the act provided funding for the cleanup of abandoned hazardous waste sites, but it was the Reagan administration taking office in January 1981 that would implement it. The official placed in charge of the superfund program was Rita Lavelle. Her appointment produced near paroxysm among environmentalists because she had worked for a company that was on EPA's priority list of hazardous waste sites ("Environmental Apoplexy," 1982). Critics complained that the program was being mismanaged (which was confirmed by an internal EPA study; see Shabecoff, 1983) and handled on a political basis. Congressional investigations into the implementation of superfund led to a confrontation between several House committees and the Reagan administration, particularly over the refusal of the administration to hand over subpoenaed documents. EPA administrator Anne Burford favored turning over the documents, but higher administration officials refused (Kurtz, 1984).[7] The result was a contempt citation issued against Burford and shortly thereafter her resignation and the resignation and firing of most of the top EPA administrators.

Other scandals rocked the agency. One was the existence and possible use of "hit lists" by EPA officials, including the possibility that scientists were evaluated on political criteria for membership in EPA's Scientific Advisory Board (see Feliciano, 1983). One of the more interesting of the allegations could be labelled "Dow and the dioxin plant." Dow Chemical, headquartered in Midland, Michigan, was the principal manufacturer of the herbicide 2,4,5-T. That herbicide contains small amounts of the highly toxic contaminant 2,3,7,8-TCDD, the most toxic form of dioxin.[8] The EPA regional office attempted to conduct a study of the wastewater from the Midland plant. Dow refused access to the plant, and the study was conducted outside the company's grounds. Researchers found that dioxin levels were considerably higher downstream from the plant as compared to upstream. However, deputy EPA administrator John Hernandez ordered the regional office to go over the report with Dow officials. The Dow officials suggested changes in the report, backed by Hernandez, that virtually emasculated it. For instance, a reference to fertility problems among wives of plant workers was deleted (*EPA: Investigation of Superfund*, 1983). Later reports, after the personnel changeovers, did indeed show higher levels of contamination downriver from the plant (Reinhold, 1983). Other instances of alterations of scientific documents during this period came to light.

In addition to the scandals, two other related factors, part of the political stream that Kingdon (1984) discusses, played a role in changing the Reagan administration's attempt to alter cancer policy. Both of those related to strong support for environmental protection in Congress and in the public at large. In the House, which remained under Democratic control after the 1980 elections, basic support for environmental protection remained strong among members and committee and subcommittee chairmen. Since the 1982 congressional elections produced a larger Democratic majority in the House, environmental concerns remained at least as strong as previously. Most of the investigative hearings on the EPA scandals were held in the House. In the Senate in 1981, the Republicans gained control for the first time in twenty-five years. However, even then supporters of strong environmental protection held key committee positions. For example, Senator Robert Stafford (R.-VT) became chairman of the Environment and Public Works Committee, the major committee with jurisdiction over EPA.

The second factor, public opinion, showed similar strong backing for environmental protection. Public opinion polls from 1970 on have consistently shown that the environment holds a high priority among a majority of Americans. Though environmental protection has almost never been the top-ranked issue, polls have demonstrated that given a choice between, say, energy development and environmental protection, the latter has been given preference. Only economic growth has been given higher priority.[9] The combination of scandals within EPA plus strong congressional and public support for continued environmental protection created an environment in which cancer policy development moved back toward the consensus (among the agencies, at any rate) enunciated during the Carter administration.

Return To Consensus

Rita Lavelle was fired by EPA administrator Anne Burford, who herself later resigned. Other resignations followed. Key replacements were William Ruckelshaus as EPA administrator and Alvin Alm as deputy administrator, the official with responsibility for day-to-day operation of the agency. Ruckelshaus had an outstanding reputation as the first administrator of EPA (from 1971 to 1973) and then as deputy attorney general, resigning that post in 1973 in what came to be called the "Saturday Night Massacre." He thus was seen as having a strong track record for environmental protection, a strong ethical posture, and his own independent status.[10]

Ruckelshaus is important to our story because of the emphasis he gave to and the initiatives he started in risk assessment and risk management. He asserted that there was indeed a consensus on risk assessment (the objective estimation of risk from a chemical substance) and that the issues had essentially been settled. He insisted on the strict separation of risk assessment and risk management, a stand which could partly be seen as a reaction to the EPA scandals (Stanfield, 1985c). He pursued consistency in risk assessment both within EPA and among regulatory agencies. From a cancer policy standpoint, that is the legacy of William Ruckelshaus.[11]

These cancer policy initiatives can be seen in a speech Ruckelshaus gave at the National Academy of Sciences in June 1983 and that was widely reprinted in scientific journals. He began his speech by pointing out the emotional atmosphere in which risk decisions arise and are made. What was needed, he said, was a resolution of the "dissonance between science and the creation of public policy" (1983, p. 1026). The basic problem, as he saw it, was that science and public policy (or law) were uneasy partners. Evoking the three-value/two-value decision-making distinctions discussed in chapter 2, Ruckelshaus said that the reason for the uneasiness was that science thrived on uncertainty but that the laws often demanded or assumed greater certainty than science could provide. He then described the problems facing EPA (and other agencies):

> We must now deal with a class of pollutants for which it is difficult, if not impossible, to establish a safe level. These pollutants interfere with genetic processes and are associated with the diseases we fear most, cancer and reproductive disorders, including birth defects. The scientific consensus is that any exposure, however small, to a genetically active substance embodies some risk of an effect. Since these substances are widespread in the environment, and since we can detect them down to very low levels, we must assume that life now takes place in a minefield of risks from hundreds, perhaps thousands, of substances. We can no longer tell the public that they have an adequate margin of safety. (Ruckelshaus, 1983, p. 1027)

Ruckelshaus indicated the uncertainties at the various stages of risk assessment and stated that the laws should reflect those uncertainties. He also called for a common statutory framework for assessing risks and benefits. He then distinguished between the two functions, risk assessment (assessing the risk) and risk management (deciding what to do about the risk).[12] The two functions should be completely separated. Risk assessment must be based, he continued, "only on scientific evidence and scientific consensus" (Ruckelshaus, 1983, p. 1027).

Ruckelshaus then made three proposals: involve the public in a more explicit manner in risk decision making;[13] form a task force to ensure consistency of risk assessment and management efforts within EPA; and begin an interagency coordinating effort.[14] He concluded:

> In sum, my goal is a government-wide process for assessing and managing environmental risks. Achieving this will take cooperation and goodwill within EPA, among Executive Branch agencies, and between Congress and the Administration, a state of affairs that may partake of the miraculous. Still, it is worth trying, and the effort is worth the wholehearted support of the scientific community. I believe such an effort touches on the maintenance of our current society, in which a democratic policy is grounded in a high-technology civilization. Without a much more successful way of handling the risks associated with the creations of science, I fear that we will have set up for ourselves a grim and unnecessary choice between the fruits of advanced technology and the blessings of democracy. (Ruckelshaus, 1983, p. 1028)

Establishing The Consensus

The EPA risk assessment initiatives, to be discussed below, were based on two reports issued in 1983–1984, one by the National Research Council (NRC) (1983), the other by the White House Office of Science and Technology Policy (OSTP) (1984). The NRC report was used by EPA to make a strong distinction between risk assessment and risk management. The OSTP report was viewed as having produced a scientific consensus on risk assessment issues.

National Research Council

The report of the National Research Council (1983) emanated from a congressional directive to the Food and Drug Administration to study the feasibility of centralized science panels.[15] FDA then commissioned the NRC study. The panel members wrote that no radical organizational changes need be made but that the process of risk assessment could be improved. The major problem the NRC panel found was the "incompleteness of data." The report consisted of three parts. Part one looked at the nature of risk assessment. Part two, discussed in the second chapter, looked at inference guidelines. The major contribution of this section was its distinction between risk assessment and risk management and its clear spelling out of the inferences and science policy decisions that are an integral and inevitable part of risk assessment. The second chapter also reviewed the development of risk assessment guidelines and the arguments for and against generic guidelines. The NRC report concluded:

1. All agencies have found it necessary to write guidelines, in part, to make their choice of inference options more evident to the public. However, the application of inference options to specific risk assessments has been marked by a general lack of explicitness. . . .

2. Agency guidelines have varied markedly in form and content. Without a deliberate coordinating effort, there is no reason to assume that guidelines will become more clearly uniform.

3. Uniform guidelines for risk assessment (except for exposure assessment) are feasible and desirable.

4. Even well-designed guidelines may be unsuccessful unless:
   * Attention is given to the process by which they are developed.
   * They can accommodate change.
   * They are viewed as valuable tools, rather than formulas for producing risk assessments (National Research Council, 1983, pp 79–81)

The National Research Council thus made a number of important recommendations. EPA adopted or attempted to adopt some of them; others are discussed in chapter 8. The NRC was calling for openness and explicitness of assumptions and procedures, uniformity, and coordination.

Office of Science and Technology Policy

The third set of risk assessment guidelines by the White House Office of Science and Technology Policy was published in the *Federal Register* in May 1984. It was the product of several years of deliberations and review (see chapter 5). This third draft articulated a set of principles for cancer policy and reviewed the "state-of-the-science" behind those principles. The purpose of the document was, in the authors' words, to "serve as the basis for consistent regulatory cancer guidelines that the Federal agencies can tailor to meet the requirements of the legislative acts they are charged to implement" (Office of Science and Technology Policy, 1984, p. 21595). Appendix A contains the principles stated in the document.

As the discussion in chapter 2 pointed out, the OSTP draft took many of the same positions on inference issues as the Carter administration guidelines, demonstrating the strong effect of the criticism and scandal discussed in the last chapter. For example, while recognizing the distinction between initiators and promoters, the document stated that for practical purposes no distinction need be made. Similarly, OSTP observed that there was no evidence to prove the existence (or lack) of thresholds. Following weight-of-the-evidence approach, it did recognize some of the criticisms made about early cancer policy documents. Note principle 4 (see appendix A) and the related discussion in chapter 1 of the OSTP document that testing regimens may overwhelm the animal's defensive systems; this metabolic overload must be evaluated. Similarly, pharmacokinetic data need to be considered in selecting highest dose levels.

The final chapter of the document, which dealt with risk assessment, presented a much more positive view of the process than did the first draft. Describing risk assessment as "a complex blend of current scientific data, reasonable assumptions and scientific judgments that permit decisions to be made in the absence of complete information" (Office of Science and Technology Policy, 1984, p. 21656), OSTP saw this final chapter as bridging the gap between the scientific foundation and the agencies.

Perhaps the most interesting part of this chapter is the discussion of dose-response models. After reviewing different models, OSTP concluded that no one model had gained universal acceptance. The draft considered related issues. The first was the question of background additivity. If there is a common mechanism of tumor induction, then all the models are essentially linear. If there is no background additivity, that is, if there are different tumor induction mechanisms (as Salzburg and Heath [1981] stated), then the models will differ considerably. If the critical dose is the biologically effective dose (the amount that actually reaches the target organ) rather than the administered dose, the relationship between the two doses is nonlinear, and pharmacokinetic data might modify low-dose estimates.

The OSTP document also discussed other estimation procedures, particularly the NOEL approach advocated in the EPA water quality draft guidelines in 1982. OSTP pointed out that while the safety factor approach was often used, a number of problems remained in its application to chronic diseases such as cancer. First, the observation of no treatment effects could be a function of the small number of test animals employed. Second, the approach ignored the shape of the dose-response curve. Third, there was no biological justification for the use of any safety factor. Finally, the approach assumed that a true population threshold exists. The problem here is that there is genetic variability among individuals. Furthermore, because of the already high background incidence of cancer in the population, any new chemical exposure might enhance an ongoing process and "produce a collective or additive exposure that exceeds the unknown threshold level" (Office of Science and Technology Policy, 1984, p. 21659). OSTP concluded by noting that there is insufficient understanding of cancer mechanisms to employ classifications schemes based on whether or not a substance acts directly on DNA.

As a final note, the report was careful to point out the uncertainties that exist in the science and, as a result, in risk assessments, inferences, and science policy decisions. Finally, the report pointed to developing areas of science that might affect risk assessment in the future. The final version of the OSTP report was published in 1985 and is virtually identical to the 1984 draft (see Office of Science and Technology Policy, 1985).

The OSTP report was subject to criticism, particularly by those favoring a more risk-tolerant position. One such critique appeared in *Regulation*. After indicating how the OSTP draft had moved closer to its desired position in some ways, the editor stated:

> Still, a close reading of the new document reveals that it has not succeeded in its professed goal of distinguishing science from "science policy." Instead, it contains instance after instance where policy masquerades as science. ("Revision Without Revolution," 1984, p. 5)

The critique then offered three examples of "policy masquerading as science": the acceptance of animal tests as predictors of human carcinogenicity, animal testing guidelines, and thresholds. The article pointed out that while bioassays have implicated hundreds of substances as carcinogens, only a few substances (between ten and twenty) have been shown to be carcinogenic in epidemiological tests. Most interesting is the discussion of thresholds. The article's complaint was that carcinogens are treated one way and other hazards another (the safety factor approach). Echoing Cornfield (1977), the article stated that since "there are no obvious differences between carcinogens and toxins in the shape of experimentally observed dose-response curves" (p. 7), why treat carcinogens differently? Their final characterization of the OSTP report saw it as virtually the same as the Carter administration guidelines, "based less on a scientific attempt to gauge the likeliest actual level of risk than on a political desire to be 'prudent' by adopting worst-case estimates" (p. 7).[16]

Ruckelshaus Initiatives

The initiatives begun by William Ruckelshaus took three interrelated paths: (1) the creation of a toxics integration task force to develop more uniformity in risk assessments and risk decisions within EPA, (2) the updating of EPA's risk assessment guidelines, and (3) the development of more uniformity in risk assessment among the various federal regulatory agencies.[17] I examine these initiatives in this section.

Toxics Integration Task Force

A toxics integration task force was established in 1983 to investigate risk assessment and risk management as it was currently practiced within EPA. One task force study of some twenty-seven decisions made by various branches within EPA found considerable inconsistency in the risk assessments and risk decisions that were reached, going beyond differences created by divergent statutory mandates (see table 3.2). The obvious solution was to ensure uniformity across program lines. This solution was accomplished in two ways. First, EPA adopted, in 1984, a set of uniform risk assessment summary forms that allowed higher level EPA personnel to assess the evidence. Second, updated guidelines, such as the cancer guidelines discussed below, were to be written. By November 1984, five of the six guidelines had been issued. A further proposal made by the task force and accepted by the agency was the creation of the Risk Assessment Forum, in which agency scientists could discuss various risk assessment issues. Finally, the new risk assessment and risk management framework produced as a result of the task force's work called for risk-benefit and cost-benefit analyses.

Guidelines

The cancer guidelines (Environmental Protection Agency, 1984c)[18] were published in the *Federal Register* in November 1984. The distinction between risk assessment and risk management was strongly asserted and was based on the NRC report. The summary of the state of knowledge and the principles set forth in the OSTP report was the basis for the guidelines. The purpose of the guidelines was to consider changes in the science, to promote consistency of risk assessments, and to inform those outside EPA of the basis for EPA decision making. It was emphasized that the guidelines did not alter any policies set down by legislation, nor could they be specific because of rapid changes in the scientific base.

In these guidelines EPA took the weight-of-the-evidence approach. The guidelines also employed a modified version of the International Agency for Cancer Research classification scheme for carcinogens, which stemmed from the draft additional water quality guidelines discussed in chapter 5. The document set forth five categories for epidemiological and bioassay data: sufficient, limited, inadequate, no evidence, and no data. Sufficient evidence from epidemiological studies is a demonstration of a causal relationship between an agent and human cancer. For bioassays, sufficient evidence of carcinogenicity (generally increased incidence of malignant or malignant and benign tumors) is evidence in multiple species or strains or in multiple experiments with preferably different routes of administration, or unusual incidence. Additional evidence could come from dose-response data and from data on chemical structure and short-term tests. The two types of evidence (human and animal) are then combined to create an overall categorization scheme. Group A is human carcinogens that have been identified by sufficient epidemiological evidence. Group B (probable human carcinogens) is divided into two subgroups: B1 (those identified by at least limited evidence of carcinogenicity from epidemiological studies) and B2 (those identified by inadequate evidence from human studies and sufficient evidence from animal studies). Group C (possible human carcinogen) includes substances for which there is limited evidence from animal data in the absence of human data. Group D (not classified) includes substances for which there is inadequate animal evidence of carcinogenicity. Group E (no evidence) includes substances for which there is no evidence from either two adequate animal tests in different species or from both human and animal data.

While moving somewhat closer to the proposed 1982 changes discussed earlier (such as the classification scheme and the heavier weight given to epidemiological evidence), the 1984 guidelines also kept the pre-1981 consensus on many of the risk assessment issues, such as the willingness to count benign and malignant tumors (except in certain situations). Of particular interest is EPA's recommendation that the linearized, multistage, low-dose extrapolation model (first recommended in the 1980 water quality guidelines) be used in most situations. It recognized that biological and statistical data might indicate the use of other models, and it specifically noted pharmacokinetic and metabolic data that might produce evidence about cancer mechanisms. The guidelines pointed out that even then estimates from the linearized model should also be presented to estimate upper-limit risk (which the guidelines say is the major estimate produced by that model).

Agency Consistency

At Ruckelshaus's urging, an Interagency Risk Management Council (IRMC) comprised of EPA, the Consumer Product Safety Commission, the Food and Drug Administration, and the Occupational Safety and Health Administration, was created. The purpose of the council was to gain uniformity of decision making across agencies, at least in terms of risk assessments.[19] It did not last long enough to make much of an impact beyond focusing attention on the problem. In late 1984 the IRMC was disbanded and its function was taken over by a cabinet level council staffed by the office of Management and Budget.

Interdisciplinary Panel

In 1983 the American Industrial Health Council (AIHC) convened an Interdisciplinary Panel on Carcinogenicity (IPC) of scientists. The council's charge was to review criteria for assessing carcinogenicity of chemicals because of what AIHC felt were new data on carcinogenesis and in other areas of cancer research. The paper (Interdisciplinary Panel on Carcinogenicity, 1984) reviewed the various types of studies (human, animal, and short-term) for strengths and weaknesses. The panel pointed out that only epidemiological studies provide direct evidence of human carcinogenicity. The panel's major point was that no general conclusions could be reached that would form the basis for guidelines and that each case should be examined individually. In addition, all the data should be considered. The panel was in some respects close to the consensus, both in its characterization of negative evidence and in its acceptance of the possibility of combining malignant and benign tumors. Its position of tentativeness is typified by the following quote:

Chemical carcinogens can, in principle, be divided into two categories. One category gives nonthreshold dose responses, is stochastic in mechanism, and may have some probability of producing carcinogenic effects at any dose. The second category gives threshold dose responses and, theoretically, has a no-effect level. A few chemicals can be placed, provisionally, in one category or the other; but for the bulk of chemical carcinogens, we are currently unable to discern in which compartment they fall. By dealing with chemicals case-by-case and by studying mechanism, we can look forward to doing better than this. (Interdisciplinary Council on Carcinogenicity, 1984, p. 685)

The panel recommended presenting most probable estimates with confidence limits for low-dose extrapolation. All the uncertainties should be included in the assessment. Taking a leave-it-to-the-scientists approach, the paper concluded that scientific impartiality, scientific experience, and judgment are necessary to weigh the evidence. These recommendations mirrored AIHC's view of cancer (see chapter 5) but had little impact because of the panel's unofficial nature.

Conclusion

The administration's efforts to restore the economy and reduce the role of government found its incarnation in the regulatory relief program (which had its roots in the Carter administration and earlier administrations). Cancer policies stemming from EPA and OSTP were attempts to combine the scientific critiques and the regulatory relief streams to produce more risk-tolerant policies. That effort was stymied both by the scandals that afflicted EPA and the continued strong support for environmental protection in Congress and in the general public. Later cancer policies by EPA and the Office of Science and Technology Policy were closer to the Carter administration consensus, with OSTP adopting the principles approach to cancer risk assessment guidelines and EPA adopting some of the ideas of the scientific critique and the earlier EPA additional water quality guidelines.

But the continued use of science to forward policy positions has not abated. Recently, the Food and Drug Administration delayed a ban on ten food and drug dyes to further study the scientific evidence ("F.D.A. Delays a Ban on Dyes, 1985).[20]

Kingdon's model of agenda building has been useful in these last four chapters in explaining changes in cancer policy development. Political events appear to be at least as strong as, and probably stronger than, scientific developments in understanding why certain choices were made and certain changes were advocated. Separating out the scientific and political elements of cancer policy, a process strongly advocated by William Ruckelshaus (at least partially for political reasons), appears to be a difficult if not impossible task. Making assumptions explicit, admitting the uncertainties that permeate the risk assessment process will, however, go a long way toward making policy choices explicit.

Although I have described cancer policy development through 1984 and into 1985 (the date of this writing), my story is not complete. considerable resources and time have gone into developing cancer policies; even more has gone into specific risk assessments and risk decisions. Has this effort made any difference? Could it make a difference? Is there really a cancer plague that needs to be addressed? Is it even possible to identify the causes of cancer? The risk assessment documents that we have looked at had one target in particular, chemicals. How important are chemicals to cancer causation? Could there possibly be other, more important factors contributing to the high cancer incidence in the United States? These and other questions form the subject of the next chapter.

7

The Challenge To Cancer Policy

We have been finding traces of that mock-scientific paridigm everywhere that we have wandered in this journey. But we now identify its precise location. *It is embedded in the official cancer prevention program.* The "apocalyptic paradigm" is a description of the mental processes of "regulatory" science when it bases itself solely on animal data, and it accounts most fully for the battle it generates. In fact, the entire conceptual structure of "cancer prevention" by animal testing alone, which has been crudely superimposed on the authentic work being done in basic research, *is* the "apocalyptic paradigm." It serves the same function in the world of cancer that it served in the "environmental" movement: Without being able to generate applicable data, without predictive power for man and in a void of scientific ignorance, it declares frightful catastrophe to be imminent, so imminent that there is no time for facts, logic, or the slow, serious development of an authentic predictive science—*if* such a predictive science is possible.

--Efron, 1984, pp. 381-382; emphasis in original

In the last four chapters, I have examined the development of, and controversies surrounding, cancer policies issued by various federal agencies. In this chapter, I move to a higher level of analysis and address two questions. First, is risk assessment necessary? Is there a problem worth worrying about and devoting public and private resources to? In its most barest form, the focus

151

of this question is on cancer rates and the causes of cancer. The other major question is whether risk assessment is genuinely possible. That section centers on one particularly disputatious work, Edith Efron's *The Apocalyptics*. The final section of the chapter will present some arguments justifying risk assessment and generic guidelines, despite the critical points made against that enterprise.

This chapter reinforces the argument of the first chapter: cancer risk assessment is a field fraught with scientific uncertainties and heavily influenced by value judgments. Those who support strict regulation of toxic chemicals assert that there is a cancer epidemic attributable (at least indirectly) to those chemicals. Those who state that strict regulation is unnecessary also maintain that there is no cancer epidemic. While it is possible to determine whether or not there is a cancer epidemic, it is much more difficult to relate cancer incidence to toxic substances. That impossibility opens the door to value judgments.

Is There a Cancer Problem?

The argument that there is a cancer epidemic and that the epidemic is due to chemicals has its origin, as Efron (1984) pointed out, in works by Carson (1962) and Commoner (1971). In *The Closing Circle*, Commoner argued that it was the development of the synthetic chemical industry after World War II that was responsible for many of the environmental problems that afflicted the country. In his view, technology was clearly the problem.[1] This line of reasoning has been accepted and extended by those advocating strict control over potential carcinogens.

As an example, one can recall the testimony by Weinstein (*Control of Carcinogens*, 1983). Weinstein, a prominent cancer scientist, began with a statement of "basic principles of environmental carcinogenesis" (p. 7). I first quote and then explore the logic of some of those principles.

> 1. *Cancer is the second leading cause of death* in the United States accounting for over 400,000 deaths per year. It is, therefore, a disease of major magnitude. . . .
>
> 2. *The majority (50-80%) of human cancers are due to environmental (i.e., exogenous) rather than hereditary factors.*

They are, therefore, in principle preventable by identifying the causative agents and reducing human exposure to them. . . .

3. *Within the past few decades there has been a marked increase in the exposure of humans to synthetic chemicals* and their various products, both in the workplace and the general environment. Although there is, thus far, no evidence that this has led to a marked increase in total cancer incidence, a number of these synthetic compounds are carcinogenic in experimental animals and several have clearly been responsible for the causation of cancers in humans. . . .

4. *There is a long lag or latent period* between exposure to carcinogens and the clinical appearance of tumors. In humans this lag is in the range of 5–30 or more years. (*Control of Carcinogens*, 1983, pp. 7–8; emphasis in original)

Weinstein, somewhat more conservative than others in that he did not directly assert a cancer epidemic, made the following points. First, cancer is an important cause of death; second, most incidences of cancer are environmentally induced. Few scientists would disagree with these first two points; indeed, they are the basis of the Doll and Peto (1981) study. But the next two points are more controversial. Third, Weinstein stated, there has been a drastic increase in exposure to synthetic chemicals, many of which have been implicated as carcinogens. While he stated that there is no direct proof that those chemicals are an important cause of cancer, this position was clearly implied by him and was stated directly by others. To that possibility he added the question of the latency period: even if there were no epidemic now, exposure to chemicals might produce one in the future. One other argument could be added to Weinstein's: most chemicals have not been adequately tested (National Research Council, 1984). Combining the latency and testing problems produces considerable uncertainty and potential for harm.

I have already addressed the problems of assessing the carcinogenicity of chemicals in previous chapters; I shall also address that problem in the next section. But is there an epidemic? Is the problem getting worse?

The Question of Cancer Rates

Rugenstein (1982) who wrote a rather polemical book looking

at the impact of chemicals on human health and the environment, stated that cancer is now the second leading cause of death (after heart attacks), up from tenth place in 1900. In addition, he asserted that the disease is the leading cause of death for young women (thirty to forty years old) and for children under ten. Furthermore, and this is a point I will return to, he indicated that less than one-third of cancer deaths is attributable to lung cancer, with the other deaths "caused by other factors, with the pervasive presence in our society of deadly chemicals thought to play a major role" (Regenstein, 1982, p. 38).

Epstein (1978) a leading cancer researcher whose *The Politics of Cancer* has been prominent in the cancer policy debates, made similar observations. "Cancer," he wrote, "is the plague of the twentieth century" (p. 15). He presented data showing that the crude cancer death rate per 100,000 population rose from 64.0 to 171.7. He also showed that most of the standardized cancer death rates by site (e.g., lung, genitals) had increased from 1937 to 1969 even when lung cancer (the most important cancer site) was not counted. He concluded (p. 21) "that there has been a real and absolute increase in cancer incidence and mortality during this century which cannot be explained away by increased life span or by smoking." He then presented evidence that most cancers (70–90 percent) are environmentally induced.

The report of the Toxic Substances Strategy Committee (TSSC) (1980), discussed in chapter 4, made similar claims. The report focused on three issues, which we shall consider both here and a little later: increasing cancer incidence, the proportion of cancers attributable to occupational exposure (based on a 1978 study by Schneiderman and others that has been severely criticized), and an estimate of the proportion of lung cancer attributable to smoking. The latter issue is of particular importance. The Karch and Schneiderman (1981) estimates of the role of smoking in causing lung cancer were considerably lower than other estimates. If they are correct, then other facts, such as toxic air pollutants, might play a greater role.

Karch and Schneiderman (1981, p. 220) presented data showing that "cancer and the obstructive lung diseases are the only major causes of death to increase throughout this century, after age, sex, and race are all taken into account." The figures offered by

Schneiderman and TSSC, however, have one major problem, the level of aggregation (looking at overall cancer rates). This point can be seen in a paper by Hodgson (1981). His figures, and Epstein's (1978), confirmed, that cancer trends, adjusted for age and by site, showed that there were many sites with increasing death rates and a few that had decreasing death rates. It is clear from the charts that lung cancer is primarily responsible for increasing cancer rates. Thus one needs to separate out the effects of lung cancer from those of other cancers.

The data clearly show that age-adjusted and crude death rates from cancer have increased. However, while Regenstein (1982) pointed to high cancer rates among children (ages 1–10), the data show that since 1950 the death rates have actually declined. In that thirty-year period, the overall death rate from cancer increased by just a little more than 7 percent. The most important site was the respiratory system, where cancer mortality rates rose 108 percent during the same period. Intriguingly, there has been a decrease in the number of smokers, the major contributor to lung cancer, but an increase in the number of heavy smokers smoking 25 or more cigarettes a day (U.S. Department of Health and Human Services, 1982).

What do we conclude? First, the cancer death rate has clearly increased over the years. This fact remains true even on an age-adjusted basis, which eliminates the aging population factor. Indeed, cancer is one of the few causes of death that have increased. Second, death rates for youngsters have decreased, a fact which eliminates the possibility of an epidemic among the young. As Regenstein asserted, such an epidemic would have made a strong argument for looking at toxic chemicals. But the data do not support such a conclusion. Third, the major contributor to the increased cancer death rate is lung cancer, which is primarily, though not entirely, due to smoking, a lifestyle factor. Factoring out lung cancer produces a *decline* in aggregate age-adjusted cancer rates over the 1950–1980 period. In fact, assuming that smoking is not as significant a factor in lung cancer as some have said, using a 75 percent figure for smoking and respiratory cancer still produces a decrease in cancer rates in that thirty-year period. If toxic substances were important, as Weinstein and others have suggested, one would expect the rates to go up. Again, we have aggregated by site. It may be that toxic chemicals are important in some types of cancers and not in others. In that case, toxics may indeed by a factor.

It is important to note, finally, that focusing on death rates is slightly misleading. Survival rates appear to have increased with advances in science, though like everything else associated with this area, they too are in contention (Boffey, 1984). The more critical statistic, but the less available and reliable one, is cancer incidence. It may be that more people are getting cancer than would appear just from death certificates. Indeed, there were 870,000 new cases of cancer and only some 450,000 cancer-related deaths in 1983 (Institute of Medicine, 1984). If this were indeed the situation, then the case for an epidemic and the role of toxic chemicals would be enhanced. The complication of incidence versus mortality, which at present remains unresolved, continues the uncertainties.[2] Focusing just on mortality rates tends to support those who state that there is no epidemic. Looking at incidence rates might support those who state that there is an epidemic and that toxics play an important role. We find here a replay of the situation discussed at length in chapter 2 (see also table 2.5). The types of cancer statistics used are related to the positions scientists take on this and other issues.

Causes of Cancer

Nearly all who study the causes of cancer agree that most cancers (50–80 percent) are environmentally (externally) induced.[3] This notion is significant for two reasons. First, it directs attention to the primary causes of cancer. If cancer is in part caused by toxic chemicals, then regulatory approaches limiting exposure to those chemicals seem justified. Second, if cancer is induced primarily by the environment, then there is strong grounds for believing that most cancers can be prevented. So the environmental causes of cancer, if appropriately identified, can lead to prevention (cheaper and less taxing on the individual than cure) and possible regulatory strategies.[4]

The question is whether the causes can indeed be correctly identified. Here again we see considerable disagreement, with studies contradicting other studies. While the overall range of environmentally induced cancer is generally agreed upon, the meaning of *environmental* is not. For some, 'environmental' refers to substances in the air, land, water, and food supply that cause cancer. This is clearly the meaning that Epstein (1978) and others use. Note the title of Regenstein's book, *The Poisoning of America.* Weinstein clearly implies this relationship.

Others, however, use 'environment' in a much broader fashion. In this use, it means anything that is external to the body; though it may include environmental insults, it is much more likely to include lifestyle factors such as smoking, diet (but not necessarily additives), drinking, and sexual behavior. This second view downplays the role of toxic chemicals and suggests alternative prevention strategies. More importantly, what is implicitly or explicitly suggested is that much of the incidence of cancer is due to personal behavior that can be changed and that does not require any regulatory intervention, apart, perhaps, from education and information. Those who view the causes of cancer as largely due to toxic chemicals see the problem as a societal one, beyond the control of individuals and requiring important regulatory interventions. Note the title of Epstein's work, *The Politics of Cancer.* The causes of cancer are known, cancer is not a biological problem but a political one, and the problem can be resolved by political activity. What then is the situation? Again, we shall see that while there is some consensus on the lifestyle factor, there is no general agreement on its weight. Those who see the need for drastic regulation state that toxics are important. Those who do not see such a need place the stress on lifestyle.

Epstein (1978) presented the strongest case for toxics as *the* most important factor in cancer causation. Part II of his book is a series of case studies in which he discusses workplace carcinogens (asbestos, vinyl chloride, bischloromethulether, and benzene),[5] consumer products (tobacco, red dyes #2 and #40, saccharin, acrylonitrile, and female sex hormones in oral contraceptives, other medical uses, and feed additives), and the general environment (pesticides and nitrosamines). He also listed chemicals known to induce cancer in humans, and substances regulated as carcinogens, and he reprinted the 1970 report of the Ad Hoc Committee to the Surgeon General (discussed in chapter 3), one of the precursors to formal cancer policies.

Epstein then addressed industry interpretations of cancer statistics.

> The American Industrial Health Council attempts to support its argument with graphs that show a decrease in cancer death rates when lung cancer (which in the general population is largely due to smoking) is excluded. The council argues that cancer is on the decline, that its present incidence can largely be attributed to smoking and diet, and that industrial chemicals are responsible for no more than 5 percent of all cancers in the United States. However, it is easy to see from industry data that two sites have accounted for most of the decrease, stomach and cervix, and that this decrease has been more than matched by increases at other sites. . . .
>
> The industry position is based on oversimplification of a complex statistical problem. Cancer is probably not one disease but a spectrum of diseases with common features but different—though proximate—causes. Cancer strikes different parts of the population with different force. Any attempt to represent the effect of cancer with a single summary statistic for many cancer sites lumped together necessarily masks the real situation. (Epstein, 1978, pp. 222–223)

One of Epstein's most critical points was that apart from smoking, "there is no reliable method for calculating the number of deaths caused by other classes of carcinogens" (p. 24). Epstein devoted considerable time to exploring cancer rates in various parts of the country and correlating high cancer rates with high levels of industrial and chemical activity. If available figures refer to known carcinogens but epidemiological studies are severely limited, then, Epstein argued, there was some unknown amount of cancer that may be caused by chemicals. This important point is based on the uncertainty of data and on a risk-averse view of cancer causation. Of course, Epstein's views are speculative and are based on a limited amount of data. This problem plagues all who delve into this field, including those with more risk-tolerant views, such as Doll and Peto (1981).

One of the more interesting cancer causation controversies surrounds the work of Marvin Schneiderman. Schneiderman, a prominent cancer researcher, a former associate director of the

National Cancer Institute, and later a member of a consulting firm, was involved with two studies that attempted to determine the role of toxic chemicals. The first was a study produced by the National Institute of Occupational Safety and Health (NIOSH), the other a study commissioned by the Natural Resources Defense Council. The earlier study (Bridbord et al., 1978) attempted to estimate the percentage of cancers attributable to occupational exposure. It stated that 20 to 38 percent of all cancers were related to occupation. Doll and Peto (1981) and others (see citations in Chemical Manufacturers Association, 1981) severely criticized the estimates. For example, the NIOSH study, on the basis of a Norwegian study, predicted 7,300 U.S. cancers from nickel exposure. Doll and Peto wrote:

> Arithmetically, this calculation is correct. . . . This calculation, however, might fairly be described as a confidence trick. It takes an estimate of risk from Norway and assumes that the same *relative* risk of respiratory cancer would apply to the United States where the normal incidence of the disease was much higher. It further assumes that the 1,400,000 workers currently "exposed to nickel" in the United States have been exposed to the same amounts as men employed in a nickel refinery, most of whom began employment under very dusty conditions . . . despite the fact that many less than 1 percent of all American nickel workers are employed in refineries, that no hazard from exposure to nickel has been demonstrated outside a refinery, and that it is uncertain which specific nickel compound is carcinogenic to humans. (Doll and Peto, 1981, p. 1305)

The second study, by Karch and Schneiderman (1981) of the consulting group Clement Associates, Inc., was commissioned by the Natural Resources Defense Council (NRDC) to reestimate the amount of lung cancers due to air pollution. The basic quandry here is that, as we saw above, lung cancer is the most prominent type of cancer and is largely responsible for the increases in overall cancer death rates. Most lung cancers are caused by smoking (and perhaps smoking in combination with exposure to other carcinogens, especially asbestos). If, however, lung cancer had other causes besides smoking, then smoking would be less important (but by no means unimportant). Doll and Peto (1981) (see below) estimated that smoking contributes to 88.5 percent of lung cancer. Karch and Schneiderman's basic point was that smoking has actually decreased and that the tar and nicotine content has also decreased (though they do not point out that those who smoke tend to smoke more than in the past). If smoking is the primary cause of lung cancer, then lung cancer rates should be decreasing in conjunction with declines in smoking; they have not. Therefore, there has to be some other factor that is keeping lung cancer rates high. That factor, labelled the "urban factor," is essentially a residual of differences between rural and urban dwellers adjusted for age, race, and smoking habits. Karch and Schneiderman's estimate was that current pollution, using three crude indicators, may produce 10 to 19 percent of future lung cancer deaths.[6] Their estimate is not incompatible with the Doll and Peto (1981) assessment for lung cancer that is attributable to smoking (88.5 percent). Whether the estimate means that pollution is reponsible for the remaining lung cancers is a different question. Note also that Karch and Schneiderman mentioned current pollution. But present cancer rates should have been caused by past pollution, and there has been a decrease in the ambient levels of some pollutants (Council on Environmental Quality, 1982); this decrease may (in Karch and Schneiderman's view) decrease the rates of respiratory cancer in the future.

The Karch and Schneiderman paper was subject to a blistering critique by the Chemical Manufacturers Association (CMA) (1981). CMA stated that Karch and Schneiderman's data failed to show a correlation between air pollution rates and lung cancer. Further, CMA charged that Karch and Schneiderman manipulated the data to produce their results. For example, CMA stated that Karch and Schneiderman aggregated lung cancer rates in urban areas and compared them to rates in rural rates. By doing so, inconsistencies in the data were masked, inconsistencies that showed that some smaller urban areas had higher lung cancer rates than other larger urban areas. Perhaps the most critical point that CMA made, about both the 1978 NIOSH and the 1981 NRDC studies, is that neither of them were published and thus were not subject to peer review.

The most comprehensive and authoritative (but by no means unanimously accepted) study of the causes of cancer is that by Doll and Peto (1981), which was commissioned by the congressional Office of Technology Assessment (1981) for its study of risk assessment. The purpose of Doll and Peto's study was to estimate the precentage of cancer deaths that were due to preventable or external causes. Doll and Peto accepted the consensus that most cancers are externally induced and therefore preventable, but they used the broader definition of 'exogenous' to include lifestyle factors. Their findings, reported in the OTA report and published both in the *JCNI* and separately as a monograph, seem to show that only a very small portion of cancers are due to exposure to toxic chemicals. Rather, lifestyle factors are considerably more important. These factors include diet, smoking, drinking, and sexual behavior. Note that their estimates of cancers from various sources are based solely on epidemiological data rather than on some combination of epidemiological and bioassay data. Their epidemiological data do appear to show that many cancers are avoidable. For instance, the incidences of specific cancers differ in different areas. Studies of migrant groups reveal that when a group with a high incidence of a particular type of cancer moves to another country, then the incidence of that cancer declines to rates close to that of the new country and the incidence of specific cancers common in the new country appear in the immigrant group.

Doll and Peto severely criticized other studies, such as the interpretations of data by Schneiderman and the report of the TSSC. They also indicated that short-term tests and bioassays were unreliable. In addition, they made heavy use of the distinction between initiators and promoters. In perhaps the best defense of the importance of this distinction, Doll and Peto (1981, p. 1214) wrote:

> Perhaps the currently emerging understanding of "initiators" will turn out to be substantially correct, with the current short-term tests picking out all the important exogenous chemicals which currently cause human cells to undergo the "early" stages of carcinogenesis (and being useful tools in the search for the preventable determinants of the endogenous synthesis of such chemicals). However, "promotion" is still very poorly understood, as are almost all the other intracellular processes in-

volved in transforming a partially altered cell into a fully cancerous one. . . . Moreover, such "late" processes may turn out to be of much greater relevance to carcinogenesis in large-bodied animals like man that have to avoid cancer for 75 years than in the small, short-lived animals that laboratory workers must necessarily study. . . . If cells must independently undergo first "early" and than "late" processes before cancer can develop, then a 50 percent reduction in *either* class of processes would halve the eventual risk of cancer . . . and the only determinant of which class is more "important" is which is more easily halved.[7]

Table 7.1 presents Doll and Peto's estimates of the contribution of various factors to cancer causation. Their best estimate is that 65 percent of all cancer deaths are due to diet and tobacco. Note, however, the tentativeness of their conclusions, particularly concerning diet. In section 5 of their study, Doll and Peto examined the various factors in the diet that might cause cancer. Neither their tables nor their discussion present estimates of the role of each factor; it is difficult, therefore, to see how they came up with their estimates. Indeed, their discussion indicated problems in making estimates. They wrote: "We have attributed the largest risk to dietary factors. . . . It must be emphasized that the figure chosen is highly speculative and chiefly refers to dietary factors which are not yet reliably identified" (Doll and Peto, 1981, p. 1258). Note the range of estimates of the dietary factor—from 10 to 70 percent. Their best estimate is essentially a midrange point, which provides considerable room for critics to disagree.

Other studies confirmed the rough estimates, or more strictly speaking, the importance of the lifestyle factors. The Doll and Peto view has been widely, though not entirely, accepted in the scientific community. Wynder and Gori (1977) pointed to the county study by Hoover (discussed by Hoover, 1979) and demonstrated that though Hoover and his colleagues found significant differences in cancer rates in counties, with industrial counties having higher rates than nonindustrial counties, smoking habits were not standardized. Like Doll and Peto, Wynder and Gori emphasized the nutritional factor, that is, the importance of either deficiencies or excesses. They also pointed out the implications of these findings. In particular, they stated that individual

Table 7.1
Proportions of Cancer Deaths Attributed to Various Factors

	Percentage of all cancer deaths	
Factor or class of factors	Best	Range of acceptable estimates
Tobacco	30	25–40
Alcohol	3	2–4
Diet	35	10–70
Food additives	<1	-5-2*
Reproductive and sexual behavior	7	1–13
Occupation	4	2–8
Pollution	2	<1–5
Industrial products	<1	<1–2
Medicines and medical procedures	1	0.5–3
Geophysical factors	3	2–4
Infection	10?	2–?
Unknown	?	?

Source: Doll and Peto (1981).
*Allows "for a possibly protective effect of antioxidants and other preservatives" (p. 1257).

lifestyle is at the root of many cases of cancers. But because most people do not want to face up to this personal responsibility, the general environmental factors are given much more importance. Public education and suitable research would then follow. Similarly, Reif (1981) stated that half of cancers are preventable and that future research can reduce incidence of cancers by 80 to 90 percent. Again, lifestyle factors were the most important.

Doll and Peto's study has been subject to criticism. Davis et al. (1983) pointed out that it neglected important increases in males 45 to 65 years old, masking this figure by including this group with the younger ones. In particular, Davis et al. demonstrated that cancers of the brain and lung and multiple myeloma have increased in the over 55 group, the group with the longest potential exposure to workplace carcinogens. In addition, they indicated that the types of lung cancers that are increasing seem to have shifted somewhat and that (like Karch and Schneideman) there is other evidence suggesting that the contribution of smoking has been overestimated. Davis et al. made the salient point that dietary changes, the decline in certain infectious diseases, and the smaller per capita workplace exposure to carcinogens has led to a decline of most cancers in the 35 to 44 age group. But they also noted that "the health effects of recent increases in chemical production and use are not likely to be fully expressed in this century. . . ." (p. 364). The evidence remains unclear.

The Doll and Peto study has also been criticized for undercounting blacks and the elderly. In addition, critics have noted that Doll and Peto attributed about 10 percent of cancers to manmade chemicals, thus arguing for the need for regulatory control (Epstein et al., 1984). Even if the Doll and Peto estimates are high, the burden of the work being done does indicate that lifestyle and natural carcinogens are important, perhaps more important than man-made carcinogens. On the other hand, lifestyle factors are largely incurred voluntarily, whereas exposure to toxic substances is generally involuntary (Slovic et al., 1978).

The most intriguing addition to the cancer causation controversy was by Bruce Ames (1983). Ames is a particularly interesting figure in our story because he was the originator of the most widely used short-term test for mutagenicity, the Ames *salmonella* test. In a 1979 article, Ames (1979) discussed the utility of this test and the validation of the linkage between mutagens and carcinogens mentioned in chapter 2. The 1983 article was a review of the literature on carcinogens and anticarcinogens in the diet. His basic point was that carcinogens and mutagens in the diet may generate oxygen radicals (free radicals) which may be responsible for degenerative diseases such as cancer. In addition, there are a number of antioxidants in the diet that may counter those free radicals (see Weinberg and Storer, 1985). This factor therefore needed further exploration and treatment, though he acknowledged that toxic substances still warrant control. In other forums, Ames has indicated that the most important factor, and the one he is now devoting more time to, is diet, and that he is downplaying the role of toxic substances (Hopson and Gurin, 1984).

Ames's 1983 article was criticized by Epstein and other scientists (including former Carter OSHA administrator Eula Bingham) in a letter to *Science*. They wrote that incidence rates for specific sites have risen in the 1970s and that this rise was "consistent with the theory that past exposure to industrial carcinogens, whose production have increased exponentially since the 1940s, are responsible for recently increasing cancer burdens" (Epstein et al., 1984, p. 660). They pointed out that Ames's assertions on the role of free radicals and the protection given by antioxidants was speculative and that Ames also downplayed the role of synthetic chemicals.

Ames's reply was that he was pointing out the importance of natural carcinogens in the diet and that standard methodologies (such as the Ames test) were employed on man-made but not natural carcinogens. In a statement that clearly evokes many of the problems discussed in this book, Ames wrote:

> Much fear of traces of man-made carcinogens is based on ignoring the natural background of carcinogens and using "worst case" assumptions in extrapolating risk from the most sensitive rodent (when the chemical is given at the maximum tolerated dose) to low-dose human exposure. This quantitative extrapolation is viewed with great unease by much of the toxicological and epidemiological community because there is little scientific support underlying it. . . . It is an extrapolation based on ideas of prudence, not on firm science . . . it is time to do the same types of worst case risk calculations on natural chemicals as well as man-made chemicals before deciding what our priorities are. (Ames, 1984a, p. 758)

Alvin Weinberg, both in a letter commenting on the Ames article (1984) and in a review of Efron's *the Apocalyptics* (1985), was clear on the implications of Ames's work. First, he wrote, the focus on small amounts of toxic chemicals was misdirected. He cited a study by Totter (1980) which showed that overall cancer mortality in various countries was not correlated with industrialization. Second, Weinberg stated that the Delaney amendment, which focused on man-made carcinogens in the food supply, was at best bad science and bad policy, given the much larger amounts of natural carcinogens in the food supply. His final point was that if cancer is a natural process (and therefore inevitable), then the major focus must be on early detection and treatment of tumors. "This, I believe, would require rethinking of the National Cancer Institute's underlying strategy, which at present seems to be dominated by the belief that cancer, unlike death itself, is a preventable disease" (Weinberg, 1984, p. 659).

While Weinberg's last point, that cancer is inevitable and that therefore a treatment strategy rather than a preventive strategy should be followed, is partially implied in Ames's work, there are other implications that can be drawn from the whole body of literature on the causes of cancer. Following Ames and Doll and Peto, one could advocate public sector policies that focus on preventing those factors that seem most important. This is the basis for the American Cancer Society (1984) and the National Academy of Sciences (1982) recommendation to modify diet, particularly dietary fat. Research strategies would also flow from this emphasis. For example, Weinstein (1983) suggested that studying the effects of beta-carotene as an anticarcinogen would be more cost effective than conducting bioassays on b-dichlorobenezene.

The Apocalyptics

In 1984 a potentially revolutionary book, Edith Efron's *The Apocalyptics: Cancer and the Big Lie; How Environmental Politics Controls What We Know About Cancer*, was published. The impact of the book was stated on the back cover by an anonymous "expert in carcinogenesis":

> I found it fascinating . . . a very accurate report of one of the sorrier aspects of our previous decade's history. . . . Many of the characters that fill the pages were not truly scientists at all. They were politicians . . . preying on the general U.S. public's respect for American science. . . . I would venture to predict . . . that the book will become one of the social documents of the era. (Efron, 1984)

Reviews of the book divided, generally speaking, along ideological lines (see Ames, 1984b; Banta, 1985; Bennet, 1984; Greenberg, 1984; Johnson, 1984; Marshall, 1984; and Weinberg, 1985). Those who criticized government cancer policies liked the book; those who supported those policies did not. Alvin Weinberg had perhaps the most balanced review in *Environment* (1985). What had Efron said that caused such an emotional reaction?

Efron's points can be readily summed up. First, there is no cancer epidemic, and therefore the concern with man-made carcinogens has been misplaced. Second, there has been little concern with natural carcinogens, an omission she rectified with two chapters that cite literature on both man-made and natural carcinogens. Her point, one also made by Ames (1983, 1984b), was that nature is not necessarily benign.

Given the absence of a cancer epidemic and the important role that natural carcinogens obviously play, what did Efron say about risk assessment? Here she spent most of her time criticizing risk assessment, essentially saying that there are so many uncertainties that little reliable knowledge can be gained. She attacked the various assumptions of risk assesment one by one, such as thresholds and the somatic (mutation) theory of cancer. Her comments are basically sound, and her exhaustive research is unexcelled. If the scientific basis of risk assessment is weak and untenable, then on what basis have decisions been made? Her answer is the use of "prudent" assumptions, assumptions that we have looked at in previous chapters.

But Efron went further. Not only is risk assessment invalid as currently practiced, but it cannot be done because of theoretical limitations. Here she set the high criterion of absolute certainty, to which we shall return (see also chapter 2). She excluded most of the risk assessment methodologies, such as short-term tests and bioassays, leaving epidemiological studies as the sole basis for making risk assessment decisions. Even here, she dismissed most types of epidemiological studies as essentially correlational in nature. What Efron was demanding is a causal explanation, the why, the mechanism by which cancer is initiated and progresses. Her final point was that given the absence of a cancer epidemic and the highly questionable validity of risk assessment techniques, there was a conspiracy among antitechnological scientists and environmental activists to foster the "big lie." (For a similar argument about antitechnologists, see Douglas and Wildavsky, 1982.)

Efron's book made quite a stir. But to state that it was well researched and that many of the points she made were well founded is not to accept everything that she said.[8] There are three basic problems with her analysis, two related to her wholesale dismissal of risk assessment. The first is her concentration on the OSHA cancer policy, and the second is her implicit assumption that the body of scientific knowledge does not change. Her last problem is the philosophical one of scientific determinism.

Efron's major example of cancer risk assessment guidelines was the OSHA 1980 policy discussed in chapter 4. In many respects, that policy was a caricature of cancer policies in that it took the most rigid stance on many of the issues, adopting a "presumption-rebuttal approach." A better example of cancer policies during the Carter administration was the Interagency Regulatory Liaison Group guidelines. On the other hand, because Efron dismissed risk assessment as an illegitimate scientific endeavor, it probably does not matter which document she chose. But as chapters 4 and 5 make clear, cancer policies did evolve. Efron took no note of that evolution.

Her second problem was her view of science as essentialy static. Risk assessment is a relatively young effort, encompassing sciences from different fields.[9] Risk assessments conducted in the early and middle 1970s were much less sophisticated than those conducted in the 1980s. Knowledge of cancer mechanisms has also improved. Science has changed, but Efron did not recognize the change.

The last comment is the most crucial. Not only is science stagnant, an implicit assumption of her book, but science has one view of epistemology, determinism. Recall the discussion in chapter 2 of the nature of science. It was noted there that science, particularly the physical sciences, had abandoned the mechanistic, deterministic philosophy originating with Newton and had replaced it with a more probabilistic one. But Efron demanded certainty; we must know whether this substance caused that cancer.[10] It is, in the end, an impossible standard of proof. There is first the difficulty of separating out the factors in a multicausal disease. Indeed, cancer itself appears to be a set of different diseases. Then there is the high background level of cancer, caused undoubtedly by the kinds of processes that Efron and Ames discussed: diet, aging, and so forth. By her standards, even the arguments made by Ames and Doll and Peto on the role of diet must be dismissed because they cannot show that a specific substance, such as dietary fat, causes a specific cancer, nor can they show what the mechanisms are. This is the major fault of her work. Its virtues are important; there clearly are problems with risk assessment. But this admission does not necessitate a view of science that was abandoned in the early years of this century at the latest.

Conclusion: Justifying Risk Assessment

Despite the uncertainties, the disagreements within the scientific community over many of the risk assessment inference options, and the attacks on the whole risk assessment enterprise, risk assessment by regulatory agencies continues. Given all these problems, what justification could there possibly be for generic risk assessment guidelines? In fact, there are a number of reasons for having a cancer policy.

The simplest justification for cancer policies is that agencies will continue to make risk assessments, and some guidance and uniformity in their decision-making processes will be helpful to those inside and outside of government. For those inside government, the guidelines provide a framework by which individual risk assessments can be conducted; an example is the standard set of summary risk assessment forms adopted by the Environmental Protection Agency in 1984.

There are other reasons for expecting that agencies will continue to engage in cancer risk assessments. The first is the presence of actual threats. Assuming that the Doll and Peto (1981) estimates of causes of cancer are accurate and reliable, that still leaves, according to the Office of Technology Assessment (1981), about 10 percent of all cancers that might be due to toxic substances. Granting that diet plays a large role in cancer causation, the uncertainty of the Doll and Peto estimates is so large, and the range of estimates so huge (10–70 percent), that the actual percentage of cancers attributable to toxic chemicals may be greater than 10 percent. If nothing else, the focus on cancer mortality (because the data are considerably more reliable) rather than on cancer incidence, which may be the more important factor, suggests that one use caution in dismissing the role of toxics. In addition, Efron (1984) identified a number of "firmly established causes" (pp. 476–477) of cancer which included a number of chemicals to which people are occupationally exposed. That there is some threat posed by toxic substances seems clear; what is in dispute is the extent of that threat.

A second factor supporting the continuing need for cancer policies is that regulatory agencies have a legislative mandate to address the risks posed by toxic substances. While agencies may vary in how they do risk assessments and what factors are considered, risk assessments are helpful in making decisions that have to be made anyway. Much of the problem with risk assessments may reside in the failure "to engage in a careful, systematic review of the available scientific evidence to determine which conclusions are appropriate" (Lave, 1982, p. 3).[11] Lave argued that quantitative risk assessment can help inform political judgments.

> Despite its limitations, quantitative risk assessment has no logical alternative. With the exception of a policy of no risk, which is impossible to implement in a modern industrial society, risk assessment is the only systematic tool for analyzing various regulatory approaches to health and safety. All other frameworks involve some sort of intuitive balancing that is inappropriate where quantitative analysis is possible and where the stakes are high. (Lave, 1982, p. 2)

A third reason for the continued use of risk assessments of toxic chemicals relates to the question of the perception of risk. The work of Slovic et al. (1978) on risk perception indicates that one of the critical dimensions is whether the risk is voluntarily engaged in or whether one is involuntarily exposed to the risk. People are willing to accept risks that they incur voluntarily, for example, by not using a seat belt, or by smoking or drinking. However, we perceive an involuntary risk as more threatening than a voluntary one. It is quite understandable, from that standpoint alone, why greater emphasis has been placed on toxics than on lifestyles. Moreover, a focus on lifestyles requires an acknowledgement of individual responsibility and a change in behaviors, both of which are not especially easy to produce. It is simpler to assume a societal responsibility for ills that afflict us.

The final reason why toxics risk assessment will endure is that the lifestyle factor itself is controversial. Weinstein (1983), in his cost-effectiveness study mentioned earlier, admitted that "countervailing objections" (p. 22) might limit the implications of his findings. As with everything else in this area, no study remains unchallenged. Evidence of the lifestyle and natural aging factors that Efron, Ames, and Weinberg mentioned rests on an uncertain basis, though it is perhaps more certain than for toxic substances. Industry interests (e.g., tobacco, meat) produce studies showing that the alleged dangers are overstated (see chapter 8). Even scientific bodies disagree among themselves. In a classic instance of such disagreement (and one that will be discussed at length in the final chapter), a 1980 panel of the National Academy of Sciences stated that there was not sufficient evidence to make judgments about diet and cancer, certainly not enough to make dietary recommendations. A 1982 NAS panel stated that the evidence for the important role of cancer was overwhelming and offered dietary advice. Such dramatic shifts create confusion and downplay the role of the lifestyle factor.

What have we learned in this chapter? Risk assessment is itself a risky undertaking, where all judgments are based on virtually insurmountable uncertainties and are subject to challenge. Even the most important question, whether there is a cancer epidemic, has not been entirely settled. Risk assessments can be challenged because of limited understanding and an insufficient data base. We have been making progress in our understanding, but not enough to say that risk assessment is going in the right direction or has identified the proper targets. Yet agencies must make decisions in the face of this uncertainty. Recall the "Broad Street Pump" example from the first chapter. There we saw that even though John Snow did not understand the mechanisms of cholera and even though there were sufficient questions raised that lent doubt to his conclusions, he was, in fact, correct. We can predict, even in the face of uncertainty, even if we do not know the "why," as Efron has challenged. That toxic substances may have only a small role in overall cancer incidence and mortality is granted. Even so, risk assessments will continue, and cancer policies are needed to guide them.

8

Mixing Truth With Power[1]

The risks from typical environmental exposures to toxic substances—unlike the touchable, visible, malodorous pollution that stimulated the initial environmental revolution—are largely constructs or projections based on scientific findings. We would know nothing at all about chronic risk attributable to most toxic substances if scientists had not detected and evaluated them. Our response to such risks, therefore, must be based on a set of scientific findings. Science, however, is hardly ever unambiguous or unanimous, especially when the data on which definitive science must be founded scarcely exist. The toxic effects on health of many of the chemicals EPA considers for regulation fall into this class.

"Risk Assessment" is the device that government agencies such as EPA have adopted to deal with this quandary. It is the attempt to quantify the degree of hazard that might result from human activities—for example, the risks to human health and the environment from industrial chemicals. Essentially, it is a kind of pretense; to avoid paralysis of protective action that would result from waiting for "definitive" data, we assume that we have greater knowledge than the scientists actually possess and make decisions based on those assumptions.

--Ruckelshaus, 1985, p. 26

Introduction

Cancer policy, as we have seen, is highly disputatious in all its manifestations. The scientific foundation for cancer risk assessment is fraught with uncertainty. Regulatory decisions necessarily demand (if not assume) greater scientific certainty than exists. The questions of whether there is a cancer epidemic or what the causes of cancer are lead to seemingly endless controversy. Whatever an agency decides to do, or not to do, it will be faced with criticism. Clearly, cancer policy making is, at least at the present, a no-win proposition.

Despite the uncertainties endemic to cancer policy, risk assessments, as Lave (1982) and Ruckelshaus (1985) have pointed out, are still conducted. It is, after all, better to make a decision based on imperfect information than on no information at all. To recognize that risk assessment is necessary is not to say that it is equally well done by all or that it cannot be shaped by societal forces.

I return then to the four themes that form the argument of this book. The first theme, scientific uncertainty, marks the field. The uncertainties include ambiguities about the fundamental knowledge of cancer mechanisms, limitations of methodologies (e.g., epidemiology and bioassays), and limitations of various types of extrapolations (e.g., mouse-to-man, high to low doses). These uncertainties lead to scientific and regulatory controversies, the second theme. In chapter 2, I examined ten inference controversies and looked at how various cancer policy documents resolved them. Regulators and scientists must make numerous assumptions and science policy decisions that will allow them to proceed with their tasks.

The uncertainties and the necessity to make inference decisions lead to the next two themes, the heart of my argument: the mixing of science and politics and the political uses of science. If there is no scientific or factual basis for choosing, say, one dose-response extrapolation model over another, then some other basis must be used. An examination of the controversies and the guidelines reveals consistent patterns (see especially table 2.5). The science policy decisions and the inferences have clear policy implications. One dose-response model implies more stringent or risk-averse regulation than another. Classifying some carcinogens as epigenetic or as promoters implies higher permissable levels of exposure, a more risk-tolerant policy.

We have examined the various guidelines and seen how the choices made reflected the values held by those writing the guidelines. Policies issued during the Carter administration resolved the inference controversies differently from those of the Reagan administration. While the Carter administration placed some emphasis on regulatory reform, its policies took "prudent," risk-averse positions. In the absence of definitive knowledge, the cancer policy guidelines issued during the 1977–1980 period were protective of public health. During the Reagan administration, the proposed guidelines took more risk-tolerant stances. Perhaps the best example of this attitude is the additional water quality guidelines (Environmental Protection Agency, 1982a). That document specifically recommended an alternative model, the no-observable-effects-level (NOEL) model, as well as other choices, that would produce less stringent regulation. This mixing of politics and science, though inevitable and possibly regrettable, is not always recognized. Guidelines issued during the entire period under discussion (1976–1984) were permeated with values, even if they were not explicit.

The fourth, and final theme, is the political use of science. None of the documents we have discussed boldly states that political values helped shape its content. Rather, the claim is made that the science was the determining factor. But in fact, the guidelines are not scientific (though scientifically based) but political or administrative documents. This truth is perhaps clearest during the early Reagan administration years. The science had changed, we were told, and regulators needed to take that change into consideration. Note the title of the Salsburg and Heath (1981) article: "When Science Progresses and Bureaucracies Lag—The Case of Cancer Research." But in fact the science was used as the rationale for the changes, to justify more or less regulation. The "window of opportunity" for agenda change in the later periods of policy development was largely, though not entirely, affected by the political stream (e.g., new administrations), which reflected value changes.

The scientific foundation of cancer research has certainly progressed. There have been astonishing breakthroughs that could not have been anticipated in the early 1970s when the War on Cancer was launched (see Roberts, 1984). Some of those changes (such as the role of diet and other lifestyle factors as causes of cancers) imply that the target of cancer policies (chemical carcinogens) may be misplaced. Other research, such as work in molecular biology and the discovery of the importance of oncogenes (cancer genes), suggests that an underlying theory of cancer may be just ahead and that chemical carcinogens, at least those that act on DNA and chromosomes (e.g., genotoxic), may be important. It is not yet clear that new research over the last ten years points us to one direction over another in cancer policy.

Case Study: Diet and Cancer

Attributing cancer to chemical substances presents difficult, and to some, insurmountable problems. Even if it could be done, many (e.g., Doll and Peto, 1981) have concluded that chemical carcinogens cause only a very small proportion of cancers. Other factors, such as lifestyle, may be more important. Still others (e.g., Ames, 1983) point to natural carcinogens and bodily processes that lead to cancers. Whatever the cause, however, conclusive proof is difficult, if not impossible, to develop.

Given the uncertain nature of the scientific foundation, it should not be surprising that there is considerable disagreement. I have spent much of my time pointing this out. One case more than any other seems to capture the problems underlying cancer policy. While my focus has been chemical carcinogens because that has been the central concern of cancer policies, the following case study reinforces the argument of the book by examining a similar controversy related to the lifestyle factor. If controversy exists here, then we should certainly expect it with chemical carcinogens, where the evidence is more troubling.

This case study is based on a General Accounting Office (GAO) (1984d) analysis of two National Academy of Sciences (NAS) reports. The first one (National Academy of Sciences, 1980), entitled *Toward Healthful Diets*, concluded that while the elements of a healthful diet could be outlined, and they recommended such a diet, the scientific basis was too uncertain to make dietary recommendations for reducing the risk of cancer. The second report (National Academy of Sciences, 1982), entitled *Diet, Nutrition, and Cancer*, concluded that the scientific basis was sufficient to make specific, interim dietary recommendations. Both reports were disputatious on their own. The first report was criticized for disagreeing with other government reports and recommendations and for ignoring evidence of the link between diet and disease. The second study was criticized, primarily by industry groups, for making recommendations on the basis of tenuous data. For our purposes what is important is the disagreement between the two reports, only two years apart, and what that disagreement tells us about the relationship of science and public policy.

First, the National Academy of Sciences viewed the two reports as completely distinct and not at all contradictory. The reports had different purposes, were written for different audiences, and had different resources. For example, *Toward Healthful Diets* contained a 1½ page section devoted to cancer and diet, whereas *Diet, Nutrition, and Cancer* was "a comprehensive evaluation of the diet and cancer scientific literature" (General Accounting Office, 1984d, p. 33). NAS also said that different conclusions can be arrived at "because science evolves and much scientific information changes" (General Accounting Office, 1984d, p. 35). Because science evolves, theories are constantly reevaluated.

> One scientist told us that one never has enough data to draw absolutely firm conclusions, so one always makes judgments based on incomplete data. Scientists' interpretations of the same data often differ. Scientists accept these differences as part of the process of science, although the public may find the differences confusing. (General Accounting Office, 1984d, pp. 35-36)

The GAO report noted that 19 percent of the literature cited in *Diet, Nutrition, and Cancer* appeared after the earlier report was written. Because of the dynamic nature of cancer research, considerable progress can be made. As has been stated by many, policy based on science should consider those changes.

From a policy standpoint, the most intriguing difference between the two reports centers on the questions of how much and what kind of evidence is needed to reach a conclusion. These are the fundamental questions facing scientists and policymakers. The two NAS reports had different views on the "how much" question, primarily because the composition of the two panels was considerably different.[2] The differences between the two panels were philosophical or epistemological.[3] "Scientists have stated that conclusions drawn by scientists from different schools of thought may differ partly because they begin with diferent assumptions and look at problems from diferent perspectives" (General Accounting Office, 1984d, p. 44).

The GAO report divided the scientists into two groups that we have seen under different guises. One group is the "possibility of benefit" school. This school reflects a "public-wide" approach by concentrating on disease incidence and searching for ways to reduce that incidence. It sees diet as a factor which may help and which people can control. Even if dietary changes have not been conclusively shown to reduce risk, the changes themselves have no risks. The advice offered is optional.

The other school of thought is the "proof of preventive benefit" approach. It has the same concerns, but in the words of the GAO authors, "scientific evidence supporting dietary recommendations as a disease prevention measure is incomplete" (General Accounting Office, 1984d, p. 45). The GAO report summarized the differences as follows:

> The difference in the two reports partly stems from disagreement among scientists about what conclusions and public recommendations can be drawn from the available evidence on the relationship between diet and chronic diseases such as cancer and heart disease. NAS officials told us that it is not uncommon for two groups of scientists to review the same scientific data and come to different but supportable conclusions. No standard has been agreed upon among scientists or government policymakers about what scientific data are needed to support suggesting public health measures, such as dietary changes, to reduce the public's risk of developing long-term diseases such as cancer. Scientists whom we interviewed stated that they do not believe a standard of evidence is feasible because scientists could never all agree on a single set of standards and because each public health problem is unique.

Because no standard exists, scientists make personal value judgments on the basis of scientific evidence which can result in legitimately different conclusions. (General Accounting Office, 1984d, p. 30)

This case study makes several important points that underscore the themes and basic argument of the book. First, there are disagreements among scientists based on, in this case, epistemological differences. Those differences by themselves would be of little concern because much of science is inherently disputatious (Campbell, 1985). However, the dispute has public policy implications, my second point. Third, of course, disagreement is possible because the evidence is inconclusive or uncertain. The fourth point, made in the above quote, is that there are no techniques or standards for deciding these issues. In short, disagreement will remain and characterize this whole field, whether the focus is on diet or chemicals as a cause of cancer.

Separating Science and Policy

This discussion returns us to the relationship between science and politics, facts and values. Since cancer policy is based on findings from regulatory science, the relationship between the two is clear. If, as we have argued, the scientific foundation is inevitably uncertain, then the policy choices that rest upon that foundation will always be tentative, subject to criticism as bad science. The question we confront is a philosophical one, concerning not just, as Lowrance (1976) and others might say, what is acceptable risk, but what is acceptable evidence. Both are important, value-laden questions. The difference is that the acceptable risk question (risk management) is conventionally seen as value laden, whereas the acceptable evidence question (risk assessment) is not.

William Ruckelshaus, during his tenure as EPA administrator, repeatedly emphasized the strict separation of risk management and risk assessment.[4] Ruckelshaus's initiatives within EPA were grounded on these distinctions. The November 1984 cancer policy guidelines issued by the agency were based on the assumption that all the risk assessment issues had been settled by the Office of Science and Technology Policy (1984) report.

In a 1985 paper, Ruckelshaus continued these distinctions, relying on the 1983 National Research Council study. The NRC report, discussed in several previous chapters, spent considerable time examining inference policy, or what we have called "risk assessment policy." The report, according to Ruckelshaus, set out guidelines for keeping the distinctions clear. Ruckelshaus wrote:

> The NRC report suggests that this problem can be substantially alleviated by the establishment of formal public rules guiding the necessary inferences and assumptions. These rules should be based on the best available information concerning the underlying scientific mechanisms. Adoption of such guidelines reduces the possibility that an EPA administrator may manipulate the findings of some risk assessment so as to avoid making the difficult, and perhaps politically unpopular, choices involved in a risk-management decision. (Ruckelshaus, 1985, p. 28)

Yet at two places, Ruckelshaus's arguments undercut the possibility of clearly distinguishing risk assessment and risk management. Just prior to the above quote, he stated that inference choices are affected by the values of the choosers. The guidelines that the NRC recommended would perhaps circumscribe the role of those values, but they would not eliminate them. Secondly, in the quote that opened this chapter, Ruckelshaus refers to risk assessment as a process that is based on a pretense of knowledge where little exists. So the choices involved in risk assessment, the objective portion of risk control, are not so casually dismissed as he implies in other places. Because of the uncertainties that inevitably remain, the value-laden nature of risk assessment cannot be avoided.

Comingling and Concurrent Development

Any science-based policy area, such as environmental policy in general and cancer policy in particular, will have interactions be tween policy and science. Those interactions have been documented in the middle four chapters (3-6) of this book.[5] There are those who seek a strict separation of policy and science. But assuming or seeking to create a strict separation of science and policy through such institutions as centralized science panels masks the reality of the relationship and thereby seek solutions that fail to address important issues. I have asserted that science and policy are related, and my closing observations and recommendations are based on this reality. In this section, I specifically examine the nature of this relationship.

Science and scientific progress are affected by policy in many ways. The purer or more basic sciences are affected by the support for science education and for scientific research. As the scientific enterprise has grown in scale, public resources have become limited and choices among projects must be made; only so many particle accelerators can be constructed. The more that applied sciences and technologies are viewed as supporting major goals (e.g., military buildup, economic growth), the more support they will receive.

Cancer research developed in this way. Until the early 1970s, it was a modest enterprise, partially because of the limited progress made, but also because of limited public funding. The happy coincidence of enhanced public funding with the War on Cancer, combined with breakthroughs in molecular biology, led to tremendous progress in this field. The funding was the product of a lobbying effort led by Mary Lasker (see chapter 3) and others who pushed for biomedical research funding in general and cancer research in particular. The scientific breakthroughs were first made possible by the work of Crick and Watson (see Watson, 1968), who discovered the nature of the genetic code and did further work at the molecular level. The coincidence was not inevitable, nor did the one development necessarily lead to the other, though public funding undoubtedly accelerated the process.

When we turn to regulatory science, the connections between policy and science become clearer. While a small carcinogenesis program had begun within the National Cancer Institute in the late 1960s, it was the environmental legislation of the early and middle 1970s that created the need for a regulatory science focused on chemical carcinogens. In a sense, one can see the development of short-term tests such as the Ames test as a response to the expense and time of the longer, classical bioassays. But the policy necessity created pressures on regulatory science, demanding greater certainty than the science could, and still can, produce. We can see this interaction of science and policy. Science (and technology) created the substances which many viewed as potentially harmful. Legislation was passed to control exposures to those substances. But some way was needed to identify appropriate targets—thus regulatory science. Regulatory science was sufficiently developed to identify potential carcinogens (though of course that too was disputed), but it was not sufficiently developed to identify cause-and-effect relationships at the level of human exposure. Science, along with scientific and technological progress, thus produced a dilemma: it was able to identify a possible problem but unable to propose definitive solutions. Thus science and policy made reciprocal demands on each other.

The two models that we employed for chapters 3–6 capture this interaction of science and policy, as well as of scientists and other policy actors. The agenda-building model of Kingdon (1984) looked at three streams—problems, policies (or solutions), and politics. At critical junctures, labelled "windows of opportunity." the three streams flowed together and created periods when policy changes were possible. Science, or regulatory science, is important to the problems and policy streams because it identifies chemical carcinogens as a potential factor. Of course, someone has to identify and define the problems and propose solutions. The solution was cancer policy, and the policy entrepreneurs included both scientists and nonscientists.

As Kingdon points out, the problems and policy streams, which are more affected by science than the political stream, dominate the early stages of policy development. The political stream becomes more important as policy development matures. Still, science continues to play a role even here. For example, the challenge to the principles approach, discussed at length in chapter 5, was based partly on science and partly on politics. The political element was the change of administration and the antiregulatory attitude of the Reagan administration. The scientific element were new developments in understanding, such as the more challengeable views on scientific mechanisms, but also theories about the importance of lifestyle and the newer literature on natural carcinogens and bodily changes. Again, science has pro-posed problems that others, both scientists and nonscientists, have interpreted as requiring policy changes.

The other model that I employed, the political arena or 'estates' model of Hamlett (1984), also supports the importance of the interaction of science and policy. The 'estates' model focuses on political actors making and influencing policy decisions. These actors included 'estates' normally involved in politics: congressional, executive, regulatory, consumerist-environmentalist, and so forth. But the model adds the academic-professional 'estate', which in the case of cancer policy is the scientist. Many of the policy entrepreneurs were prominent scientists. When they argued, either explicitly or implicitly, for a particular policy, they stepped out of their traditional role of neutral scientist, no longer the "apolitical elite" that Robert Woods (1969) wrote about some years ago, but fully political actors. Some may serve directly as administrators in regulatory or research agencies. Others may serve the interests of the corporate-managerial 'estate'. It is especially noteworthy that the vast bulk of participants in the OSHA hearings were scientists—some representing agencies, some representing environmental groups, some representing industry. The scientists, and the science, were surrogates for arguing over political values.

It is no coincidence that the views of industry scientists on the various issues went in one direction, while those of agency and environmental scientists took different positions. For example, Saffiotti, Epstein, and Schneiderman were three scientists who argued for risk-averse cancer policies. Roe, Gori, Gehring, and Williams argued for more risk-tolerant policies. Bruce Ames, in perhaps the most illuminating case, went from concentrating on chemical carcinogens to asserting the importance of diet and natural processes. That he should do so is somewhat unusual but does not by itself make him a political actor. On the other hand, when he steps out of the role of scientist to discuss his findings and looks at the implications of those findings, then he is no longer disinterested and apolitical. Weisburger and Williams, as well as Squire, did this even more explicitly by recommending frameworks for regulatory action, just as much as Saffiotti and Weinstein did for seeking to base cancer policies on a set of "scientific" principles.

Thus, at a variety of levels, science and policy mix: the scientist is a policy entrepreneur, science poses problems, politics uses science to justify policy actions or policy changes, scientific research receives public funding, and regulatory science comes into being. In the next and final section, I offer some comments and recommendations about cancer policy based on the nature of regulatory science and the explicit acknowledgement of the mixing of truth with power.

Final Observations and Recommendations

First, we should recognize that cancer is not a single disease with only a single cause. Cancer differs by site and has many different causes. Therefore the one cause or set of causes pinpointed by cancer policy is only one cause and perhaps not even the most important. It may be that some other factors (natural carcinogens, lifestyle, and bodily processes) are more important than chemical carcinogens. This does not mean, however, that we should neglect the latter. Chemical carcinogens are responsible for some proportion of cancers, and government can act more directly against them than against the other factors.

Second, we should recognize that zero-risk is unachievable. Some risk will remain, and efforts to eliminate all possible risk will prove both fruitless and costly. However, to acknowledge that some risk will inevitably remain does not mean that we should tolerate every and any risk. Not all economic behavior is worth the risk. This may seem like an obvious point, but the case of the herbicide 2,4,5-T demonstrates its significance. 2,4,5-T has been used for silviculture, that is, the removal of competitor shrubs, plants, and trees from economically significant ones. The argument in favor of the use of 2,4,5-T was that it was the most efficient method for clearing competitors. Those opposed to the herbicide's use suggested alternatives and further stated that its economic benefits were significantly less than industry groups claimed. An analysis by economist Jan Newton substantiated that claim. She presented her findings in congressional testimony and waited for the countertestimony from industry that would destroy her evidence. It never came. Industry failed to make the case that 2,4,5-T had any economic benefits or was effective in reducing competition (Newton, 1983–1984). In such cases, where the cost-benefit analysis is loaded against a product that apparently has few benefits, the product should be discontinued even if the risk from its use is small or difficult to prove. In such a case, no risk from a product that produces no benefits seems warranted.

Another important consideration is that the vast majority of risk analyses, formal or informal, assume that the only important exposure is to the target substance. However, we live in a sea of carcinogens, natural and man-made, and any substance should be seen as an addition or increment to that sea. This is the rationale behind EPA's recommending that the linearized, multihit, dose-response model be used. Although there may be a threshold for a particular substance, given interactive or synergistic effects, such a threshold cannot be safely assumed. Thus, this recommendation supports both Ruckelshaus (1985) and Weinberg (1985) in looking at background levels, for example of radiation or chemical exposure, but it also recognizes that any single substance is an addition to that background level.

Third, risk assessments and generic guidelines should take a weight-of-the-evidence approach. Most of the guidelines do so. By explicitly following this path, the guidelines ensure that science will not be "frozen" at a particular point of development. All the evidence should be considered.

But such a consideration has a twofold meaning. On the one hand, it means looking at metabolic and pharmacokinetic, as well as other, data. Such a position would tend to produce a somewhat more risk-tolerant policy. Whether administered doses cause physical damage that produces tumors or overcomes bodily defenses should certainly be considered. On the other hand, a weight-of-the-evidence approach would also examine the general direction of the studies. Even if no one study met all criteria for a well-conducted project, if the totality of the studies pointed a certain way, then the weight-of-the-evidence approach would suggest that we follow that direction. It would allow an agency to take action (including a decision not to take action) in the absence of definitive evidence.

A fourth, and related, point is that the guidelines should be flexible. They should not lock an agency into a set position, unable to consider additional evidence that may warrant reconsideration of positions. The EPA guidelines are a model of this because they state that the linearized model will be used unless evidence suggests a different one. Even here, flexibility would suggest that both the linearized and an alternative model be presented.

The fifth point also follows. Recall the recommendations of the White House Office of Science and Technology Policy in their 1980 report (Calkins et al., 1980) and the critique of the IRLG report by the American Industrial Health Council (1979). Both recommended that the most likely estimates rather than the upper limits be presented. The upper limits present a level below which effects are likely to appear. The most likely estimate presents a point estimate of likely effects, accompanied by confidence levels (how likely the estimate is to be within the true range). Point estimates, however, presume a level of certainty unwarranted by the data (Behn and Vaupel, 1982). A more appropriate approach is to present the most likely estimate plus the range (including the upper limits) of risk or exposure, and to include a discussion of the confidence of the most likely estimate. The Doll and Peto (1981) study took this approach but provided no basis for judging the point estimate that it made.

A sixth, and again related, point is that risk assessment should be explicit about uncertainties and the assumptions made to bridge them. As Ruckelshaus pointed out, the National Research Council provides guidelines for making the inference assumptions. Frankly admitting and carrying forward those uncertainties may make it difficult for agencies to act, since all sides in a particular dispute will point to the inadequacies of risk assessment to support their position. But an unwillingness to admit the existence of uncertainties makes for less realistic policy making.

Seventh, there is a role for qualitative and quantitative risk assessment. Qualitative risk assessment can demonstrate that a substance is a mammalian carcinogen and potentially a human one. Quantitative risk assesment, which looks at the potency of a possible carcinogen, presents nearly insurmountable problems in extrapolation. However, it can compare the potency of one substance with the potency of another. This data, combined with exposure data, can be used to set priorities for regulation.

Eighth, despite the disparity of legislation, consistent risk assessment policy across and within programs and agencies would be very helpful. Again, this was a Ruckelshaus initiative, particularly the use of standardized risk assessment forms. Similar models and assumptions across agencies and programs ought to be used. Even though different legislation provide for different degrees of protection and define risk differently, the risk assessments are not constrained by the legislation, and uniformity ought to be encouraged.

Generic policies that incorporated the recommendations of this chapter would help ensure uniformity of assessment while taking into account all the evidence and the dynamic nature of regulatory science. Risk assessments are necessary, even if limited in quality, because it is better to have some information with which to make decisions than none. By making uncertainties and assumptions explicit, by recognizing that uncertainies may allow risk assessments to be shaped in a particular direction, risk assessments will serve a public purpose.

Finally, some procedural changes could be suggested that would take into account new scientific developments in risk assessment methodologies and the mixing of science and politics. The idea of having periodic reviews of the state of the art in cancer research is an excellent one. Some institution, and here I would suggest both the White House Office of Science and Technology Policy (OSTP) and a committee of the National Academy of Sciences/National Research Council, should conduct such a review, which should include a discussion of the implications of those new developments. These examinations should be peer reviewed (as was the OSTP reports) and published in the *Federal Register* and perhaps elsewhere (e.g., *JCNI*, formerly the *Journal of the National Cancer Institute*).

The other part of this suggested change (and the one that explicitly recognizes the mixing of science and politics) is to convene an ongoing "consensus dialogue" among the affected parties (e.g., industry groups, environmental groups, and agency representatives).[6] The purpose of such a dialogue would be to produce an agreement among the various disputants on inferences, assumptions, and so on, taking into considerations the scientific review mentioned above. The goal of the dialogue would be to reduce conflict among the various parties and to enable regulatory agencies to carry out their missions. The purpose (agreement) may not be fully achieved (consensus on the various inference issues) but the process itself, a nonadversarial setting where antagonists can talk with one another, may reduce tension and controversy. That by itself would be a worthy goal.

Appendix A.
Risk Assessment Principles

I. Principles Derived from the Mechanisms of Carcinogenesis

1. Carcinogenesis is a multistage phenomenon that may involve the genome both directly and indirectly. These stages of carcinogenesis may be, to a varying degree, influenced by a number of variables, such as age at exposure, diet, hormonal status, intra- and inter-species variability, which should be considered when trying to predict human response to potentially carcinogenic agents.

2. Appropriate *in vitro* and *in vivo* tests can indicate that an agent has a certain action such as genetic toxicity or promotion. Such information may be useful in evaluating mechanism(s) of cancer induction. However, in the evaluation of human risk, the attribution of observed findings of carcinogenicity to a particular biological effect must rest upon sound evidence that the effect is responsible for the cancer induction. It must be kept in mind that a chemical may contribute to carcinogenesis in multiple ways.

3. At the present stage of knowledge, mechanistic considerations, such as DNA repair and other biological responses, in general do not prove the existence of, the lack of existence of, or the location of, a threshold for carcinogenesis. The presence of a threshold for one step of the carcinogenic process does not necessarily determine the presence or absence of a threshold for the whole process. For example, there is strong evidence that the existence of DNA repair will not result in a threshold for the accumulation of DNA damage; however, the consequences of this for a threshold for carcinogenesis is unclear.

4. The carcinogenic effects of agents may be influenced by non-physiological responses induced in the model systems. Testing regiments

189

inducing these responses, such as extensive organ damage, saturation of metabolic pathways, saturation of DNA repair with functional loss of the system, should be evaluated for their relevance to the human response to the agent and evidence from such a study, whether positive or negative, must be carefully reviewed.

II. Principles for Tests for Cancer Induction

A. Short-Term Tests

5. Short-term tests, such as assays for point mutations, chromosomal aberrations, DNA damage, and *in vitro* transformation are useful in: (1) screening for potential carcinogens; (2) supporting a judgment on the carcinogenicity of a chemical; and (3) providing information on carcinogenic mechanisms.

6. At the present, short-term tests are limited in their ability to predict carcinogenicity and cannot supplant data from epidemiological investigations or long-term animal studies since the tests do not necessarily screen for all potential means of cancer induction and do not necessarily mimic all reactions that would occur *in vivo*. Additional research is required to improve existing tests and develop ones that identify chemicals which act by genetic mechanisms not yet detected or which act by other, non-genetic, mechanisms.

7. Short-term tests should be carefully selected to ensure they have been adequately validated. Several tests with different endpoints may be required to characterize a chemical's spectrum of response.

B. Long-Term Animal Tests

8. In the context of the result from a long-term test, the term carcinogen should be used in a broad sense, i.e., a substance or process capable of increasing the incidence of neoplasms (combining benign and malignant when scientifically defensible) or decreasing the time it takes for them to develop. Agents found carcinogenic in animal studies, subject to the considerations discussed in Principles 4 and 14, are considered suspect human carcinogens.

9. Some experimental animal models normally have high incidences of certain tumors. The evaluation of tumor data from such animals can pose special problems. For example, the interpretation of cancer incidence in some strains of rats with testicular or mammary tumors, or in some strains of mice with lung or liver tumors must be approached carefully in the light of other biological evidence bearing on potential carcinogenicity.

10. Protocols for long-term tests should be designed to achieve an appropriate balance between the two essential characteristics of a biological assay: adequate biological and statistical sensitivity (a low false negative rate) and adequate biological and statistical specificity (a low false positive rate). The absence of biases in selection and allocation of animals between control and treatment groups as regards diet, husbandry, necropsy, and pathology is crucial.

11. It is appropriate to use test doses that generally exceed human exposure levels in order to overcome the inherent insensitivity of the traditional design of the long-term animal test. The highest dose should be selected after an adequate prechronic study and after evaluating other information, e.g., pharmacokinetic data, as necessary to determine the highest dose consistent with predicted minimal target organ toxicity and normal lifespan, except as a consequence of the possible induction of cancer.

12. The diagnosis of pathologic lesions is complicated and requires judgment and appropriate experience. Diagnoses can differ depending on the tissue and species involved and can change with time as techniques improve and data on bioassay accumulate. Accurate interpretation of tumor data is contingent upon careful attention to gross observation, tissue sampling, slide preparation and histologic examination. Diagnosis of tumors should be guided by evidence of their histogenic origin and stage of progression.

13. Appropriate statistical analysis should be performed on data from long-term studies to help determine whether the effects are treatment related or possibly due to chance. These should include a statistical test for trend and a test based on pairwise comparisons, including appropriate correction for differences in survival. The weight to be given to the level of statistical significance (the p-value) and to other available pieces of information is a matter of overall scientific judgments.

14. Decisions on the carcinogenicity of chemicals in animals should be based on consideration of relevant biological and biochemical data, including the following:

(a) Use of background or recent historical control incidence of tissue specific tumors can be an aid in the evaluation of tumor data. Care should be exercised when combining different control groups to avoid inappropriate combinations of such groups.

(b) Evidence of probable reproducibility is important. This evidence can consist of independent confirmation of the original findings or may be derived from intergroup comparisons of tumor incidence data, between dose groups, sexes, strains or species.

(c) Evidence of dose response increases confidence that the effect is treatment related; similarly the lack of an observed dose-response may reduce the likelihood that the effect is associated with the treatment.

(d) Confidence is increased when: (1) The incidence of tumors is markedly elevated in the treated groups compared to controls, particularly when the tumors in controls are infrequent; (2) tumor incidence is significantly increased at multiple anatomical sites; and (3) tumor latency is reduced.

(e) In addition to tumor incidence at specific tumor sites, the stage in the development of neoplasia should be evaluated. For example, the finding that the majority of neoplastic lesions at a specific tissue site is more advanced in a treated group compared to its control may provide additional evidence of a treatment related effect. Conversely, the finding that the control group lesions are more advanced might argue that a marginal evaluation of tumor incidence is not treatment related.

(f) The incidence of preneoplastic lesions in treatment or control groups may, in certain instances, provide evidence for the biological plausibility of a neoplastic response and contribute to the interpretation of a bioassay.

(g) Identification from prechronic studies, or other toxic studies of effects in the target organ(s), can assist in evaluating whether or not differences in tumor incidences are treatment related.

(h) Information on the activity of chemicals at the physiological, cellular and molecular level may be important to the evaluation of carcinogenicity data on a case-by-case basis.

III. Principles for Epidemiology

15. The strength of the epidemiological method is that it is the only means of assessing directly the carcinogenic risk of environmental agents in humans; however, because of the limitations of the available information, e.g., the elements discussed in Principle 18 as well as the paucity of data, primary reliance is often placed on animal testing.

16. Descriptive epidemiological studies (based on the measurement of disease rates for various populations), including correlational studies (in which the rate of disease in a population is compared with the spatial or temporal distribution of suspected risk factors), are useful to generate and refine hypotheses, or provide supporting evidence in evaluating relationships detected by other means, but rarely, if ever, provide information allowing a practical causal inference.

17. Well-designed, conducted and evaluated analytic epidemiological investigations of either case-control or cohort variety

can provide the basis for practical (causal) inferences especially useful for public health decisions.

18. Elements in interpreting the likely practical causality of epidemiological observations include the magnitude of the risk estimates (strength of the associations); the possibility of their being due to chance (statistical significance); the rigor of the study design to avoid various kinds of bias, including those related to selection, confounding, classification and measurement; dose-response relationships; the temporal relationships between exposure and disease; the specificity of the associations; their biological plausibility; and the reproducibility of the findings.

19. A high quality negative epidemiologicl study, while useful, cannot prove the absence of an association between chemical exposure and human cancer. Within the scope of the study, specifically for the populations studied (including concomitant exposures), for the levels and durations of exposure to the agent evaluated, and for the time assessed following exposure, the likely upper bounds on the estimates of risk can be made and the statistical likelihood of the study to detect an effect can be assessed.

IV. Principles for Exposure Assessment

20. It is desirable that exposure routes employed in animal health effects studies are comparable to human exposure routes both for the simplification of risk assessment and because there may be important route dependent differences in molecular, biochemical and physical parameters in organs.

21. At present, a single generally applicable procedure for a complete exposure assessment does not exist. Therefore, in the near term, it is expected that integrated exposure assessments (utilizing monitoring data results from physical and chemical models, and consideration of all routes of exposure through all media) will be conducted on a case-by-case basis.

22. The depth and accuracy of an exposure assessment should be tailored to provide the degree of knowledge required to support analytical needs. A preliminary assessment using available crude data can often shed light on the upper or lower bounds of potential risks.

23. An exposure assessment should describe the strengths, limitations and uncertainties of the available data and should indicate the assumptions made to derive the exposure estimates.

24. In general, an array or range of exposure values is preferable to a single numerical estimate.

V. Principles for Risk Assessment

25. Decisions on the carcinogenicity of chemicals in humans should be based on considerations of relevant data, whether they are indicative of a positive or a negative response and should use sound biological and statistical principles. This weight of evidence approach can include consideration of the following factors and should give appropriate weight to each on a case-by-case basis:

(a) Findings from long-term animal studies (See Principle 14);

(b) Results from epidemiological studies (see Principles 16–18);

(c) *In vivo* and *in vitro* short-term tests;

(d) Structure-activity relationships of chemicals;

(e) Known metabolic differences between animals and humans.

26. No single mathematical procedure is recognized as the most appropriate for low dose extrapolation in carcinogenesis. When relevant biological evidence on mechanism of action (e.g., pharmacokinetics) exists, the models or procedures employed should be consistent with the evidence. However, when data and information are limited, as is the usual case, and when much uncertainty exists regarding the mechanism of carcinogenic action, models or procedures which incorporate low-dose linearity are preferred.

27. The quantitification of the various sources of uncertainty involved in cancer risk assessment can be as important as the projection of the risk estimate itself. The sources that might be addressed include:

(a) The statistical uncertainty associated with a given risk estimate;

(b) The variability introduced by the selection of a particular low-dose extrapolation procedure;

(c) When risk estimation is based on laboratory generated data, the biological variability associated with the use of a particular test organism and its scaling or extrapolation to man.

28. An estimate of cancer risk for humans exposed to an agent can be no more accurate than an exposure assessment that it utilizes. Lack of adequate exposure data is frequently a major limiting factor in evaluation of carcinogenic risks in humans.

29. While several considerations often enter the risk assessment process, it is important to try to maintain a clear distinction among facts (statements supported by data), consensus (statements generally held in the scientific community), assumptions (statements made to fill data gaps), and science policy decisions (statements made to resolve points of current controversy).

30. Differences in human susceptibility, and variable and extreme exposures to chemicals suggest the likelihood that there are subpopula-

tions that are at greater than average risk. Increased consideration should be given to the identification of high risk populations.

31. Because of the uncertainties associated with risk assessment, full evaluation of risk to humans should include a qualitative consideration of the basic strengths and weaknesses of the available hazard and exposure data in addition to any estimations that are made.

Source: Office of Science and Technology Policy (1984), pp. 21597–21600.

Appendix B.
Inference Choices

Hazard Identification

Epidemiologic Data

• What relative weights should be given to studies with differing results? For example, should positive results outweigh negative results if the studies that yield them are comparable? Should a study be weighted in accord with its statistical power?

• What relative weights should be given to results of different types of epidemiologic studies? For example, should the findings of a prospective study supersede those of a case-control study, or those of a case-control study those of an ecologic study?

• What statistical significance should be required for results to be considered positive?

• Does a study have special characteristics (such as the questionable appropriateness of a control group) that lead one to question the validity of its results?

• What is the significance of a positive finding in a study in which the route of exposure is different from that of a population at potential risk?

• Should evidence on different types of response be weighted or combined (e.g., data on different tumor sites and data on benign versus malignant tumors)?

Animal-Bioassay Data

• What degree of confirmation of positive results should be necessary? Is a positive result from a single animal study sufficient, or should positive results from two or more animal studies be required? Should negative results be disregarded or given less weight?

• How should evidence of different metabolic pathways or vastly different metabolic rates between animals and humans be factored into a risk assessment?

• How should the occurrence of rare tumors be treated? Should the appearance of rare tumors in a treated group be considered evidence of carcinogenicity even if the finding is not statistically significant?

• How should experimental-animal data be used when the exposure routes in experimental animals and humans are different?

• Should a dose-related increase in tumors be discounted when the tumors in question have high or extremely variable spontaneous rates?

• What statistical significance is required for results to be considered positive?

• Does an experiment have special characteristics (e.g., the presence of carcinogenic contaminants in the test substance) that lead one to question the validity of its results?

• How should the findings of tissue damage or other toxic effects be used in the interpretation of tumor data? Should evidence that tumors may have resulted from these effects be taken to mean that they would not be expected to occur at lower doses?

• Should benign and malignant lesions be counted equally?

• Into what categories should tumors be grouped for statistical purposes?

• Should only increases in the numbers of tumors be considered, or should a decrease in the latent period for tumor occurrence also be used as evidence of carcinogenicity?

Short-Term Test Data

• How much weight should be placed on the results of various short-term tests?

• What degree of confidence do short-term tests add to the results of animal bioassays in the evaluation of carcinogenic risks for humans?

• Should in vitro transformation tests be accorded more weight than bacterial mutagenicity tests in seeking evidence of a possible carcinogenic effect?

• What statistical significance should be required for results to be considered positive?

• How should different results of comparable tests be weighted? Should positive results be accorded greater weight than negative results?

Structural Similarity to Known Carcinogens

• What additional weight does structural similarity add to the results of animal bioassays in the evaluation of carcinogenic risks for humans?

General

• What is the overall weight of the evidence of carcinogenicity? (This determination must include a judgment of the *quality* of the data presented in the preceding sections.)

Dose-Response Assessment

Epidemiologic Data

• What dose-response models should be used to extrapolate from observed doses to relevant doses?

• Should dose-response relations be extrapolated according to best estimates or according to upper confidence limits?

• How should risk estimates be adjusted to account for a comparatively short follow-up period in an epidemiologic study?

• For what range of health effects should response be tabulated? For example, should risk estimates be made only for specific types of cancer that are unequivocally related to exposure, or should they apply to all types of cancers?

• How should exposures to other carcinogens, such as cigarette smoke, be taken into consideration?

• How should one deal with different temporal exposure patterns in the study population and in the population for which risk estimates are required? For example, should one assume that lifetime risk is only a function of total dose, irrespective of whether the dose was received in early childhood or in old age? Should recent doses be weighted less than earlier doses?

• How should physiologic characteristics be factored into the dose-response relation? For example, is there something about the study group that distinguished its response from that of the general population?

Animal-Bioassay Data

• What mathematical models should be used to extrapolate from experimental doses to human exposures?

• Should dose-response relations be extrapolated according to best estimates or according to upper confidence limits? If the latter, what confidence limits should be used?

• What factor should be used for interspecies conversion of dose from animals to humans?

• How should information on comparative metabolic processes and rates in experimental animals and humans be used?

• If data are available on more than one nonhuman species or genetic strain, how should they be used? Should only data on the most sensitive species or strain be used to derive a dose-response function, or should the data be combined? If data on different species and strains are to be combined, how should this be accomplished?

• How should data on different types of tumors in a single study be combined? Should the assessment be based on the tumor type that was affected the most (in some sense) by exposure? Should data on all tumor types that exhibit a statistically significant dose-related increase be used? If so, how? What interpretation should be given to statistically significant *decreases* in tumor incidence at specific sites?

Exposure Assessment

• How should one extrapolate exposure measurements from a small segment of a population to the entire population?

• How should one predict dispersion of air pollutants into the atmosphere due to convection, wind currents, etc., or predict seepage rates of toxic chemicals into soils and groundwater?

• How should dietary habits and other variations in lifestyle, hobbies, and other human activity patterns be taken into account?

• Should point estimates or a distribution be used?

• What is the proper unit of dose?

• How should one estimate the size and nature of the population likely to be exposed?

• How should exposures of special risk groups, such as pregnant women and young children, be estimated?

Risk Characterization

• What are the statistical uncertainties in estimating the extent of health effects? How are these uncertainties to be computed and presented?

- What are the biologic uncertainties in estimating the extent of health effects? What is their origin? How will they be estimated? How will uncertainties be described to agency decision-makers?
- Which dose-response assessments and exposure assessments should be used?
- Which population groups should be the primary targets for protection, and which provide the most meaningful expression of the health risk?

Source: National Research Council (1983), pp. 29-34.

Appendix C.
Chronology

1958	Delaney Amendment to the Food, Drug and Cosmetic Act
1969	"Report of the Secretary's Commission on Pesticides and Their Relationship to Environmental Health," DHEW (Mrak commission)
1970	creation of Environmental Protection Agency (EPA) by executive order
1970	Occupational Safety and Health Act (OSHA)
1970	"Evaluation of Chemical Carcinogens," report to the Surgeon General
1971	*Toxic Substances*, Council on Environmental Quality
1972	Consumer Product Safety Act (CPSC)
1976	Toxic Substances Control Act
1976	"Interim Procedures of Health Risk and Economic Impact Assessments of Suspected Carcinogens," EPA
1977	Carter environmental message
1977	creation of Toxic Substances Strategy Committee (TSSC)
1977	OSHA issues draft cancer policy
1977	"General Criteria for Assessing the Evidence for Carcinogenicity of Chemical Substances," National Cancer Advisory Board
1977	formation of Interagency Regulatory Liaison Group (IRLG)
1978	"Interim Policy and Procedure for Classifying, Evaluating and Regulating Carcinogens in Consumer Products," CPSC
1978	Executive Order 12044

1978	creation of Regulatory Analysis Review Group
1978	formation of Regulatory Council
1978	creation of National Toxicology Program
1979	"Chemical Compounds in Food Producing Animals: Criteria and Procedures for Carcinogenic Residues," FDA
1979	Scientific Bases for Identification of Potential Carcinogens and Estimation of Risks," IRLG
1979	"Identification and Control of Potential Carcinogens: a Framework for Federal Decisionmaking," OSTP
1979	CPSC withdraws guidelines
1979	"National Emission Standards for Hazardous Air Pollutants," EPA
1980	"Water Quality Criteria documents," EPA
1980	"Toxic Chemicals and the Public," TSSC
1980	OSHA issues final generic cancer policy guidelines
1980	Supreme Court decides benzene case
1980	Reagan elected president
1980	*Mandate for Leadership*—Heritage Foundation
1980	Stockman "Manifesto"
1981	establishment of President's Task Force on Regulatory Relief
1981	abolition of IRLG, Regulatory Council, Regulatory Analysis Review Group, and Council on Wage and Price Stabilty
1981	Executive Order 12291
1981	OSHA amendments to generic cancer policy
1981	*Assessment of Technologies for Determining Cancer Risks from the Environment*, OTA
1981	Supreme Court decides cotton dust case
1982	"Additional U.S. Environmental Protection Agency Guidance for the Health Assessment of Suspect Carcinogens with Specific Reference to Water Quality Criteria," EPA
1982	"Review of Data Available to the Administrator Concerning Formaldehyde and d-(2-ethylhexyl) Phthalate (DEHP)," Todhunter memorandum
1982	"Review on the Mechanisms of Effect and Detection of Chemical Carcinogens," first draft, OSTP
1983	"Review on the Mechanisms of Effect and Detection of Chemical Carcinogens," second draft, OSTP
1983	*Risk Assessment in the Federal Government: Managing the Process*, National Research Council

1983	William Ruckelshaus appointed as EPA administrator
1983	establishment of Interagency Risk Management Council (IRMC)
1983	creation of Toxics Integration Task Force within EPA
1984	"Chemical Carcinogens; Review of the Science and its Associated Principles," OSTP
1984	"Criteria for Evidence of Chemical Carcinogens," Interdisciplinary Panel on Carcinogenesis
1984	abolition of IRMC
1984	Reagan reelected
1984	"Proposed Guidelines for Carcinogen Risk Assessment," EPA
1985	Office of Management and Budget given additional responsibility over regulatory process
1985	"Chemical Carcinogens; Review of the Science and its Associated Principles," OSTP, final version
1985	"A Strategy to Reduce Risks to Public Health from Air Toxics," EPA

Appendix D.
Acronyms

AIHC	American Industrial Health Council
BEIR	biological effects of ionizing radiation
CAG	Carcinogen Assessment Group
CEQ	Council on Environmental Quality
CIIT	Chemical Industry Institute of Toxicology
CPSC	Consumer Product Safety Commission
EPA	Environmental Protection Agency
FDA	Food and Drug Administration
HEW	Health, Education, and Welfare
IARC	International Agency for Research on Cancer
IPC	Interdisciplinary Panel on Carcinogenesis
IRLG	Interagency Regulatory Liaison Group
IRMC	Interagency Risk Management Council
MTD	maximally tolerated dose
NAS	National Academy of Sciences
NCAB	National Cancer Advisory Board
NCI	National Cancer Institute
NIH	National Institutes of Health
NIOSH	National Institute of Occupational Safety and Health
NOEL	no-observable-effects level
NRC	National Research Council
NRDC	Natural Resources Defense Council
NTP	National Toxicology Program
OMB	Office of Management and Budget
OSHA	Occupational Safety and Health Administration
OSTP	Office of Science and Technology Policy
OTA	Office of Technology Assessment
RARG	Regulatory Analysis Review Group
TSCA	Toxic Substances Control Act
TSSC	Toxic Substances Strategy Committee

Notes

Chapter 1. Science, Uncertainty, and Politics

1. The term *generic*, according to *Webster's Seventh New Collegiate Dictionary*, means "relating to or characteristic of a whole group or class." In the case of risk assessment guidelines, generic means that an agency will answer the same questions that arise in different cases in the same ways. The assumptions, inferences, and science policy decisions that are made will cover the whole class of chemical carcinogens.

2. For example, carcinogens may act upon DNA, chromosomes, hormones, and so forth. Radiation acts upon DNA, and this feature has also been seen in many, but not all, chemical carcinogens. Cole (1985) has pointed out that as we learned more about the effects of radiation, exposure standards were dramatically tightened. Is it possible that in this respect, too, cancer policy will mimic radiation policy?

3. The linear dose-response model suggests that the response of humans or animals is proportionately related to dose. This, in its various forms, is the most risk-averse model. The quadratic model suggests, by the shape of the curve (see diagram 1.2), that at lower doses there will be proportionately less response or incidence in animals or humans. It is therefore somewhat more risk tolerant. The compromise model, the linear quadratic model, suggests a linear response at low doses and a quadratic response at higher doses; this combination translates as a greater response at high doses but a smaller response at lower doses than is implied by the linear model. The relatively small difference between the linear and linear quadratic models illustrates how polarized disputes can become. I will return to the discussion of models in chapter 2.

4. For similar definitions of risk control activities, see Conservation Foundation (1984), Kates (1978), Lowrance (1976), and Rowe (1977).

5. The OSTP (1984) report has recently been criticized precisely for including inferences and assumptions that are unsupported by data. See "Revision without Revolution" (1984).

6. One important exception was the case of formaldehyde. In that instance, it was the industry-funded Chemical Industry Institute of Toxicology that first developed evidence that formaldehyde might be a carcinogen. See Ashford et al. (1983b) and Rushefsky (1984.)

Chapter 2. Science and Regulatory Science

1. Some have argued that the case against asbestos has been overstated. See Mosher (1984).

2. For a discussion of determinism, see Nagel (1961).

3. For a recent example of the advisor-expert role in defense policy, see Broad (1985), who describes the meetings between President Reagan and J. Edward Teller that led to the Strategic Defense Initiative effort, more popularly known as Star Wars.

4. Ashford ("Examining the Role," 1983) suggests that regulators and science advisory panels should take a Bayesian approach to the question of the sufficiency of evidence. Under such an approach, all the data would be examined. Possibly no one study would be conclusive by itself because of data limitations, but the totality of all the studies might point in a certain direction, and weighing all of that evidence might lead to a particular decision. In this scheme, there are clear differences between scientific standards of proof and the evidence needed to justify a decision.

5. In scientific language, we are attempting to distinguish the *signal* (cancer from the suspect substance) from the *noise* (background or overall cancer incidence).

6. For a critique of this validation, see Efron (1984).

7. The list is not a long one, and many chemicals have been either inadequately tested or not tested at all. See National Research Council (1984).

8. As mentioned earlier in the chapter, the body of scientific evidence is constantly changing. Research is moving us closer to an underlying cancer theory. See Hattis (1985) and Schmeck (1984).

9. The IRLG report was used by the Occupational Safety and Health Administration, the Food and Drug Administration, and the Consumer Product Safety Commission in developing their cancer regulations. See Clark (1979). The Environmental Protection Agency used the 1984 OSTP report in the development of its 1984 guidelines. See chapters 4 and 6 for more discussion on this point.

10. In other words, such a decision would involve concentrated costs (to industry) with rather diffuse benefits (to exposed populations). Those are always difficult decisions. For a discussion of the regulatory burden of costs and benefits, see Wilson (1980).

11. One of the problems in cancer risk assessment is defining a carcinogen. The Office of Science and Technology Policy (1984, p. 21635) report stated the following:

> Several attempts have been made over the last 10 years to construct a suitable operational definition for a chemical carcinogen. . . . Though none of these have succeeded fully, there is common agreement that a chemical carcinogen is a substance which induces cancer by some chemical/biological mechanism. A chemical carcinogen may be a substance which either significantly increases the incidence of cancer in animals or humans or significantly decreases the time it takes a naturally-occurring (spontaneous) tumor to develop relative to an appropriate background or control group. Either phenomenon is said to represent the effects of a carcinogen.

12. Recall the earlier discussion about the importance of probability in science. Note also that there are multiple opportunities to obtain statistically significant results because one can obtain data at each of the cancer target sites (lung, liver, etc.). This possibility creates the complication (as if more were needed) of multiple comparisons. I thank Dale Hattis for pointing this fact out to me, though of course any misinterpretation is mine.

13. *Upper limits* refers to how much risk may occur at a particular dose level; it is the upper confidence level of risk at a particular dose. *Lower limits* refers to the least exposure or dose corresponding to a particular risk. Risk levels are expressed as the number of cancers per number of people, e.g., 10 cancers per million people. Again, I thank Dale Hattis for pointing this fact out to me, and again, any misinterpretation is mine.

14. The IRLG report can be reasonably characterized as prudent. There are other statements throughout the report that are similar to the

last sentence in the quote. This viewpoint was the basis for the industry objection that the report was mixing scientific and policy considerations (see chapter 4).

15. An *order of magnitude change* describes a change, up or down, of ten times. In scientific notation, a one order of magnitude increase might be from 1 in 10,000 (1×10^4) to 1 in 100,00 (1×10^5).

16. I thank Nicholas Ashford for pointing out this fact.

17. For a discussion of independent, centralized scientific panels, see Ashford (1984) and Rushefsky (1984b).

Chapter 3. Origins of Cancer Policy

1. The public agenda consists of those issues meriting public attention and considered legitimate for government action. The institutional agenda are those issues seriously being considered by policymakers. See Cobb and Elder (1972) for a discussion of these two types of agendas. For a discussion of the entire policy process, see Jones (1984).

2. As examples of policy entrepreneurs in another field, note the work of Paul Ellwood and Alain Enthoven, who vigorously advocated competition in the delivery and financing of health care. See Falkson (1980) and Enthoven (1980).

3. Lowi (1964) distinguishes among distributive, regulatory, and redistributive policy 'arenas'. These 'arenas' are characterized by different levels of policy making, visibility, interest group involvement, and levels of conflict.

4. For a discussion of corporatism, see Schmitter and Lehmbruch (1979).

5. Hamlett (1984) mentions in passing one other 'estate' or 'arena', the judiciary. He argues that the judiciary has, at present, only a minor role in technology development, the subject of his article. While the courts have also had a minor role in cancer policy development, they have played an important role in the general environmental area and occasionally in risk assessment. See Matheny and Williams (1984), Melnick (1983), and Vig (1984a).

6. Organized labor is in an ambivalent position. On the one hand, it is interested in occupational safety and health legislation and regulation, and has been a strong supporter of OSHA. On the other hand,

when environmental regulations, such as the risk assessment guidelines, threaten jobs, labor is less supportive.

7. For a discussion of the first environmental (or, more accurately, conservationist) period, see Culhane (1981). For a discussion of pre-1970 environmental legislation, see Davies (1975), Esposito (1970), Turner (1970), and Wellford (1972).

8. As an indication of the paucity of federal environmental legislation at the time of the Santa Barbara spill, Secretary of the Interior Walter C. Hickel was able to close down the platform only because of a clause in the lease which forbad wasting oil. See Hickel (1971).

9. The environmental movement, in its early stages, was seen as white and elitist. Blacks in particular opposed the philosophy of the movement because it emphasized restricted economic growth. See Hallow (1970) and Wildavsky (1976).

10. Downs (1972) argues that the public's attention to issues is not constant but grows and declines. While the "issue attention cycle" certainly does exist, in the environmental area the polls showed that a strong basis of public support remained even though environmental issues did not hold quite the same importance as they did during the late 1960s and early 1970s. This topic is discussed more in chapter 5.

11. The 1960s and 1970s were the periods of greatest growth in 'social' regulation. Social regulation, or the 'new' regulation, is concerned with environmental and worker protection and the safety of consumer products, concerns that cut across industries. 'Economic,' or 'old,' regulation concerns more traditional market behavior, such as prices and market entry, and is limited to specific industries. For a discussion of the two types, see White (1981).

12. The risk frameworks and degrees of protection discussed here are based on Office of Technology Assessment (1981). For other discussions of risk frameworks, see Lave (1981), Matheny and Williams (1984), and Rogers (1980).

13. The Resource Conservation and Recovery Act (RCRA) passed the same year and had the same anticipatory features as TSCA. Indeed, one should see both bills as part of an overall strategy to control toxic substances, though this interpretation may be granting more credit to Congress than is warranted. TSCA controlled chemicals at the point of their initial use. RCRA controlled chemicals at the point of their disposal. To a lesser extent, other legislation, such as the Clean Air Act,

the Water Pollution Control Act, and the Safe Drinking Water Act, focused on chemicals that find their way into those media.

14. For a discussion of "unreasonable risk" in TSCA, see Davies et al. (1979).

15. Note that Maguire is using the term *environment* in a narrow sense to refer to man-made substances that might be in the air, water, and food supply. As we shall see, while the overall attribution of cancer to environmental causes is correct, "environment" in the broader sense includes anything exogenous or external to a person. This broader definition includes not only chemicals, but also smoking, drinking, and eating habits. These latter lifestyle factors are given considerably more weight than narrowly defined environmental factors. The implications of the two definitions (broad and narrow) for cancer policy will be discussed in chapter 7.

16. Note that this approach was first seen in the Ad Hoc Committee's report and that the principles were put together by lawyers rather than by scientists.

17. This is one of the major points of criticism by those opposed to the principles approach to cancer policy. Critics say that such a definition fails to distinguish those substances that cause tumors (tumorigens) from those that cause malignant tumors (carcinogens). While carcinogens are clearly life threatening, tumorigens are not necessarily so worrisome.

18. This is the two-stage model discussed in chapter 1.

Chapter 4. Maturation of Cancer Policy

1. The emphasis on regulatory reform and coordination was not a new one (see March and Olson, 1983). The Ash Council during the Nixon administration suggested a number of changes. The Ford administration saw regulatory reform as a key part of its anti-inflation program (See Gottron, 1982).

2. The Carter executive order was greatly expanded during the Reagan administration. This topic is discussed in chapter 5.

3. Members included the Department of Agriculture and its Food Safety and Quality Service; the Departments of Commerce, Energy, State, Interior, and Transportation; the Department of Health and Human Services (then Health, Education, and Welfare) and some of its

components, such as the Food and Drug Administration and the National Cancer Institute; the Consumer Product Safety Commission; the Environmental Protection Agency; the Nuclear Regulatory Commission; and observers and ex-officio members from the Office of Management and Budget, the Interagency Regulatory Liaison Group, the Office of Science and Technology Policy, the Domestic Policy Staff, and the President's Reorganization Project.

4. Delays in implementation typify administration in this area. The regulations for the Resource Conservation and Recovery Act took over three years to write. Recently, the General Accounting Office (GAO) issued two reports (1984a, 1984b) complaining about delays in implementing TSCA, eight years after its passage.

5. This paragraph is based on McGarity (1983).

6. This topic is discussed at length in White (1981). A similar but considerably more centralized process occurred during the Reagan administration. That administration eliminated many of these agencies (such as the Interagency Regulatory Liaison Group, the Regulatory Council, the Council on Wage and Price Stability, and the Regulatory Analysis Review Group) and replaced them with the Office of Management and Budget. Chapter 5 discusses these changes.

7. Not everything that AIHC representatives said was reasonable. Note the statement by Dr. Francis Roe, submitted as part of the OSHA hearings record:

> Cancer in its many forms is undoubtedly a natural disease. It is probably one of Nature's many ways of eliminating sexually effete individuals who would otherwise, in Nature's view, compete for available food resources without advantage to the species as a whole. (Occupational Safety and Health Administration, 1980, p. 5026)

8. Among other changes, the automatic reduction of potential carcinogens to their lowest feasible levels was deleted and the significance of risk was included (Occupational Safety and Health Administration, 1981). In 1982 OSHA proposed that some parts of its cancer policy be reconsidered. For a discussion of risk assessment and the Supreme Court's decisions in the two cases, see Matheny and Williams (1984).

9. The emphasis of the OSTP 1980 report (and the AIHC critiques) on the "most likely value" is as deceptively simple as selecting a high estimate recommended in risk-averse cancer policies. The high value may overestimate real risk but is accepted by agencies that are cautious and

that place high priority on protecting public health and on not making mistakes. Its defense is based on policy rather than on science. But the "most-likely value" has only a quasi-scientific base. Any single estimate (even one accompanied by confidence intervals) gives a false sense of precision, particularly given all the attendant uncertainties of risk assessment. It would be more appropriate to provide as much information as possible, including a range of values and a discussion of high estimates, most likely values, and confidence intervals. EPA's exposure guidelines (1984d), for example, take the reasonable stance that because no one exposure value can be defended, then one must assume that all values are equally likely. The result is a curve that is somewhat more risk-tolerant than high estimates (though still relatively risk-averse) and more informative than simply providing extreme values.

10. The one-hit model suggests that any exposure to a carcinogen increases the risk of getting cancer. The linearized, multistage model suggests that carcinogenesis consists of at least two stages and also suggests a somewhat smaller risk of cancer. Both models are linear in that they view the relationship between dose and response as essentially proportional. For a discussion of models, see Whittemore and Keller (1978).

11. Like other risk assessment documents, the airborne cancer policy was subject to criticism. AIHC made the following five comments on the proposed policy: (1) the policy listed chemicals as hazardous without fully assessing risk; (2) the policy listed chemicals without giving an economic analysis or assessing the degree of risk; (3) the policy made no attempt to state why the rules were necessary; (4) there is no serious problem related to airborne carcinogens; and (5) there is no significant increase in cancer rates since 1937. See "EPA's Proposed Air Cancer Policy" (1979). The Regulatory Analysis Review Group also chipped in with its suggestions for change. See "Interagency Group" (1980).

Chapter 5. The Reagan Administration: Challenge and Change

1. The reader is referred to the extensive references in the Interagency Regulatory Liaison Group (1979) risk assessment guidelines.

2. For a discussion of the incorporation of pharmacokinetic models, see Brown and Koziol (1983) and Hoel et al. (1983).

3. Recall that many of the guidelines stated that the two different types of carcinogens could not be distinguished experimentally.

4. See Dunkel (1983) for a discussion of the variety of endpoints for short-term tests.

5. *In vivo* refers to testing inside a living organism, as in the standard animal bioassays.

6. This is a reference to the "qualitative" evaluation of carcinogenicity, that is, whether or not a substance is a carcinogen.

7. Other factors included overloading the policy agenda with many comprehensive proposals, poor legislative liaison, the "second oil shock" of 1978–1980, the Iranian hostage crisis, and unfortunately for Carter, economic conditions (high interest and inflation rates and a badly timed recession).

8. For a discussion of possible reforms within EPA, see Crandall and Portney (1984). They argue that much change was needed within EPA but that the Reagan administration avoided reforms and made draconic cuts as part of its regulatory relief program.

9. For a discussion of the Heritage Foundation report and its impact on EPA, see Belsky (1984).

10. For a discussion of the effect of EO 12291 and benefit-cost analysis on regulation, see Belsky (1984) and Whittington and Grubb (1984). Note that benefit-cost analysis is applied with a bias toward less regulation. We can see the importance of OMB's new role and the bias of regulatory reform by considering some recent events associated with the regulation of asbestos. In early 1985, EPA, which has been considering a ban on asbestos, decided, under OMB prodding, to transfer regulatory responsibility to the Occupational Safety and Health Administration and the Consumer Product Safety Commission. Such transfers are permitted under the 1976 Toxic Substances Control Act. EPA staff people did not believe that either of those two agencies could effectively regulate the substance. Further, CPSC and OSHA had not been afflicted by scandals as had EPA and might be more amenable to a risk-tolerant position. EPA later rescinded the action after it became public knowledge (see Stanfield, 1985a and 1985b). In a related matter, OMB urged that EPA weigh the value of a human life in performing a benefit-cost analysis for asbestos regulations. OMB suggested that each life be valued at $1 million but that the value be discounted by 10 percent for every year that asbestos-related diseases remained dormant. Because many of those diseases, such as cancer, have long latency periods, such discounting could effectively reduce the value of lives saved to zero (see Shabecoff, 1985b).

11. Both the emphasis on regulatory reform in general and the specific emphasis on regulatory impact analysis have its origins in earlier administrations, particularly the Carter administration. See Gottron (1982).

12. This is a position taken by the Interdisciplinary Panel (1984) and is discussed in chapter 6.

13. This is an example of what Belsky (1984) labels "cooperative regulation."

14. For details of these events, see Ashford et al. (1983a, 1983b) and Rushefsky (1984a).

15. Crump is one of the leading researchers of low-dose extrapolation models. For a discussion of his work, see Brown and Koziol (1983) and the references cited to Crump's work.

16. This is scientific notation indicating that the range of cancer is from 1 in a million (1×10^{-6}) to one in ten thousand (1×10^{-4}).

17. The Todhunter memorandum (and the other 1982 documents discussed in this chapter) was quite controversial and the subject of heated debate in the scientific literature (see letters in *Science*, vol. 224, May 11, 1984, pp. 550–556, in response to Ashford et al. 1983b, and the letters reprinted in *Control of Carcinogens*, 1983, pp. 219–221) as well as in congressional hearings (*Control of Carcinogens*, 1983; *Formaldehyde*, 1982).

18. This means that the guidelines assumed a 10 percent response or incidence of cancer, even if there may not be any cancer response, and then applied a safety factor as a precaution.

19. The maximum likelihood value (also recommended by the American Industrial Health Council) was discussed in the previous chapter. The dose conversion factor mentioned in the water quality document makes those guidelines more risk-tolerant than using surface area conversion.

20. The OSTP guidelines went through four drafts altogether, evolving by the third and published draft into a set of guidelines and principles considerably different from the first draft. The second draft was closer to the third than to the first draft. The third draft will be discussed in chapter 6. The final is virtually identical to the third.

21. The term *beliefs* is intriguing in the context of a scientific document. There is an implication that the basis for those beliefs is unscien-

tific, perhaps consisting more of value judgments. An alternative wording might have been *consensus*. Note that 'belief' is the subheading, but 'consensus' is used in the body of the document. The reader might wish to compare those beliefs with appendix A, the statement of principles from the third draft. The change between the two drafts is significant.

22. This is a point made by Ames (1983). It also implies that there is little that might be done to reverse the progression. In the words of Francis Roe (quoted in Occupational Health and Safety Administration, 1980, p. 5026), cancer may indeed be a "natural process."

23. Delays still mark that program (as well as other environmental programs). See General Accounting Office (1984b, 1984c).

24. The contribution of air toxics to cancer is, again, very controversial. Attempts to estimate and survey the effects are caught up in politics. A July 1984 EPA draft study estimated that some 2,000 cancer cases were caused by air toxics. The report was later held up for peer review (See Environmental Protection Agency, 1984b, and "EPA Decides Against Releasing," 1984). A subsequent survey of 80 chemical companies found that toxic air emissions were much higher than anyone had estimated. Partially as a result, the chemical industries urged that stricter air toxics rules be issued. See Diamond (1985) and Shabecoff (1985a).

Chapter 6. Scandal, Critique, and Consensus

1. It is useful to point out here that these scientists are "visible" (see Goodell, 1977) and that they are stepping out of the traditional role of scientists to advocate policy.

2. Weinstein does not directly state, but implies, a possible and future relationship between exposure to synthetic chemicals and cancer. It is clearly a prudent policy that Weinstein is defending, one based on assumptions.

3. This is the same position taken by the Interdisciplinary Panel on Carcinogenicity (1984) commissioned by AIHC.

4. For a critique of OSTP's first draft, see Perera's comments in *Control of Carcinogens*, 1983, pp. 121–145.

5. Similar reviews of EPA decisions can be found in other congressional hearings (see *Formaldehyde*, 1982; and *PCB and Dioxin Cases*, 1982).

6. This was the basis for EPA's choice of the linearized, multistage model. See Environmental Protection Agency (1984c).

7. The refusal to turn over documents continued into 1984 (see "EPA Data Withheld," 1984).

8. Dioxin is considered a promoter and an epigenetic carcinogen, but its potency is so high that it argues against using those categories to assess risk. See Wines (1983).

9. For a discussion of public opinion polls and the environment, see Anthony (1982), Keeter (1983), and Mitchell (1984).

10. There was some queasiness among environmentalists about Ruckelshaus. He was a vice-president of the Weyerhauser Corporation, a major timber products company, before returning to EPA.

11. Ruckelshaus also meant more than that, obviously. Morale was poor at EPA during the Burford years, and Ruckelshaus restored it. Budget cuts were also repaired, though in real dollar terms EPA was still worse off than in 1980. There were attempts, not always successful, to address controversial issues that the administration preferred to defer, such as acid rain.

12. Thus Ruckelshaus was a strong proponent of the two-stage model of risk control discussed in chapter 1. This viewpoint can also be seen in his criticism of a panel of scientists, convened by the White House Office of Science and Technology Policy, which recommended decreases in sulfur dioxide emissions to reduce acid rain. Ruckelshaus stated that the scientists had gone beyond risk assessment and were now making policy recommendations that were the responsibility of policymakers. See "Authors of White House Acid Rain Report" (1984). Ruckelshaus was correct in his interpretation, but one must note that scientists have been going beyond risk assessment since at least 1970; Saffiotti, Schneiderman, Cornfield, and Squire are examples. This point will be considered in the last chapter.

13. The prototype of increased public involvement were the hearings held in Tacoma, Washington, in 1984 to educate the public and gather input on allowable arsenic emissions from the Asarco copper-smelting plant. See "Hearings on Arsenic Output" (1983) and Kalikow (1984).

14. A fourth initiative mentioned in the speech was the sharing of information with other countries.

15. For a discussion of centralized science panels, see Rushefsky (1984b).

16. The emphasis on "worst-case estimates" is interesting. Such estimates are commonly used in defense policy; by assuming the worst, one protects against that possibility and provides the most protection. In an intriguing parallel, recent debates about the existence of "yellow rain" in southeast Asia raised the question of how much evidence is needed to reach a policy conclusion. "Yellow rain," according to the Reagan admnistration, is evidence that chemical warfare is being used by the Vietnamese in Cambodia and Laos. The data are several leaf samples. Others, such as Meselson, assert that the "yellow rain" is no more than bee pollen. The point is that the Reagan administration is willing to accept a much lower level of evidence ("worst-case") for yellow rain than for carcinogens. This is a perfect example of the mixture of science and politics on both sides. See Eimer (1984) and Wade (1983, 1984).

17. A fourth initiative was public involvement in risk decisions. Again, the Tacoma case is the prototype of this initiative.

18. The carcinogen guidelines, the subject of this section, were one of the six to be written and recommended by the toxics integration task force. Five of the six guidelines were published at the same time.

19. The IRMC can be considered a successor, both in participants and mission, to the IRLG established during the Carter administration. Both groups suffered the same fate during the Reagan administration.

20. It should be noted that the delay was just one of a series of delays, the twenty-seventh in the last twenty-two years.

Chapter 7. The Challenge to Cancer Policy

1. Even among environmentalists, such a view was controversial. Note the bitter dialogues between Commoner and Paul Ehrlich, who saw rapid population growth as the root cause of our environmental problems. For a balanced and more complex view of this issue, see Miller (1984).

2. Doll and Peto (1981) addressed this issue, stating that mortality figures are much more reliable than incidence rates. The data are much better for mortality than incidence, but this point just begs the question.

3. There is new evidence that certain factors within the body, such as free oxygen radicals and oncogenes, also play a significant role. See Ames (1983), Boffey (1984), Cerutti (1985), and Institute of Medicine (1984).

4. In the context of the public policy literature, the subject under discussion is problem perception and definition (see chapter 3); it is critical to cancer policy development. First, as Lindblom (1980) has pointed out, there is no such thing as a given problem. Someone has to perceive that something is happening (for example, trends in cancer mortality rates) and define that event, give meaning to it. Are the rates going up or down? Are they attributable to this set of causes or that one? Jones (1984) discusses the importance of perception and definition in structuring the rest of the policy process. How a problem is perceived and defined can help determine what, if any, solutions will be proposed. A view that toxics are an important cause leads to regulatory solutions. A view that lifestyle factors are the most important cause leads to proposals for information dissemination. A view tht natural bodily processes are the prime factors leads to a concern for cures.

5. The workplace provides perhaps the best potential evidence for the role of toxics in causing cancer. Here we are looking at a limited population with relatively well-defined and limited exposure to chemicals. In principle, epidemiological studies are the easiest to conduct in this setting. In reality, such studies are as much in dispute here as elsewhere.

6. Note that the Karch and Schneideman paper contains many instances where they say "we believe." These beliefs form the assumptions under which their calculations were made. Again, the question can be raised as to whether their value judgments led them to make the kind of estimates that they did.

7. The importance of concentrating on promoters as a strategy for cancer prevention is also supported by Day and Brown (1980).

8. Several points Efron made discredit her arguments—for example, the notion that there was a conspiracy. That, as Weinberg (1985) pointed out, was not the case. To Efron, the conspiracy was so strong that most scientists who reviewed her book prior to publication would not allow attribution. Yet as has been pointed out in chapter 5, and indeed as Efron herself pointed out, there was opposition even among the academic scientists (which she focused on to avoid an industry bias), let alone among other scientists. Because there was published opposition and questioning of the direction of cancer policy, it is hard to understand why the fear of attribution would exist.

9. For an historical perspective on risk control, see Covello and Mumpower (1985).

10. The deterministic view of science and the demand for causality that Efron asserted would have aborted much progress in science. Consider the case of fluoridation. Studies over the last forty years have shown that fluoridation reduces the number of cavities by 60 percent. Yet no one knows how it works, and a number of different explanations have been offered. By Efron's standard, we should not have undertaken fluoridation because we do not know the causal mechanism. Yet fluoridation works. See Morgan (1984).

11. Greenwood (1984a, 1984b) argues that the scientific ineptness of regulatory agencies has been drastically overstated.

Chapter 8. Mixing Truth with Power

1. With apologies to Aaron Wildavsky (1979).

2. For a detailed discussion of the National Academy of Sciences and particularly the importance of the composition of scientific panels, see Boffey (1975).

3. For a discussion of epistemological differences, see Lynn (1983), Robbins and Johnston (1976), and Rushefsky (1982).

4. Stanfield (1985c) maintains that Ruckelshaus's insistence on the strict separation of risk assessment and risk management was meant to defuse the political problems that afflicted the Environmental Protection Agency.

5. There is yet one more example of the mixing of science and politics that is worth noting. In September 1985 a draft report of a National Academy of Sciences committee recommended lower nutritional dietary allowances. Nutritional allowances are used in planning meals in schools and for federal welfare programs such as food stamps. The reaction was immediate and strong. Lowered requirements would mean, for example, that cutbacks could be made in this welfare program. As a result of the public furor, the report was deferred. See Pear (1985a, 1985b).

6. For a discussion of consensus dialogues and regulatory negotiation, see Rushefsky (1984b). A consensus dialogue was employed in the National Coal Policy Project; see *Regulatory Negotiation* (1980).

References

"Administrator's Job has Shifted in 10 Years to Public Health Problems, Ruckelshaus Says" (1984). *Environmental Reporter* 14 (November 11): 1291–1292.

Alm, Alvin M. (1975). "Environmental Protection Agency Memorandum on Agency Approach to Cancer Policy." *Environmental Reporter* 6 (October 24): 1144–1146.

American Cancer Society (1984). *Cancer Facts & Figures 1984.* New York: American Cancer Society.

American Industrial Health Council (1978). *AIHC Recommended Alternatives to OSHA's Generic Carcinogen Proposal.* Scarsdale, NY: American Industrial Health Council

———(1979). *AIHC Comments on: A Report of the Interagency Regulatory Liaison Group (IRLG), Work Group on Risk Assessment Entitled "Scientific Bases for Identification of Potential Carcinogens and Estimation of Risks".* Scarsdale, NY: American Industrial Health Council

Ames, Bruce N. (1979). "Identifying Environmental Chemicals Causing Mutations and Cancer." *Science* 204 (May 11): 587–593.

———(1983). "Dietary Carcinogens and Anticarcinogens." *Science* 221 (September 23): 1256–1264.

———(1984a). "Letter: Reply, Diet and Cancer." *Science* 224 (May 18): 668–670, 757–760.

———(1984b). "Mother Nature is Meaner than You Think: Review of *The Apocalyptics.*" *Science* 84 5 (July–August): 98–99.

Anderson, Elizabeth L., et al. (1983). "Quantitative Approaches in Use to Assess Cancer Risk." *Risk Analysis* 3 (December): 277–295.

Anthony, Richard (1982). "Polls, Pollution and Politics." *Environment* 24 (May): 14–20, 33–34.

Arundel, Anthony, and Theodor Sterling (1984). "What is an Epidemiological Study and Just How Useful is the Epidemiology of Pesticides?" *NCAP News* 4 (Spring): 2–5.

Ashford, Nicholas A. (1984). "Advisory Committees in OSHA and EPA: Their Use in Regulatory Decisionmaking." *Science, Technology, & Human Values* 9 (Winter): 72–82.

Ashford, Nicholas A., et al. (1983a). "A Hard Look at Federal Regulation of Formaldehyde: A Departure from Reasoned Decisionmaking." *Harvard Environmental Law Review* 7: 297–370.

————(1983b). "Law and Science Policy in Federal Regulation of Formaldehyde." *Science* 222 (November 25): 894–900.

"Authors of White House Acid Rain Report Went Beyond their Role, Ruckelshaus Asserts" (1984). *Environmental Reporter* 15 (August 31): 690.

Banta, H. David (1985). Review of *The Apocalyptics*, by Edith Efron. *Issues in Science and Technology* 1 (Spring): 130.

Barber, Bernard (1952). *Science and the Social Order*. New York: MacMillan Publishing Company.

Bauman, Patricia (1984). "Why Should We Regulate Chemicals?" *Conservation Foundation Newsletter* (September–October): 2.

Beebe, Gilbert W. (1982). "Ionizing Radiation and Health." *American Scientist* 70 (January–February): 35–44.

Behn, Robert D., and James W. Vaupel (1982). *Quick Analysis for Busy Decision Makers*. New York: Basic Books, Inc.

"BEIR Report on Radiation Hazards Comes Unglued" (1979). *Science* 204 (June 8): 1062.

Belsky, Martin H. (1984). "Environmental Policy Law in the 1980's: Shifting Back the Burden of Proof." *Ecology Law Quarterly* 12: 1–88.

Bennett, William (1984). "The Politics of Prevention." Review of *The Apocalyptics*, by Edith Efron. *The Washington Post National Weekly Edition* (September 3).

Berenblum, I. (1941). "The Mechanism of Carcinogenesis: A Study of the Significance of Cocarcinogenic Action and Related Phenomena." *Cancer Research* 1: 807-814.

————(1978). "Established Principles and Unresolved Problems of Carcinogenesis." *Journal of the National Cancer Institute* 60 (April): 723-726.

Boffey, Phillip M. (1975). *The Brain Bank of America: An Inquiry into the Politics of Science.* New York: McGraw-Hill.

————(1984). "After Years of Cancer Alarms, Progress Amid the Mistakes." *The New York Times* (March 20).

Bridbord, K., et al. (1978). "Estimates of the Fraction of Cancer in the United States Related to Occupational Factors." Washington, DC: National Institute of Occupational Safety and Health.

Broad, William J. (1985). "Reagan's 'Star Wars' Bid: Many Ideas Converging." *The New York Times* (March 4).

Broad, William, and Nicholas Wade (1982). *Betrayers of the Truth.* New York: Simon and Schuster.

Brown, Charles C., and James A. Koziol (1983). "Statistical Aspects of the Estimation of Human Risk from Suspected Environmental Carcinogens." *SIAM Review* 25 (April): 151-181.

Burnham, David (1985). "Reagan Authorizes a Wider Role for Budget Office on New Rules." *The New York Times* (January 5).

Cairns, John (1978). *Cancer: Science and Society.* San Francisco: W. H. Freeman and Company.

Calkins, D.R., et al. (1980). "Identification, Characterization, and Control of Potential Human Carcinogens: A Framework for Federal Decision-Making." *JCNI* 64 (January); 169-176.

Campbell, Donald T. (1985). "A Seminar: Toward an Epistemologically Relevant Sociology of Science." *Science, Technology, and Human Values* 10 (Winter): 38-48.

Carson, Rachel (1962). *Silent Spring.* Boston: Houghton Mifflin Co.

Carter, Jimmy (1977). "Protection of the Environment." Pp. 30E-37E in *1977 Congressional Quarterly Almanac.* Washington, DC: Congressional Quarterly Press.

Carter, Luther J. (1974). *The Florida Experience: Land and Water Policy, in a Growth State.* Baltimore: The Johns Hopkins University Press.

Cerutti, Peter A. (1985). "Prooxidant States and Tumor Promotion." *Science* 227 (January 25): 375–381.

Chemical Manufacturers Association (1981). "Response to Natural Resources Defense Council Report, 'Explaining the Urban Factor in Lung Cancer Mortality,' by N.J. Karch and M.A. Schneiderman. Reprinted in *Clean Air Act (Part 2)*, December 16, pp. 588–616.

Clark, Timothy B. (1978). "Cracking Down on the Causes of Cancer." *National Journal* 10 (December 30): 2056–2060.

——(1979). "A Battle Plan for the War on Cancer." *National Journal* 11 (October 27): 1808–1811.

Clean Air Act (Part 2) (1981). Hearings before the Subcommittee on Health and the Environment of the Committee on Energy and Commerce, U.S. House of Representatives, 97th Congress, 1st session, November–December.

Cobb, Roger W., and Charles D. Elder (1972). *Participation in American Politics: The Dynamics of Agenda-Building*. Boston: Allyn & Bacon.

Cole, Leonard A. (1985). "Facts, Values, and Policies." *Politics and the Life Sciences* 4 (August): 45–47.

Commoner, Barry (1971). *The Closing Circle: Nature, Man & Technology*. New York: Bantam Books.

Conservation Foundation (1982). *State of the Environment 1982*. Washington, DC: The Conservation Foundation.

——(1984). *State of the Environment: An Assessment at Mid-Decade*. Washington, DC: The Conservation Foundation.

——(1985). "Air Toxics Problems Leave EPA Gasping." *Conservation Foundation Letter* (July–August): 1–7.

Control of Carcinogens in the Environment (1983). Hearings before the Subcommittee on Commerce, Transportation, and Tourism of the Committee on Energy and Commerce, U.S. House of Representatives, 98th Congress, 1st session, March 17.

Cornfield, Jerome (1977). "Carcinogenic Risk Assessment." *Science* 198 (November 18): 693–699.

Council on Environmental Quality (1971). *Toxic Substances*. Washington, DC: Council on Environmental Quality.

————(1978). *Environmental Quality 1978.* Washington, DC: Council on Environmental Quality.

————(1982). *Environmental Quality 1981.* Washington, DC: Council on Environmental Quality.

Covello, Vincent T., and Jeryl Mumpower (1985). "Risk Analysis and Risk Management: An Historical Perspective." *Risk Analysis* 5 (June): 103–120.

Crandall, Robert W., and Paul R. Portney (1984). "Environmental Policy." Pp. 47–81 in Paul R. Portney (ed.), *Natural Resources and the Environment: The Reagan Approach*, Washington, DC: The Urban Institute Press.

Culhane, Paul J. (1981). *Public Land Politics: Interest Group Influence on the Forest Service and the Bureau of Land Management.* Baltimore: The Johns Hopkins University Press.

Davies, Clarence J., III (1975). *The Politics of Pollution.* 2nd ed. New York: Pegasus Press.

Davies, Clarence J., III et al. (1979) "An Issue Report: Determining Unreasonable Risk under the Toxic Substances Control Act." Washington, DC: The Conservation Foundation.

Davis, Devra Lee, et al. (1983). "Cancer Prevention: Assessing Causes, Exposures, and Recent Trends in Mortality for U.S. Males, 1968–1978." *International Journal of Health Services* 13: 337–372.

Davis, Earon S. (1984). "Public Perception: The Environment is 'Moving.' " *Environmental Forum* 3 (December): 29–33.

Day, Nicholas E., and Charles C. Brown. (1980). "Multistage Models and Primary Prevention of Cancer." *JCNI* 64 (April): 977–989.

Diamond, Stuart (1985). "Very High Levels of Toxic Material are Found in Air." *The New York Times* (March 26).

Dodge, Christopher H., and Robert L. Civiak (1981). "Risk Assessment and Regulatory Policy." Washington, DC: Congressional Research Service, Issue Brief No. 1B81019.

Doll, Richard, and Richard Peto (1981). *The Causes of Cancer: Quantitative Estimates of Avoidable Risks of Cancer in the United States Today.* Oxford: Oxford University Press.

Douglas, Mary, and Aaron Wildavsky (1982). *Risk and Culture: An Essay on the Selection of Technical and Environmental Dangers.* Berkeley: University of California Press.

Downs, Anthony (1972). "Up and Down with Ecology—the 'Issue-Attention' Cycle." *The Public Interest* 28 (Summer): 38–50.

Dunkel, Virginia C. (1983). "Biological Significance of End Points." Pp. 34–41 in Williams et al.

Efron, Edith (1984). *The Apocalyptics: Cancer and the Big Lie; How Environmental Politics Controls What We Know About Cancer.* New York: Simon and Schuster.

Eimer, M. (1984). "Letter: Yellow Rain Evidence That Cannot be Ignored." *The New York Times* (March 10).

Elder, Charles D., and Roger W. Cobb (1984). "Agenda-Building and the Politics of Aging." *Policy Studies Journal* 13 (September): 115–129.

Enthoven, Alain (1980). *Health Plan.* Reading, MA: Addison-Wesley.

"Environmental Apoplexy" (1982). *The New York Times* (February 22).

Environmental Causes of Cancer (1976). Hearing before the Subcommittee on Oversight and Investigations of the Committee on Interstate and Foreign Commerce, U.S. House of Representatives, 94th Congress, 2nd session, May 28.

Environmental Forum (1984). "Reviewing 'The Apocalyptics.' " 3 (November): 32–39.

Environmental Protection Agency (1976). "Health Risk and Economic Impact Assessments of Suspected Carcinogens: Interim Procedures and Guidelines." *Federal Register* 41 (May 25): 21402–21405.

———(1979). "National Emission Standards for Hazardous Air Pollutants; Policy and Procedures for Identifying, Assessing, and Regulation of Airborne Substances Posing a Risk of Cancer." *Federal Register* 44 (October 10): 58642–58662.

———(1980). "Water Quality Criteria Documents. Availability (Final)." *Federal Register* 45 (November 28): 79318–79379.

———(1982a). "Additional U.S. Environmental Protection Agency Guidance for the Health Assessment of Suspect Carcinogens with Specific Reference to Water Quality." Pp. 105–124 in *PCB and Dioxin Cases.*

————(1982b). "EPA Air Program's Draft Toxic Air Pollutant Strategy." *Environmental Reporter* 13 (November 26): 1183–1186.

————(1982c). "EPA Draft Guidelines for Performing Regulatory Impact Analyses under Executive Order 12291." *Environmental Reporter* 13 (July 16): 385–392.

————(1983a). "Fourth Draft of EPA's Hazardous Air Pollutant Strategy." *Environmental Reporter* 13 (January 21): 2282–2288.

————(1983b). "EPA Draft Document Requesting Public Comment on 'Process for Evaluation and Control of Toxic Air Pollutants.' " *Environmental Reporter* 13 (April 8): 1632–1636.

————(1984a). "Risk Management: The New Program at EPA." Proceedings of a conference held June 7 at Arlington, VA. Washington, DC: Environmental Protection Agency.

————(1984b). "Summary of Data on Specific Pollutants and Cancer Risk Estimates Excerpted from EPA Draft Study on Air Toxics Problem in United States." *Environmental Reporter* 15 (August 10): 616–618.

————(1984c). "Proposed Guidelines for Carcinogen Risk Assessment." *Federal Register* 49 (November 23): 46294–46301.

————(1984d). "Proposed Guidelines for Exposure Assessment." *Federal Register* 49 (November 23): 46305–46312.

————(1984e). "Report of the Toxics Integration Task Force." Washington, DC: Environmental Protection Agency.

————(1984f). "Risk Assessment and Management: Framework for Decision Making." Washington, DC: Environmental Protection Agency.

————(1985). "A Strategy to Reduce Risks to Public Health from Air Toxics." Washington, DC: Environmental Protection Agency.

"EPA Data Withheld, Panel Asserts" (1984). *The New York Times* (April 31).

"EPA Decides Against Releasing Toxics Study Until Peer Review Undertaken, Officials Say" (1984). *Environmental Reporter* 15 (September 7): 722–723.

EPA: Investigation of Superfund and Agency Abuses (Part 1) (1983). Hearings before the Subcommittee on Oversight and Investigations of the Committee on Energy and Commerce, U.S. House of Representatives, 98th Congress, 1st session, February–March.

"EPA Wrongfully Used Definitions of Cancer, Carcinogens Meeting Told" (1976). *Environmental Reporter* 6 (March 19): 1954–1955.

"EPA's Proposed Air Cancer Policy Draws Sharp Criticism from Industry" (1979). *Environmental Reporter* 10 (October 12): 1335.

Epstein, Samuel S. (1978). *The Politics of Cancer.* San Francisco: Sierra Club Books.

Epstein, Samuel S., et al. (1984). "Letter: Cancer and Diet." *Science* 224 (May 18): 660–668.

Esposito, John C. (1970). *Vanishing Air.* New York: Grossman Publishers.

"Evaluation of Environmental Carcinogens" (1970). Report to the Surgeon General, United States Public Health Service, April 22, Ad Hoc Committee on the Evaluation of Low Levels of Environmental Chemical Carcinogens, National Cancer Institute. Reprinted in *Chemicals and the Future of Man*, Hearings before the Subcommittee on Executive Reorganization and Government Research of the Committee on Government Operations, U.S. Senate, 92nd Congress, 1st session, April 6–7, 1971, Pp. 180–198.

"Examining the Role of Science in the Regulatory Process" (1983). *Environment* 25 (June): 6–14, 33–40.

Falkson, Joseph L. (1980). *HMOs and the Politics of Health System Reform.* Bowie, MD: Robert J. Brady Co.

"F.D.A. Delays a Ban on Dyes" (1985). *The New York Times* (April 3).

Feliciano, Donald V. (1983). "The U.S. Environmental Protection Agency: An Analysis of its Controversies." Washington, DC: Congressional Research Service, Report No. 83–114 ENR.

Formaldehyde: Review of Scientific Basis of EPA's Carcinogenic Risk Assessment (1982). Hearings before the Subcommittee on Investigations and Oversight of the Committee on Science and Technology, U.S. House of Representatives, 97th Congress, 2nd session, May 20.

Gehring, P.J., et al. (1977). "The Relevance of Dose-Dependent Pharmacokinetics in the Assesment of Carcinogenic Hazard of Chemicals." Pp. 187–203 in H.H. Hiatt et al. (eds.), *Origins of Human Cancer*; Book A: *Incidence of Cancer in Humans*. New York: Cold Spring Harbor Laboratory.

General Accounting Office (1976). *Federal Efforts to Protect Public From Cancer-Causing Chemicals Are Not Very Effective*. Washington, DC: General Accounting Office.

————(1984a). *Assessment of New Chemical Regulation under the Toxic Substances Control Act*. Washington, DC: General Accounting Office.

————(1984b). *Delays in EPA's Regulation of Hazardous Air Pollutants*. Washington, DC: General Accounting Office.

————(1984c). *EPA's Efforts to Identify and Control Harmful Chemicals in Use*. Washington, DC: General Accounting Office.

————(1984d). *National Academy of Sciences' Reports on Diet and Health—Are They Credible and Consistent?* Washington, DC: General Accounting Office.

Giere, Ronald N. (1979). *Understanding Scientific Reasoning*. New York: Holt, Rinehart and Winston.

Goldstein, Martin, and Inge F. Goldstein (1978). *How We Know: An Exploration of the Scientific Process*. New York: Plenum Press.

Goodell, Rae (1977). *The Visible Scientists*. Boston: Little, Brown & Co.

Gori, Gio Batta (1980). "The Regulation of Carcinogenic Hazards." *Science* 208 (April 18): 256–261.

Gottron, Martha V. (1982). *Regulation: Process and Politics*. Washington, DC: Congressional Quarterly Press.

Graham, Frank, Jr. (1970). *Since Silent Spring*. Boston: Houghton Mifflin Co.

Greenberg, Daniel S. (1984) "Cancer, Chemicals and 'Conspirary' ". Review of *the Apocalyptics*, by Edith Efron. *The New York Times*.

Greenwood, Ted (1984a). "The Myth of Scientific Incompetence of Regulatory Agencies." *Science, Technology, & Human Values* 9 (Winter): 83–96.

————(1984b). *Knowledge and Discretion in Government Regulation.* New York: Praeger Publishers.

Hadden, Susan G., ed. (1984). *Risk Analysis, Institutions, and Public Policy.* Port Washington, NY: Associated Faculty Press.

Hallow, Ralph Z. (1970). "The Blacks Cry Genocide," Reprinted in Walt Anderson (ed.), *Politics and Environment: a Reader in Ecological Crisis,* Pacific Palisades, CA: Goodyear Publishing Company, Pp. 22–25.

Hamlett, Patrick W. (1984). "Understanding Technological Development: A Decisionmaking Approach." *Science, Technology, & Human Values* 9 (Summer): 33–46.

Hattis, Dale B. (1982). *Analyzing the Benefits of Health, Safety, and Environmental Regulations.* Cambridge, MA: Center for Policy Alternatives, Massachusetts Institute of Technology.

Hattis, Dale B., and John A. Smith, Jr. (1985). "What's Wrong with Quantitative Risk Assessment?" Paper prepared for presentation at Georgia State University, September 26–28.

"Hearings on Arsenic Output Seek to Protect Job Interests" (1983). *The New York Times* (November 3).

Heclo, Hugh (1978). "Issue Networks and the Executive Establishment." Pp. 87–124 in Anthony King (ed.), *The New American Political System.* Washington, DC: American Enterprise Institute.

Hickel, Walter J. (1971). *Who Owns America.* Englewood Cliffs, NJ: Prentice-Hall, Inc.

Hodgson, Thomas A. (1981). "Social and Economic Implications of Cancer in the United States." Pp. 189–204 in William J. Nicholson (ed.), *Management of Assessed Risk for Carcinogens,* vol. 363, New York Academy of Sciences.

Hoel, David G., et al. (1983). "Implications of Nonlinear Kinetics on Risk Estimation in Carcinogenesis." *Science* 219 (March 4): 1032–1037.

Homburger, F. (1983a). "Introduction: Workshop on Skin Painting." *Progress in Experimental Tumor Research* 26: 1–4.

————(1983b). "Introduction: Carcinogenesis Bioassay in Historical Perspective." *Progress in Experimental Tumor Research* 26: 182–186.

Hoover, Robert (1979). "Environmental Cancer." Pp. 50–60 in E. Cuyler Hammond and Irving J. Selikoff (eds.), *Public Controls of Environmental Health Hazards*, vol. 329, New York Academy of Sciences.

Hopson, Janet, and Joel Gurin (1984). "Diet and Cancer Round 2." *American Health* 3 (November): 72–83.

Institute of Medicine (1984). *Cancer Today: Origins, Prevention, and Treatment.* Washington, DC: National Academy Press.

"Interagency Group Urges EPA to Weigh Costs, Benefits of the Air Cancer Policy" (1980). *Environmental Reporter* 10 (February 29): 2059–2060.

Interagency Regulatory Liaison Group (1979). "Scientific Bases for Identification of Potential Carcinogens and Estimation of Risks." *JCNI* 63: 241–268. Reprinted in *Control of Carcinogens*, pp. 191–218.

Interdisciplinary Panel on Carcinogenicity (1984). "Criteria for Evidence of Chemical Carcinogenicity." *Science* 225 (August 17): 682–687.

Johnson, Paul (1984). "This Side of Apocalypse". Review of *The Apocalyptics*, by Edith Efron. *National Review* XXXVI (June 29): 41–44.

Jones, Charles O. (1974). "Speculative Augmentation in Federal Air Pollution Policy-Making." *Journal of Politics* 36 (May): 438–464.

——(1984). *An Introduction to the Study of Public Policy.* 3rd ed. Monterey, CA: Brooks/Cole Publishing Company.

Kalikow, Barnett N. (1984). "Environmental Risk: Power to the People." *Technology Review* 7 (October): 54–61.

Karch, Nathan J., and Marvin A. Schneiderman (1981). "Explaining the Urban Factor in Lung Cancer Mortality." Report to the Natural Resources Defense Council. Pp. 491–572 in *Clean Air Act (Part 2)*, December 16.

Kates, Robert W. (1978). *Risk Assessment of Environmental Hazard.* New York: John Wiley & Sons.

Keeter, Scott (1983). "Problematic Pollution Polls: Validity in the Measurement of Public Opinion on Environmental Issues." Paper prepared for the annual meeting of the Midwest Political Science Association, Chicago, April 20–23.

Kingdon, John W. (1984). *Agendas, Alternatives, and Public Policies.* Boston: Little, Brown & Co.

Kirschten, Dick (1977). "The New War on Cancer—Carter Team Seeks Causes, Not Cures." *National Journal* 9 (August 6): 1220–1225.

Kotelchuck, David (1984). "OSHA Under Fire." *Health PAC Bulletin* 15 (May–June): 21–22.

Kraft, Michael E. (1984). "A New Environmental Policy Agenda: The 1980 Presidential Campaign and Its Aftermath." Pp. 29–50 in Vig and Kraft.

Kuhn, Thomas S. (1970). *The Structure of Scientific Revolutions.* 2nd ed. Chicago: University of Chicago Press.

Kurtz, Howard (1984). "The Day Anne Burford Was 'Hung Out to Dry.' " *The Washington Post National Edition* 2 (December 31): 14.

Lave, Lester B., (1981). *The Strategy of Social Regulation: Decision Frameworks for Policy.* Washington, DC: The Brookings Institution.

———(1982). *Quantitative Risk Assessment in Regulation.* Washington, DC: The Brookings Institution.

Levine, Adeline Gordon (1982). *Love Canal: Science, Politics, and People.* Lexington, MA: D.C. Heath and Company.

Light, Paul C. (1985). "Social Security and the Politics of Assumptions." *Public Administration Review* 45 (May–June): 363–371.

Lindblom, Charles (1980). *The Policy-Making Process* 2nd ed. Englewood Cliffs, NJ: Prentice-Hall, Inc.

Lowi, Theodore J. (1964). "American Business, Public Policy, Case-Studies, and Political Theory." *World Politics* 16 (July): 677–715.

Lowrance, William O. (1976). *Of Acceptable Risk: Science and the Determination of Safety.* Los Altos, CA: William Kaufmann.

Lynn, Frances M. (1983). "The Interplay of Science and Values in Assessing Environmental Risks." Ph.D. dissertation, University of North Carolina at Chapel Hill.

McGarity, Thomas O. (1979). "Substantive and Procedural Discretion in Administrative Resolution of Science Policy Questions: Regulating Carcinogens in EPA and OSHA." *Georgetown Law Review* 67 (February): 729–810.

————(1983). "OSHA's Generic Carcinogen Policy: Rule Making Under Scientific and Legal Uncertainty." Pp. 55–105 in J.D. Nyhart and Milton W. Carrow (eds.), *Law and Science in Collaboration: Resolving Regulatory Issues in Science and Technology.* Lexington, MA: D.C. Heath and Company.

Mack, T.M., et al. (1977). "Epidemiologic Methods for Human Risk Assessment. Pp. 1749–1763 in H.H. Hiatt et al. (eds.), *Origins of Human Cancer; Book D: Human Risk Assessment.* New York: Cold Spring Harbor Laboratory.

McNeil, Mary (1981). *Environment and Health.* Washington, DC: Congressional Quarterly Press.

Majone, Giandomenico (1984). "Regulation and Science." *Science, Technology, & Human Values* 9 (Winter): 23–38.

March, James G., and Johan P. Olson (1983). "What Administrative Reorganization Tells Us about Governing." *American Political Science Review* 77 (June): 281–296.

Marshall, Eliot (1979). "NAS Study on Radiation takes the Middle Road." *Science* 204 (May 18): 711, 713–714.

————(1983). "EPA's High-Risk Carcinogen Policy." Reprinted in *Control of Carcinogens,* Pp. 538–541.

————(1984). "Topic of Cancer". Review of *The Apocalyptics,* by Edith Efron. *The New Republic* 190 (May 14): 33–36.

Matheny, Albert R., and Bruce A. Williams (1984). "Regulation, Risk Assessment, and the Supreme Court: The Case of OSHA's Cancer Policy." *Law and Policy* 6 (October): 425–449.

Mazur, Allan (1973). "Disputes Between Experts." *Minerva* XI (April): 243–262.

Melnick, R. Shep (1983). *Regulation and the Courts: The Case of the Clean Air Act.* Washington, DC: The Brookings Institution.

Merton, Robert K. (1968). *Social Theory and Social Structure.* New York: The Free Press.

Miller, G. Tyler, Jr. (1984). *Living in the Environment* 4th ed. Belmont, CA: Wadsworth Publishing Company.

Mitchell, Robert Cameron (1984). "Public Opinion and Environmental Politics in the 1970s and 1980s." Pp. 51-74 in Vig and Kraft.

Mitroff, Ian S. (1974). *The Subjective Side of Science: A Philosophical Inquiry into the Psychology of the Apollo Moon Scientists.* Amsterdam: Elsevier Scientific Publishing Company.

Morgan, Diana (1984). "How Does Fluoride Fight Decay?" *Science84* 5 (December): 27.

Mosher, Lawrence (1980). "The Environmental Movement Faces the '80s." *National Journal* 12 (December 13): 2116-2121.

———(1981). "Taking Aim at EPA." *National Journal* 13 (February 14): 256-259.

———(1984). "Asbestos Scare?" *National Journal* 16 (October 13): 1928-1929.

Nagel, Ernest (1961). *The Structure of Science: Problems in the Logic of Scientific Explanation.* New York: Harcourt, Brace & World, Inc.

Nathan, Richard P. (1983). *The Administrative Presidency.* New York: John Wiley & sons.

National Academy of Sciences (1980). *Toward Healthful Diets.* Washington, DC: National Academy Press.

———(1982). *Diet, Nutrition, and Cancer.* Washington, DC: National Academy Press.

National Cancer Advisory Board (1976). "General Criteria for Assessing the Evidence for Carcinogenicity of Chemical Substances." Report of the Subcommittee on Environmental Carcinogenesis. Pp. 542-554 in *Control of Carcinogens.*

National Research Council (1983). *Risk Management in the Federal Government: Managing the Process.* Washington, DC: National Academy Press.

———(1984). *Toxicity Testing: Strategies to Determine Needs and Priorities.* Washington, DC: National Academy Press.

Newton, Jan M. (1983-1984). "Herbicides and Economics." *NCAP News* 3 (Fall-Winter): 10-11.

Nixon, Richard (1970). "Message on Environment." Pp. 22A-27A in *1970 CQ Almanac.* Washington, DC: Congressional Quarterly Press.

Occupational Safety and Health Administration (1980). "Identification, Classification and Regulation of Potential Occupational Carcinogens." *Federal Register* 45 (January 22): 5002–5296.

———(1981). "Identification, Classification and Regulation of Potential Occupational Carcinogens; Conforming Deletions." *Federal Register* 46 (January 21): 5878–5880.

Office of Science and Technology Policy (1982). "Review on the Mechanisms of Effect and Detection of Chemical Carcinogens." 1st draft. Washington, DC: Executive Office of the President.

———(1983). "Review on the Mechanisms of Effect and Detection of Chemical Carcinogens." 2nd draft. Washington, DC: Executive Office of the President.

———(1984). "Chemical Carcinogens; Review of the Science and its Associated Principles." *Federal Register* 49 (May 22): 21594–21661.

———(1985). "Chemical Carcinogens; Review of the Science and its Associated Principles, February 1985." *Federal Register* 50 (March 14): 10372–10442.

Office of Technology Assessment (1981). *Assessment of Technologies for Determining Cancer Risks from the Environment.* Washington, DC: Office of Technology Assesment.

Pastor, Robert (1984). "Continuity and Change in U.S. Foreign Policy: Carter and Reagan on El Salvador." *Journal of Policy Analysis and Management* 3 (Winter): 175–190.

PCB and Dioxin Cases (1982). Hearing before the Subcommittee on Oversight and Investigations of the Committee on Energy and Commerce, U.S. House of Representatives, 97th Congress, 2nd session, November 19.

Pear, Robert (1985a). "Lower Nutrient Levels Proposed in Draft Report on American Diet." *The New York Times* (September 23).

———(1985b). "Impasse Delays Proposal to Cut Diet Guidelines." *The New York Times* (October 8).

Pelham, Ann (1978). "Government Tackles Tricky Question of How to Regulate Carcinogens." *Congressional Quarterly Weekly Report* (April 22): 957–963.

Perera, Frederica P. (1984). "The Genotoxic/Epigenetic Distinction: Relevance to Cancer Policy." *Environmental Research* 34: 175–191.

Price, Don K. (1965). *The Scientific Estate*. Cambridge, MA: The Belknap Press of Harvard University Press.

Randall, Ronald (1979). "Presidential Power versus Bureaucratic Intransigence: The Influence of the Nixon Administration on Welfare Policy." *American Political Science Review* 73 (September): 795–810.

Rayner, Steve (1984). "Disagreeing about Risk: The Institutional Cultures of Risk Management and Planning for Future Generations." Pp. 150–168 in Hadden.

Regenstein, Lewis (1982). *America the Poisoned: How Deadly Chemicals are Destroying our Environment, Our Wildlife, Ourselves and—HOW WE CAN SURVIVE!* Washington, DC: Acropolis Books, Ltd.

Regulatory Council (1979). "Regulatory Council Statement of How to Regulate Chemical Carcinogens." *Environmental Reporter* 10 (November 30): 201–213.

Regulatory Negotiation (1980). Joint hearings before the Select Committee on Small Business and the Subcommittee on Oversight of Government Management of the Committee on Governmental Affairs, U.S. Senate, 96th Congress, 2nd session, July 29–30.

Reif, Arnold E. (1981). "The Causes of Cancer." *American Scientist* 69 (July–August): 437–447.

Reinhold, Robert (1980). "Science Unit Revises Study on Radiation's Cancer Risk." *The New York Times* (July 30).

———(1983). "E.P.A.'s Dow Test Find High Toxicity." *The New York Times* (July 30).

Report of the Secretary's Commission on Pesticides and Their Relationship to Environmental Health (1969). Washington, DC: U.S. Department of Health, Education, and Welfare.

Report on Departments of Labor, and Health, Education, and Welfare, and Related Agencies Appropriations Bill, 1977 (1976). Committee on Appropriations, U.S. House of Representatives, 94th Congress, 2nd session, June 8, Report No. 94-1219.

Rettig, Richard A. (1977). *The Cancer Crusade: The Story of the National Cancer Act of 1971*. Princeton, NJ: Princeton University Press.

"Revision without Revolution in Carcinogen Policy" (1984). *Regulation* 8 (July–August): 5–7.

Robbins, David, and Ron Johnston (1976). "The Role of Cognitive and Occupational Differentiation in Scientific Controversies." *Social Studies of Science* 6 (Fall); 349–368.

Roberts, Leslie (1984). *Cancer Today: Origins, Prevention, and Treatment.* Washington, DC: National Academy Press.

Rogers, William H., Jr. (1980). "Benefits, Costs, and Risks: Oversight of Health and Environmental Decisionmaking." *Harvard Environmental Law Review* 4: 191–226.

Rosenbaum, Walter A. (1977). *The Politics of Environmental Concern.* 2nd ed. New York: Praeger Publishers.

————(1985). *Environmental Politics and Policy.* Washington, DC: Congressional Quarterly Press.

Rowe, William D. (1977). *An Anatomy of Risk.* New York: John Wiley & Sons.

Rubin, Harry (1980). "Is Somatic Mutation the Major Mechanism of Malignant Transformation?" *JCNI* 64 (May): 995–1000.

Ruckelshaus, William D. (1983). "Science, Risk, and Public Policy." *Science* 221 (September 9): 1026–1028.

————(1985). "Risk, Science, and Democracy." *Issues in Science and Technology* 1 (Spring): 19–38.

Rushefsky, Mark E. (1977). "Organic Farming: Science and Ideology in a Technological Dispute." Ph.D. dissertation, State University of New York at Binghamton.

————(1982). "Technical Disputes: Why Experts Disagree." *Policy Studies Review* 1 (May): 676–685.

————(1984a). "The Misuse of Science in Governmental Decisionmaking." *Science, Technology, & Human Values* 9 (Summer): 47–59.

————(1984b). "Institutional Mechanisms for Resolving Risk Controversies." Pp. 133–149 in Hadden.

————(1985). "Assuming the Conclusions: Risk Assessment in the Development of Cancer Policy." *Politics and the Life Sciences* 4 (August): 31–44.

Saffiotti, Umberto (1977). "Carcinogenesis, 1957–1977: Notes for a Historical Review." *Journal of the National Cancer Institute* 59 (August): 617–622.

Salsburg, David, and Andrew Heath (1981). "When Science Progresses and Bureaucracies Lag—The Case of Cancer Research." *The Public Interest* 65: 30–39.

Schmandt, Jurgen, and James E. Katz (1981). "Research Project on the Scientific State: A Report and a Proposal." Austin, TX: Lyndon B. Johnson School of Public Affairs, University of Texas, mimeo.

Schmeck, Harold, M., Jr. (1984). "Researchers Describe Cancer Genes as Having a Jekyll and Hyde Role." *The New York Times* (November 6).

Schmitter, Phillipe C., and Gerhard Lehmbruch, eds. (1979). *Trends Toward Corporatist Intermediation.* Beverly Hills, CA: Sage Publications.

Shabecoff, Philip (1983). "Internal E.P.A. Review Criticizes Mismanagement in Toxic Cleanup." *The New York Times* (May 11).

——(1985a). "Companies Say Toxic Emissions Need U.S. Curb. *The New York Times* (March 27).

——(1985b). "U.S. Budget Office Disputed on Cost Basis for Asbestos." *The New York Times* (April 17).

Slovic, Paul, et al. (1978). "Rating the Risks." *Environment* 21 (April): 14–20, 36–38.

"Special Issue on Epidemiology" (1984). *NCAP News* 4 (Spring): 1–29.

"Spectrum: Nine Point Program" (1981). *Environment* 23 (September): 21.

Squire, Robert A. (1981). "Ranking Animal Carcinogens: A Proposed Regulatory Approach." *Science* 214: 877–880. Reprinted in *Control of Carcinogens*, pp. 222–225.

Stanfield, Rochelle L. (1985a). "EPA's Withdrawal from Asbestos Regulation Prompts Complaints of Industry Pressure." *National Journal* 17 (March 9): 542–543.

——(1985b). "EPA Reverses on Asbestos." *National Journal* 17 (March 16): 597.

————(1985c). "What's the Risk?" *National Journal* 17 (March 30): 721.

Stockman, David (1980). "The Stockman Manifesto." *The Washington Post* (December 14).

Strickland, Stephen P. (1972). *Politics, Science, and Dread Disease: A Short History of United States Medical Research Policy.* Cambridge, MA: Harvard University Press.

Todhunter, John A. (1982). "Review of Data Available to the Administrator Concerning Formaldehyde and di (2-ethylhexyl) Phthalate (DEHP). Pp. 248–271 in *Formaldehyde: Review of Scientific Basis.*

————(1984). "Letter: Formaldehyde Regulation." *Science* 224 (May 11): 550–551.

Totter, John R. (1980). "Spontaneous Cancer and its Possible Relationship to Oxygen Metabolism." *Proceedings of the National Academy of Sciences* 77: 1763–1767.

Toxic Substances Strategy Committee (1980). *Toxic Chemicals and Public Protection.* Washington, DC: Council on Environmental Quality.

Turner, James S. (1970). *The Chemical Feast.* New York: Grossman Publishers.

U.S. Department of Health and Human Services (1982). *Health— United States 1982.* Washington, DC: Department of Health and Human Services.

Van Strum, Carol (1983). *A Bitter Fog: Herbicides and Human Rights.* San Francisco: Sierra Club Books.

Vig, Norman J. (1984a). "The Courts: Judicial Review and Risk Assessments." Pp. 60–79 in Hadden.

————(1984b). "The President and the Environment: Revolution or Retreat? Pp. 77–95 in Vig and Kraft.

Vig, Norman J., and Michael E. Kraft, eds. (1984). *Environmental Policy in the 1980's: Reagan's New Agenda.* Washington, DC: Congressional Quarterly Press.

von Hippel, Frank, and Joel Primack (1971). "Scientists and the Politics of Technology." *Applied Spectroscopy* 25 (November): 403–413.

Wade, Nicholas (1983). "Editorial Notebook: The Embarrassment of 'Yellow Rain.' " *The New York Times* (November 28).

———(1984). "Editorial Notebook: The White House's Misuse of Science." *The New York Times* (February 14).

Wagner, Sheldon L., et al. (1979). *A Scientific Critique of the EPA Alsea II Study and Report: Summary.* Corvalis, OR: Environmental Health Sciences Center, Oregon State University.

Watson, James D. (1968). *The Double Helix: A Personal Account of the Discovery of the Structure of DNA.* New York: Atheneum Press.

Weinberg, Alvin M. (1972). "Science and Trans-Science." *Minerva* 10 (April): 209–222.

———(1984). "Letter: Diet and Cancer." *Science* 224 (May 18): 659.

———(1985). "Review: *The Apocalyptics* by Edith Efron." *Environment* 27 (January–February 1985): 28–30.

Weinberg, Alvin M., and John B. Storer (1985). "Ambiguous Carcinogens and Their Regulation." *Risk Analysis* 5 (June): 151–156.

Weinstein, Milton C. (1983). "Cost-Effective Priorities for Cancer Prevention." *Science* 221 (July 1): 17–23.

Weisburger, Elizabeth K. (1983). "History of the Bioassay Program of the National Cancer Institute." *Progress in Experimental Tumor Research* 26: 187–201.

Weisburger, John H., and Gary M. Williams (1981). "Carcinogen Testing: Current Problems and New Approaches." *Science* 214 (October 23): 401–407.

Wellford, Harrison (1972). *Sowing the Wind.* New York: Grossman Publishers.

Wessel, Milton R. (1980). *Science and Conscience.* New York: Columbia University Press.

Whitaker, John C. (1976). *Striking a Balance: Environment and Natural Resources Policy in the Nixon-Ford Years.* Washington, DC: American Enterprise Institute.

White, Lawrence, J. (1981). *Reforming Regulation: Processes and Problems.* Englewood Cliffs, NJ: Prentice-Hall, Inc.

Whittemore, Alice S. (1983). "Facts and Values in Risk Analysis for Environmental Toxicants." *Risk Analysis* 3 (March): 23-33.

Whittemore, Alice S., and Joseph B. Keller (1978). "Quantitative Theories of Carcinogenesis." *SIAM Review* 20 (January): 1-30.

Whittington, Dale, and W. Norton Grubb (1984). "Economic Analysis in Regulatory Decisions: The Implications of Executive Order 12291." *Science, Technology, & Human Values* 9 (Winter): 63-71.

Wildavsky, Aaron B. (1976). "Aesthetic Power or the Triumph of the Sensitive Minority over the Vulgar Mass." *Daedalus* 96 (Fall): 1115-1128.

———(1979). *Speaking Truth to Power: The Art and Craft of Policy Analysis.* Boston: Little, Brown and Co.

Williams, Gary M. (1983). "Genotoxic and Epigenetic Carcinogens: Their Identification and Significance." Pp. 328-333 in Williams et al. (1983).

Williams, G.M., et al., eds. (1983). "Cellular Systems for Toxicity Testing." *Annals of the New York Academy of Science*, vol. 407.

Wilson, James Q. (1980). "The Politics of Regulation." Pp. 357-394 in James Q. Wilson (ed.), *The Politics of Regulation*, New York: Basic Books.

Wines, Michael (1983). "Reagan's Cancer War." *National Journal* 15: 1264-1269.

Wynder, Ernst L., and Gio B. Gori (1977). "Contribution of the Environment to Cancer Incidence: An Epidemiologic Exercise." *Journal of the National Cancer Institute* 54 (April): 825-832.

Ziman, John (1978). *Reliable Knowledge: An Exploration of the Grounds for Belief in Science.* Cambridge: Cambridge University Press.

Index

83 146